THE OUTDOOR WOMAN

Patricia Hubbard

THE OUTDOOR WOMAN

A HANDBOOK TO ADVENTURE

PATRICIA HUBBARD
and STAN WASS

MasterMedia Limited
New York

Copyright © 1992 by Patricia F. Hubbard and Stan Wass
All rights reserved, including the right of reproduction in
whole or in part in any form.
Published by MasterMedia Limited.
MASTERMEDIA and colophon are registered trademarks of
MasterMedia Limited.

Library of Congress Cataloging-in-Publication Data

Hubbard, Patricia.
    The outdoor woman : a handbook to adventure /
Patricia Hubbard and Stan Wass.
        p.   cm.
    Includes bibliographical references (p. 223).
    ISBN 0-942361-36-9
    1. Outdoor recreation for women—United States—
Handbooks, manuals, etc. I. Wass, Stan. II. Title.
GV191.64.H83 1992
796'.0194—dc20   92-11536
                                                      CIP

Designed by Jacqueline Schuman
Production services by Martin Cook Associates, Ltd.
Manufactured in the United States of America

10 9 8 7 6 5 4 3 2 1

ACKNOWLEDGEMENTS

First and foremost we would like to thank Susan Stautberg for encouraging us to write this book and then for gently prodding us along to the finish. Thanks also to Nick and Lisa Dyslin, Dick Weber, Ed and Margy Eveleth, and Tamsin Venn. Special thanks to Gordon Nash, Pete Sparhawk, Dr. Ned Frederick of Exeter Research, Rebecca Busselle, Cliff Crase, Sugar Ferris, Janet Robertson, Sherry Jagerson, Carol Poster, Bev Wessel, Susan Rogers, Sallie Greenwood, and Mary Scott, all of whom generously shared their time, research, and expertise.

And most especially we thank those outdoor women who have inspired and encouraged us by generously sharing their tales of adventure. Without their moxie, their strength, their humor and spirit, there would be no stories to tell.

CONTENTS

THE OUTDOOR WOMAN

INTRODUCTION

Today's outdoor woman is accepting more and greater challenges. She is standing atop the world's highest peaks, racing sailboats through the "Roaring Forties," kicking her way up the slickest ice cliffs, and paddling the toughest rivers. But, for all her high adventures, she started with the easy stuff—a sail on a lake, a hike in the hills, or a scramble up an intriguing boulder.

Your first step into the great outdoors will probably be a trip to a local sporting-goods store for the proper clothes and equipment. You'll be greeted by a friendly salesperson who will tell you all about things like "suspension systems" and "lumbar pads," "expanded polystyrene," "high performance," "function specific," and "compression straps." That's only the beginning. There's "quick-drying gear" with "wicking capabilities," possessing special pockets and zippers that resist rips and tears, that is lightweight, rainproof, water-resistant, and made from 100 percent "environmentally friendly" fabrics. Likely as not, you will wander around the store, trying on backpacks, thumping canoes, staring in dumb amazement at the shelves of freeze-dried foods, wondering if you should buy cotton or polypro underwear, pondering the difference between drysuits, wetsuits, and rainwear. You'll ask yourself: can rainwear really be "breathable" and still resist and repell water? After three hours of this god-awful process you will probably stumble out to your car in complete exhaustion, having bought nothing at all. It's enough to make you scrap all plans for an outdoor trip and buy a video game instead. Of course, this is a worst-case scenario, but it is not unusual—so if it happens to you, don't despair.

"Unisex is just another word for men's," says Sally McCoy, Director of Marketing for The North Face. So be aware that most items advertised as sized for women are actually scaled-down men's sizes. Women 5'4" and under will have an especially difficult search. But take heart . . . One major outdoor-equipment company is launching a line of women's technical outerwear. Another is focusing on "gender-specific" clothing, completely replacing their unisex sizing. Our guess is that savvy manufacturers will follow this trend, producing more and better-fitting items made for a woman's figure. This handbook will guide you through the process of outfitting yourself for comfort in the outdoors; supplying you with information on the "bare essentials" that will make your outdoor experience a pleasure; ensuring that you'll venture out again.

While traditionally the outdoors has been perceived as being a man's world, women are claiming their place in greater numbers and in such varied sports as white-water canoe and kayak racing, cross-country biking, long-distance hiking, mountaineering, and fly fishing, just to name a few. Because outdoor magazines focus on the male audience, male role models abound, both editorially and through advertising, while female heroes in both categories are scant, at best. Every road biker aspires to be Greg LeMond; he's the guy next door. But with whom do women bikers identify? When was the last time you saw a mountain bike ad showing a grinning, sweat-soaked, mud-spattered woman careening down a mountain path on some hot new bike? Not lately, I bet. It would lead one to believe that there are no serious female athletes out there, wouldn't it? But there are. While advertisers sometimes use world-class athletes such as rock climber Lynn Hill, mountaineer Stacy Allison, polar explorer Helen Thayer, or sled dog racer Susan Butcher, to display their products, it is rare.

The purpose of this book is to provide a vehicle through which we can share the stories of the typical outdoor woman. Who is she? She is a woman like you; she could be single or married, a student, a mother, or a grandmother. In the following chapters you will be introduced to accomplished women of all ages, sizes, and abilities who are hooks for us all to grab onto; a way to identify our outdoor selves.

Women who love the outdoor life face a paradoxical existence. On one hand, feeling comfortable and confident outdoors conveys a message to the world that she is strong, independent-minded, a risk-taker, able to cope with periods of isolation or hardship, and at the same time can experience great happiness and joy (media-translation:

You don't need a man!). Summing up the attitude of most of us outdoor women, one Idaho mountain guide said that although women guides work like "one of the guys, we still feel it's important to remember we *aren't* literally one of the guys. We're proud to be strong women." You'll find that the role models presented in this book are women who are proud of and maintain their womanhood while reveling in outdoor adventures.

The reasons why women venture outdoors are as varied as the backgrounds and interests of the women themselves; but, basically, it's for the same reasons that men do: for rest, camaraderie, and a chance to commune with nature. When asked why she participates in Iditasport (a 200-mile bike ride across Alaska in the snow), one woman replied, "As a forty-year-old mother of two strong-willed daughters who are only beginning to face the challenges of life, I believe in role models." You may not ride a bike or paddle a canoe, but you will identify with the women in this book. Achieving even the smallest degree of success in the outdoors is empowering. It gives your spirit a lift, puts a bounce in your stride and a mile-wide smile on your face!

This book encourages women to find and utilize their own unique strengths, and not just copy a man's. While it's true that in the past men have been the primary teachers and the mentors, and while it's only natural to watch and mimic your teacher we are physiologically different, and so possess different physical strengths. It doesn't take long for a novice rock climber, for example, to learn that her strength lies in balance and agility, not upper body muscle.

Above all, *The Outdoor Woman: A Handbook to Adventure* is about power. Self-confidence and the ability to trust in yourself and others adds up to one thing—power. The big "P" word is not part of most female conversations, but you'll notice that each woman profiled in this book constantly reaffirms and validates her power through outdoor sports. Power is a glorious feeling, a feeling you will want to experience too!

You are going to read about women who derive abundant joy from their sports. But remember, they were all beginners once too. Our outdoor heroes will encourage you, challenge you, make you grin a lot, maybe shed a tear or two. I bet you'll want to shout from the rafters, "I'm glad I'm a woman!"

GETTING DOWN TO BASICS

Our friends Kip and Norm have a special closet in their house that they call their Play Closet, and opening the door to this wonderful room is like stepping into an outdoor sports store. All their sports equipment is displayed in an easy-to-find manner, either hanging on hooks from the ceiling or stacked neatly on floor-to-ceiling shelves. You'll find everything in this closet, including foul-weather gear, down parkas and vests, snowshoes, downhill and cross-country skis, canoe paddles, sleeping bags, tents, cooking gear, hiking boots, mountaineering equipment (including ropes, crampons, and ice axes), and life jackets. Posted neatly on the wall just inside the closet door are several lists, each one containing the basic gear needed for each individual sport. When it's time for an adventure, they simply consult the appropriate list and quickly put together a kit for that particular trip.

Kip and Norm's lists are the result of years of enjoying many different sports. Although a sport may require its own unique equipment, they have learned that whether they go for a single-night canoe trip or a three-week backpacking trip, the basics are essentially the same. Lists not only serve as a reminder to pack those necessary items but eliminate excess weight and bulk as well. It's easy to think that "just one more item" won't hurt, but those ounces add up to pounds.

For instance, we've been conditioned to believe that a clean change of clothes is necessary for each day. Not so—in the outdoors extra clothes are needed for changing weather conditions or if you get wet. Our experience has been that people take far too much clothing on outdoor adventures, and carrying all that extra weight doesn't necessarily mean greater comfort, it only means more weight. As an example, if you are going on an overnight canoe-camping trip in the summer, you will probably need two outfits and a change of underclothing, that's all—the gear that you paddle in (which can be worn for the entire trip) and the extra outfit in case of drastically changing weather (this same outfit can be used for cool evenings around camp), or if you get wet. On every trip you should take extra pairs of socks. There's nothing quite as comforting as changing into clean, dry socks at the end of the day. After a day of paddling, your shoes will be wet, squishy, and cold; a pair of camp shoes (old running shoes are fine) is a necessity. Evenings may be cool, so put together a few items that will make you feel cozy and warm around camp (this can also be your second set of clothes). For example, pants, sweater, and hat made of lightweight pile are always a good choice. The new synthetics are easy to stuff into packs, they're warm, and dry quickly when wet. Don't forget a pair of gloves; lightweight liner gloves work well in warm weather. What if it rains, you ask? My rainsuit travels with me everywhere, on every outdoor adventure. It's always number one on the list.

For more detailed information and suggestions for formulating your own list, read the What Am I Going to Wear? chapter and refer to the Bibliography.

FUNDAMENTALS

Let's talk about the basic items that every play closet has, those items that are fundamental to making your outdoor adventures safe and comfortable.

Shelters: When we think shelters we think of either a tent or a tarp. Most campers prefer a tent and, while it's not the lightest-weight option, it does offer more protection from the weather and bugs. The current crop of tents are lightweight, compact, and easy to carry. As far as we're concerned there is one basic criterion for choosing a tent— weight. Buy a tent using the same premise as when buying a canoe. It won't do you any good if you can't carry it! Don't forget that it does make some difference what sport you will use the tent for. For instance, a tent for bike touring must be carried in a very small space even if it is split between two riders. On the other hand, if canoeing is your sport, you have the option of carrying a slightly roomier model. Larger tents offer more living space and on rainy days are easier to play cards in, but don't choose space over weight. And make sure you know how to set up the tent before you take off on your trip. Sometimes it isn't as easy as it looks.

Canoeing on the Susquehanna River in Pennsylvania recently, our only choice of campsite was a rock-strewn gravel beach. We couldn't have put a stake in the ground with a sledgehammer. This situation is not uncommon in any backcountry trip, so when you're considering buying a tent, go for the self-standing styles. They don't require stakes or guy lines for support. Domes and rounded-top tents such as the pricey but classic nine-pound, three-person, VE 24 from North Face or the less expensive six-pound, two-person Eureka Dome offer lots of room and are popular examples. At the other end of the design and price spectrum are the A-frame models, an example of which is the Timberline from Eureka. Designed with two poles at each end and a connecting cross pole, A-frames provide less room but a cheaper price. In between those two styles is an amazing variety of sizes and models. Quest, Walrus, and Sierra Design all make excellent lines of tents, ranging from large expedition and family-camping styles to one-person shelters that hardly qualify for the name tent.

Constructed of nylon, the tent body consists of a waterproof floor and a breathable top. Breathable means that moisture and heat produced by your body escape through the walls of the tent, otherwise condensing on the inside, soaking you, your sleeping bag, and other possessions. In the winter this condensation freezes and in the summer you get showers of rain every time you move. Breathable tents come equipped with a fly for repelling rain and snow.

Beware of size ratings on tents. For instance, a three- or four-person tent is perfect for two people with some extra room for gear. When shopping for a tent, check out the size of a floor model by getting inside. Ask the salesperson to lay out a couple of sleeping bags; that's the best way to tell if the tent is sized to fit your needs.

Lightweight tarps come in handy in any rainy situation, to cook or to sleep under. If bugs don't bug you, then sleeping under a tarp is lots of fun. It's a way to sleep outdoors without being totally exposed.

Packs: Packs are covered in the Hiking/Backpacking chapter.

Sleeping Pads: Sleeping pads are very personal items and frequently the subject of debate. Some folks can sleep on a bed of nails or rocks, but we love our Therm-a-Rest inflatable pads, a self-inflating combination of foam and air channels. At the time of purchase I figured I could save weight by buying a three-quarter-length pad—that was a mistake. It's miserable having your lower legs hang off the end of the mat, especially in cold or wet weather. Therm-a-Rest provides the most insulation and cushioning for the weight, but there is one thing wrong with inflatable mats—they're slippery. Try what's called a Spider Mat, a great new gimmick that wraps around the pad and helps keep you from sliding off. It also anchors the mat to the floor of the tent. A less expensive sleeping-pad option is the solid closed-cell foam pad. They come in thicknesses of 1½ to 2 inches and are comfortable in most situations.

Sleeping Bags: What makes a good sleeping bag? Quality bags have nylon outer and inner layers with insulation in between. Before you run out and spend lots of money on a sleeping bag, determine what kind of weather you'll be camping in. A strictly summer bag is no good for winter and, likewise, a strictly winter bag is no good for summer. I bought a three-season goose-down bag and it really is too warm for most low-altitude summer camping. This problem of over-heating is relieved somewhat by a zipper that can be opened at the foot of the bag.

Believe it or not, research has shown that a woman's body temperature drops quicker than a man's and is noticed first in the extremities, especially the feet. Kelty has designed a bag called Hot Foot to address this problem. Available in long or regular lengths, this 2-pound, 13-ounce Quallofil bag is designed with extra insulation and a felt-like liner around the foot, keeping your feet cozy and warm.

Sleeping bags are insulated either with artificial fiber or down filling. Down filling is the most expensive and provides the greatest loft for weight. When I shopped for a bag I crawled in and out of at least ten bags on the floor of the outdoor store. The artificial bags were nice and fat, filled with fibers such as Hollofill, Quallofil, and PolarGuard, and appeared warm, but so did the goose-down bags. The artificial bags dry faster when damp or wet, are lower in price but slightly heavier. What actually sold me on the goose-down bag was watching the salesperson stuff that huge fluffy bag into a tiny little sack. Down has the most compressibility and, on arriving at camp, shakes out to be the loftiest. So, after witnessing the magic of the stuff sack I opted for down and have never regretted it. If you choose down, just be aware that it requires more care and maintenance than the artificial fiber–filled bags. I'm extremely careful to keep my down bag dry and after a campout air the bag well before storing it away.

KITCHEN EQUIPMENT

Stoves: The trusty two-burner Coleman stove is still the best bet if you are cooking in a campground and living out of your car. With two burners you can cook several items at once, providing a variety of eating options. However, almost everyone living out of a pack, off a bike, or out of a canoe or kayak chooses a one-burner gas stove. One-burner stove technology is constantly being updated and improved. The three stoves we're most familiar with are Coleman's Peak I—a compact little stove weighing 22.7 ounces (without fuel), available in models that burn white gas, unleaded gas, or kerosene. You can boil almost 30 quarts of water with one pint of fuel and the flame can be adjusted from high to low. This little stove has a lot of power even in cold weather.

Another great stove, which we find to be most appropriate for warm-weather camping, is the Gaz. Operating on a butane cartridge, these nifty little blue stoves are compact, lightweight, and need little maintenance. They don't require priming and start as easily as your gas stove at home. A few years ago I purchased the Gaz Globe Trotter model, which included two small pots that also serve as the carrying case for the stove. I was impressed by the compact package and the easy operation of the Globe Trotter. However, I found that on days when the temperature hovers between freezing and 50 degrees, the stove is less efficient, requiring a lot of time and fuel to boil water. Butane becomes a less efficient fuel as the temperature drops. Be aware also that Gaz stoves operate on disposable butane cartridges. The cartridges must be packed out and recycled.

MSR stoves have been standard on major expeditions for years. These little fire-breathing monsters come in versions that will burn any fuel, including kerosene, unleaded gas, aviation gas, Stoddard Solvent #1, diesel fuel, or number-one stove oil. After my experience with the Gaz stove, I went to the opposite end of the spectrum and bought an MSR X-GK II stove. The darn thing is like a blow torch. I get a cup of tea or soup in seconds but it's difficult, if not impossible, to simmer or slow-cook anything. But I love it. Most meals cooked outdoors require boiling water anyway. It's great for cooking fast meals for a few people or a crowd.

Cooking Pots: One-pot meals are best for backcountry trips. I bought a two-quart aluminum pot at a yard sale for less than a dollar. It has loop handles (that's right, just like the pots your mother used) and rides in the very bottom of my pack, stuffed with my sleeping bag. The pot is thin and heats fast, is large enough for a one-pot meal for two people, and is a perfect size for doing the dishes.

It is important when choosing a pot that it be large enough to hold enough water to hydrate your meals. As for other cooking gear, take a mitt for handling hot pots, a large spoon for stirring and serving, a few spices, and your favorite camping food. We're not going to get into camp food in this book. There are dozens of wonderful outdoor cookbooks available that offer tasty recipes (and food is a very important part of your outdoor comfort), menu suggestions, kitchen equipment necessities, and outdoor nutrition. Check the Bibliography.

Tea Kettle: A small, closed pot heats water quickly for making coffee, tea, and soup. This is an optional piece of equipment that many find very convenient.

Water Purification: In even the most remote spots in the world, drinking water cannot be entirely trusted. For that reason, every backcountry visitor must use some method of water purification. The most popular methods used are iodine tablets and water-filtering pumps. Iodine tablets leave the water tasting peculiar, even after adding flavored drink mixes. But water-filter pump technology improves every day. The three or four brands currently on the market are lightweight, extremely reliable, and easy to operate. These filters will remove Giardia cysts (the most common North American problem), parasitic tapeworms, asbestos fibers, herbicides, pesticides, and other organic contaminants. Weighing 12 ounces and costing $40, my First Need filter has been a real lifesaver. Getting a late start on a recent canoe trip, we had to overnight beside a brackish inlet. Iodine tablets in that case would have done no good, even if we had strained the water. Using the First Need pump, the water filtered out to be clear and delicious.

We were all astonished at the efficiency of this little filter and the quality of the water it produced—certainly worth every penny of its price. Filters range in price from $40 to $240.

Miscellaneous Kitchen Gear: Funnel for transferring stove fuel, eyedropper for priming stove, lots of matches in a waterproof container, personal eating tools (insulated plastic bowl and large mug, fork, and spoon), and dishwashing paraphernalia.

Plastic Water Bottles: A one-quart bottle or two should be sufficient. Wide-mouth bottles are easier to fill, especially when you use a water-filtering pump. If you own a backpack with side pockets, you will obviously choose water bottles to fit those pockets.

Tools: A really neat little tool is the Leatherman Mini Tool which comes with full-size pliers, knife, wire cutters, ruler, can and bottle opener, file, and screwdrivers and is the basis for your repair kit. Also include in that kit a few short pieces of nylon cord, a small roll of duct tape, a short piece of bailing wire, and one or two nails and small wood screws. All these items can fit into a very tiny stuff sack, weighing only a few ounces.

Flashlight: A small lightweight model will serve you well. Be sure to take extra batteries and an extra bulb. If you are planning to spend time out at night, an alternative to a flashlight is a headlamp. It leaves your hands free to perform camp chores, cook, read, or write in your journal.

First-aid Kit: Adhesive pads of various sizes, butterfly bandages for closing small wounds, large-size gauze pads, roller bandage to hold the pads in place, aspirin, bandage compress, ace bandage, adhesive tape, iodine, antibiotic ointment, wire splint, Band-aids, moleskin or mole foam for covering blisters, antiseptic towelettes, safety pins, razor blade, needle, tweezers, decongestant pills, triangular bandage for use as an arm sling or large bandage, bandage scissors, and low-reading thermometer. We know this seems like a long list but it really isn't. These items fit into a very tiny stuff sack. If you're traveling with a group, obviously everyone doesn't have to take her own complete kit, but there may be some very personal items that you wish to take on your own. Outdoor Research offers prepackaged kits in various prices and sizes. Check Resources.

Personal: Extra eyeglasses or contact lens and lens solutions, bug dope, sunscreen, lip balm, toothbrush, toothpaste, small chunk of soap, comb, moisturizer, and floss. Many supermarkets and drugstores carry sample-size personal-care items. They're perfect for outdoor trips. Don't forget a plastic trowel for digging toilet facilities, toilet paper, and, if needed, lots of tampons and self-locking plastic bags for packing out used tampons.

The above information will give you a starting place in putting together your own basic outdoor list. Everything in your kit is entirely a personal choice. We feel that the above items are the very basic components for your comfort and safety. Remember, only through experience can you decide what is necessary for you.

WHAT AM I GOING TO WEAR?

Dressing properly is an important prerequisite to enjoying your outdoor experience, and let's face it, "looking the part" is half the fun. How many times have you opened a magazine and right there, before your eyes, straddling a bike you would die for, is a gorgeous model—perfect hair, perfect skin, perfect long glossy nails, and wearing the latest fantastic Lycra outfit—makes you want to gag, doesn't it? She looks like she's never broken a sweat or swatted off a horde of hungry black flies or struggled into camp after dark with two kids in tow who only have making S'mores in mind. The media bombards us with "the perfect woman," but the truth is, when you're outdoors and "looking the part," most probably you will be sweaty, mud splattered, have hair that is frizzed or bedraggled to the max, have blisters, splinters, and smelly socks. You'll also have a grin on your face a mile wide.

Nature is wonderful and mysterious—harsh as a driving hail storm and gentle as a raindrop—and we must deal with her on her terms, not our own. So it is necessary to dress for the outdoors in comfortable, appropriate clothes. Learning to regulate and maintain your body temperature while dealing with sun, rain, wind, or snow—all natural occurrences that are beyond your control—just takes practice. As a beginner, it is difficult to know what clothing is appropriate and necessary. A word of caution: Make a list of the items you *really* need before you sally off to the outdoor store, or chances are you'll spend an agonizing few hours just roaming around the store wondering what to buy, totally at the mercy of a sales clerk who'll sell you every expensive thing you *don't* need. While the latest, trendy outdoor fashions are wonderful and we all can just picture ourselves wearing them, go slowly and develop your own style. Once you've found a comfort level in the outdoors that allows the physical you to develop—who knows—you may throw your pumps away forever!

Chances are, if your outdoor adventures take place in the spring, summer, or fall, with a few exceptions, many of the items you need to get started are hanging in your closet: loose-fitting cotton-blend or synthetic fiber pants or shorts; lightweight wool cardigan; long-sleeve, cotton-blend or synthetic fiber button-down shirt; and cotton T-shirts. I'm happy to report that skirts are once again reclaiming their place in the outdoors. Full skirts are comfortable and cool and great for all but boulder climbing or difficult maneuvering over ledges or steep passes. Hikers particularly tell me they find skirts ideal for desert hiking. They're cool, nonrestrictive, and airy, and for pee-breaks they're the best—fluff out your skirt and anywhere you're standing is private. Edie Iglehart of Single Track Design in Maine has even designed a biking skirt (see Catalogs and Mail Order in Resources) that she also recommends for roller-skating, tennis, and hiking.

Whatever you decide to wear, a good general rule to follow is: "Keep it simple." Your first few trips outdoors will be an experiment. Everyone's body responds to the elements in different ways and it's only through trial and error that can you determine what it takes to make you comfortable. In most instances those truly necessary items that you don't already possess require a relatively small investment and in all but a few exceptions, you don't need any of them to get outside the first few times. For instance, it only took hiking one muddy, boulder-strewn trail in a pair of high-top sneakers to convince the bottoms of my feet that hiking boots were the way to go. There are a few particular items, though, that will make your life in the outdoors easier, safer, and more comfortable. Let's talk about those.

UNDERWEAR

Time and again, I have heard women say that no single item has given a woman more freedom and comfort in sports or outdoor activities than the sports bra. How did we live so long without it? Any woman, no matter what her breast size, who participates in any competitive or low- to high-impact sport needs a sports bra. Remember the bad old days when a good workout meant aching breasts and irritated nipples? Those days are gone. Now there are four or five companies that manufacture sports bras in a variety of sizes, colors, styles, and fabrics. Many can be worn alone and are great for running, biking, hiking, climbing, canoeing—you name it. Depending on your body size and personal style preference, there *is* a sports bra for you.

Then again, there are women who prefer wearing no bra at all. The outdoors is the greatest source of freedom from physical and emotional restraints and women are heading outdoors in droves, reclaiming their physical selves. Throughout history we have been cinched, zipped, and laced into all sorts of restrictive underclothing. Now we have a choice: sports bra, regular bra, or no bra at all. This is your personal decision and, obviously, no one's concern but your own.

Panties should be comfortable, nonrestricting, and, above all, possess wicking qualities. While many women find cotton panties comfortable for regular wear, after a half hour of working up a sweat, cotton hangs cold and damp on your body. Try some of the new fabrics such as Coolmax or Supplex. Even while drenched with sweat, those fabrics wick the water off your body and leave you with the feeling of dryness. Many of the new women's sports shorts have built-in underpants and some styles feature a soft knitted-in panty with terry crotch. These are comfortable and worth the small added expense. Andiamo (see Catalogs and Mail Order in Resources) makes panties with padded crotch and seat—great for biking or rowing.

SHOES

I know we just finished telling you that you'll probably find many items appropriate for the outdoors hanging in your closet, but footwear is the one area that is *very* specialized and does require an investment of research, shopping time, and money. No matter what sport you participate in, you'll need specialized footwear. There is nothing worse than aching, blistered feet. Consider this expense an investment in your health and comfort. While you'll find that some shoes are perfectly adaptable to a few activities, others are not. It's difficult to paddle a canoe efficiently wearing a pair of hiking boots. By the same token, it would be pretty near impossible to negotiate a boulder-strewn, muddy trail, carrying 40 pounds on your back, and wearing a pair of Aqua Socks. Proper footwear is essential.

While the local department store may provide you with casual footwear, don't expect to find products for serious athletic pursuits on their shelves. A specialty sports shop or reputable sporting-goods store is the place to go. Thumb through any magazine and you'll read ads extolling the technological breakthroughs and inherent benefits of athletic shoes: gels, "super flexible, nonslip, ultragrip traction," "double density Shock Foam," and "stable heel counters." What does it all mean? It means, before you go shopping, do some research and have an idea of what you want. *Walking, Runners World, Backpacker,* and *Outside* magazines offer a footwear buyers guide once a year. Various sports shoes and boots are reviewed, helping you to determine the best shoe for your needs.

For instance, running and walking shoes need to be supportive in width, length, and ankle height and extra cushioning is important in any shoe worn on a hard surface. When I first started running, I wore aerobic shoes. They didn't offer nearly enough support. My body felt beaten up after a run, my legs and knees were racked with pain and could have suffered permanent damage. I was astounded at how much better I felt and performed in a proper pair of running shoes.

A few years ago a colorful pair of lightweight hiking boots caught my eye. It was summer and I was headed for the Big Horn Mountains in Wyoming for a few weeks of hiking and didn't feel like wearing my heavy leather hiking boots (although they are still my favorites). Lightweights are wonderful for day hikes (when you're carrying a small pack) or for overnight backpacking trips and they require little or no break-in time. In fact, I wore them right out onto the trail with no break-in period at all and experienced no problems. Lightweights are cooler than leather and when wet, dry fast. They come in fantastic color combinations, possess soles that are less destructive to the environment, and, best of all, are less expensive than leather boots. But, before purchasing a pair of boots, determine their use—day hikes, overnight backpacking, two-week expeditions? Your idea of hiking may be strolling along essentially flat to slightly hilly terrain and running shoes may be all you'll need. Use determines the style and weight of the boot.

Specialized hiking, biking, sailing, and other water shoes will be covered in the chapters on those subjects.

SOCKS

Socks perform several functions: they provide cushioning from stress and pounding, add insulation, and keep feet dry. One-hundred-per-cent cotton might make for comfortable casual footwear, but cotton has no place on active feet. When wet and damp it loses its cushioning and insulation value quickly. Of course, new products come on the market every day and some of the new Coolmax, Thermax, or cotton-blend socks are terrific and may be right for you. When race walking I've found that cotton-blend socks are great, but if it's raining or cold, wool is the best. Wool stays warm even when wet and, unlike cotton, doesn't bunch up or cause friction spots. For hiking, skiing, snowshoe-ing, and other cold-weather sports, wool is still the best sock material. Its resilience is far superior to any of the new artificial fibers and it comes in varying thicknesses, from thick hiking socks down to the very thinnest socks that fit under the tightest cycling shoes.

Most people I know wear two pairs of socks, especially with hiking boots, ski boots, or Sorels. The innermost sock is called a liner sock and acts as a wicking agent, absorbing moisture from active feet and distributing it to the outer sock where it can evaporate. While many active women prefer synthetic materials as their choice in liner socks, I've found that, especially in warm weather, artificial fibers frequently cause hot spots, especially on the bottoms of the feet. Wool is natural; it feels soft and quickly wicks sweat away from your feet and into the outer sock, leaving feet feeling dry. Socks come in a variety of heights, from ankle length to knee high, and your purchase depends entirely on your personal preference.

LAYERING

Layering has become a buzzword in the outdoor business, and justifi-ably so. Playing outdoors, your body works hard to maintain its core temperature. Through what is called layering you can help your body cool off quickly when it becomes overheated and, conversely, warm up quickly when it becomes too cool. Layering is the concept of wearing multiple lightweight layers of clothing, rather than one or more heavier ones. These multilayers act as insulation, trapping warm air between the layers and helping your body maintain its core temperature. This concept is extremely important in the winter but is equally necessary in other seasons as well. You'll be surprised at how easy it is. Layering usually consists of a very light, innermost layer, such as silk or polypropylene underwear in the winter, or a singlet, sports bra, cotton-blend or synthetic fiber shirt in the summer. This layer wicks the moisture away from your body, keeping you dry and comfortable.

The second layer is an insulating layer whose main function is warmth. It pulls moisture from the inner layer out and away from your skin and spreads the moisture around, thus allowing the inner layer to dry quickly, preventing chilling. This layer could be a wool shirt, a lightweight wool or acrylic sweater, or a Thermax turtleneck, lightweight pile jacket, or vest. The third layer is usually a windproof or waterproof shell. In the summer, a simple, inexpensive windbreaker may be just right, but cold weather may call for an anorak or a parka. If overheating becomes a problem, take off a layer or two; conversely, add one or two for warmth when you stop for a snack or a rest. You will find the new artificial fibers superior for layering clothes.

The First Layer

If you enjoy being outdoors in cool or inclement weather, a good set of long underwear is very important. A few years ago it was all but impossible for a woman to find a set of long underwear that fit properly—that is, unless you bought a pair with a fly front. Even then, women with ample hips or breasts, or long arms or legs were out of luck. Now, however, manufacturers of outdoor clothing recognize that women are a growing segment of their market and long underwear designed for a woman's body is available in just about any color and fabric. Beyond Sportswear (see Catalogs and Mail Order in Resources) has developed Long Jaynes, polypro long underwear that incorporates a layered crotch, allowing pit stops without disrobing. Their line also includes hiking shorts and wind pants that contain the same feature. Remember, unisex means it is designed for a man.

Long underwear comes in three different weights: lightweight, medium weight, and heavy or expedition weight. Lightweight styles provide a moisture-moving layer designed to wick moisture away from the skin, making you feel warmer instantly. Except for extreme conditions, lightweights are ideal for any high-energy sport, and they also work as a primary layer in cold or damp weather when you are doing stop-and-go sports. A medium-weight fabric can be worn separately as a jersey or in colder weather under a windbreaker for more protection. The heavyweights (sometimes called expedition weight) are for activities in very cold weather, subzero temperatures, or sitting around at slightly warmer temperatures. They provide the most insulation and work well around camp after a day of exercise. Heavyweight fabric is similar to sweatshirt material in weight and can be used as a primary layer when you are looking for a sweater-like garment. It's instant comfort after a hard day on the trail or paddling.

The material used in long underwear is Thermax, polypropylene, Capilene, Prolite, or Polarplus, to name just a few. They all work and your decision is based more on color, design and *feel* than the name of the cloth. After you practice your sport, you'll see what works best for you at different temperatures.

The Second Layer

The second or insulating layer is often sports specific. Tights for cross-country skiing, race walking, biking, or rock climbing; dry suits for paddling; wool or wool-blend pants or knickers for hiking or cross-country skiing. And don't forget Synchilla or down vests. Vests are wonderful for any sport and can be worn either as a second or third layer, depending on weather conditions. Except for tights and bike shorts, sports clothing should be loose fitting. Tight clothing that binds or causes you more work or discomfort is worthless. Cotton is by far the most comfortable for outerwear in warm weather but if you sweat a lot or stand any chance of getting wet, it will be worthless. In cold and windy conditions wet cotton stays wet and can be dangerous, robbing your body of heat.

Artificial fibers are perfect for second layers. Remember polyester pile, that furry stuff that lined your winter jacket when you were a kid? Well, polyester has undergone some wild changes since then. Now it is cottony soft and, like underwear, comes in different weights. Polarplus, Polartec, Polarlite, Chinella Lite, Synchilla, and a variety of other names are used to describe piles of different weights. Garments made of these fabrics are often wind resistant, breathable, and very cozy. I carry a medium-weight pile jacket for winter hiking. It slips easily over my long underwear and under a parka, keeping me warm in the coldest weather.

After a little experimenting, you'll determine what works best for your body temperatures. For instance, I wouldn't go anywhere, in any season, without my second layer—an old moth-eaten, red wool sweater, purchased in a thrift shop for 50 cents. On a fall hike, it's perfect to slip on over a sweaty shirt at a rest stop, adding just the right amount of warmth. It's very thin and a perfect cover for polypropylene underwear in the winter. In fact, in the winter, unless conditions are sub-zero or very windy, I hike in my polypro undershirt and throw on the red sweater and sometimes a fleece jacket at rest stops or on exposed slopes. That little bit of layering makes a tremendous difference. When putting your outdoor gear together, try to buy clothing that can be used in a variety of sports. For example, the rain gear you use for backpacking can also be used for canoeing, walking, sailing, or even kayaking.

The Outer Layer

The outer layer is your protective shell, the block against wind, rain, and cold. Windbreaker jackets and pants have their place in this clothing scene, as do shells, anoraks, parkas, and medium- to heavyweight pile jackets and pants. A lightweight shell won't keep much rain off but it will keep the wind out and increase your warmth without adding the bulk of additional insulating layers.

Artificial fibers are the answer at all times when you have to respond to a changing environment. But, responding to the weather, particularly rain, requires some preparation. The fact is that if you love being outdoors, you will encounter rain. Rain throws many people off. Think back: when you told your friends about your camping or backpacking trip, was the first thing they asked, "What did you do when it rained?" Most people run inside when it rains—I run outdoors. Dressed properly, there is no greater wonder than walking, paddling, running, or gardening in the rain, but you have to be prepared. If you are properly dressed—layered properly—and have the appropriate rain gear, doing anything outdoors in the rain is wonderful.

It is possible to buy rain gear that will keep you dry regardless of how heavy the deluge. Rubberized materials are totally waterproof.

The drawback is that they are heavy and difficult to move in and have no breathability. At the other end of the spectrum is Gore-Tex, light-weight, breathable, and *very* expensive. The simplest Gore-Tex rain jacket will cost well over $200. Don't despair, there are many alternatives. Before you invest, ask your friends what they wear. Browse through sports shops and catalogs such as Patagonia and R.E.I. (see Resources). Keep an eye out for sales—search through thrift shops and tag sales. My rain suit was purchased in the hunting-clothes section of a sporting-goods store. Besides being very lightweight, waterproof, windproof, breathable, and quick drying, I was attracted by its color—its deep, dark green blends easily into the forests of the Northeast. On a hard hike it's a little hot, but then again, I get hot in anything but my undershirt anyway. For bird-watching, fishing, and camp wear, it's perfect.

Rain jackets should be cut large enough to fit over undergarments, giving you plenty of freedom of movement and allowing evaporation of moisture. An important feature to consider when purchasing a rain jacket is an underarm zipper. Protected from rain by the arms, this zipper allows greater flexibility in temperature control. Front zippers should be covered by a flap with snap or Velcro closures. If it is not raining hard you can just use the Velcro or snaps, affording greater ventilation. Sleeve closures are often snaps or Velcro strips, but one real plus for paddlers is the use of neoprene cuffs for a tighter seal. This is very helpful when you are portaging canoes or paddling kayaks. Anytime your arm is above your head, the water will slide down the canoe hull or paddle and run up your arm, hitting you in the pit. Ouch! Important: determine the use of your rain gear before you purchase.

The hood should move with your head and keep water off your face with a visor. Jackets should be hip length or just under the tips of your finger with your hand at your sides. Pockets offer a spot for your gear and a place to warm your hands. Kokatat rain gear lines their pockets with toasty pile for cold hands.

Rain pants can be waist length or bibs. The less expensive ones have ankle closures with few other features, but they are just fine for most activities. At their fanciest, rain pants have full leg zippers, making them easy to pull on over boots or shoes. Bibs offer a double layer of protection around your chest, helping to keep your core warm.

There is a saying on the trail, "If your feet are cold, put your hat on." It's true. Conversely, if you start perspiring too much, take your hat off. A hat is the first best heat regulator—not only does it keep your ears warm but it prevents heat loss as well. Wool hats are still standard for outdoor people but they are fast being replaced by pile. Patagonia makes a hat that is wool on the outside and Capilene on the inside. The Capilene wicks moisture away from your head and out into the air where it can evaporate.

Besides hats, headgear includes balaclavas and helmets, headbands, face masks, and neck gaiters. The balaclava is a one-piece garment that covers your head and neck and is ideal for really severe weather conditions. The face mask is extra protection for windy, snowy, extreme conditions. Headbands are great for winter sports where you produce a lot of heat and want to keep your ears warm but your head cool. Synchilla or wool/polypro blend headbands are perfect. Neck gaiters are great. Winter hiking and snowshoeing is a sport where one can become overheated quickly. If you're wearing polypro or Capilene underwear in cool weather, a neck gaiter can be that perfect touch, without adding a second layer. When you get too warm, simply pull the gaiter up over your ears like a headband. Pull it down around your neck again when you get chilled. I don't know why it is, but if my neck stays warm, I'm fine. Neck gaiters are underrated.

Even your hands are included in this layering system. Gloves and mittens are made of the same high-tech materials. Polypropylene, Thermax, and Capilene are used in liner gloves. Available in most colors, liner gloves are handy to use under mittens or gloves, adding warmth without bulk. If you are interested in taking pictures, thin liner gloves allow flexibility without your fingers freezing. Of course, there is no alternative to fuzzy warm mittens (with glove liners). But when your hands get too warm, wearing glove liners alone does the trick. At a rest stop, slip on the mittens again and you'll feel fine.

There, now you have all the basic information you'll ever need to know about dressing for the elements. Of course, weather conditions determine the clothing you'll wear but dressing properly for any weather conditions is simply learning how to layer appropriate fabrics to regulate your core body heat.

Now it's time for you to get outdoors. We can't stress enough that whatever you do, be good to yourself. Address your outdoor needs as you would those of your mate or your children. Some women only wear cast-offs from their spouse and children and while there is nothing wrong with that, making it a habit ignores the you whose style you want to develop—the physical you who's headed for adventure! You are important too!

CANOEING AND KAYAKING

It wasn't that I needed to get away, I needed to get to—to that wild, mountain country, to simplicity. I wanted to be lean and hard and brown and kind. I felt fat and soft and white and mean.
—*Audrey Sutherland*

At one time or another, almost every woman who reads this book has had similar thoughts. Many of us wonder how to "get to" that place in our heart. Some strap on a backpack and head for the hills, but others find a little boat to be the perfect vehicle.

If you have never paddled but have determined that paddling is a sport that you would like to know more about, networking within your community can turn up lots of ways to get started, and, best of all, networking is fun! All you need to do is to make contact with one person who knows about the sport. Through that contact you can reach out to find places to learn, people to paddle with, and water to paddle on. The paddling community is a wonderfully friendly group that is quick to offer advice and encouragement. Start by checking the activities listing in your local newspaper for outdoor groups. People who love the outdoors know others who do also and even if the one person you contact does not paddle, he or she more than likely knows someone who does or someone who knows someone who does.

Other leads include the bulletin board in your local sports shop, paddling schools and canoe race listings, the YMCA, or call your local American Red Cross office (they give lessons). Taking a paddling holiday—a canoe-camping vacation—affords the opportunity to meet others who have similar interests, receive instruction, and play around in various canoes and kayaks before you decide if paddling is the sport for you. Attend weekend symposiums such as the annual L.L. Bean

North American Canoe Symposium, where you have a chance to test-drive equipment, talk to other paddlers, attend lectures, and have fun. Write to the American Canoe Association (check Resource chapter) for information on paddler gatherings around the country.

After you have had the opportunity to try the sport and have determined that paddling is for you, the next step is to purchase your own equipment. This chapter will help identify the best possible first boat and accessories for you. Most people, if they haven't done much paddling, will find it very difficult to determine what the primary use of their craft will be, and, once recognized, that use may change. Sound confusing? Well, for instance, you may begin your search with flat-water paddling being your only goal and through the process discover that you're actually a wild white-water woman!

A canoe or a kayak is not only an investment in fun but an investment that, regardless of size, if taken care of, will hold its monetary value as well. Therefore, it is necessary to buy wisely and to take care of your craft. Luckily, most modern construction materials are so durable and problem-free that it is practically impossible to damage a boat enough to lessen its value.

YOUR CANOE AND YOU

When you think paddle sports, more than likely you think canoe so let's talk about canoes first. Canoes that have the greatest lasting value are those designed and built by established, reliable companies. While there is no hard-and-fast rule that says a new company can't design and manufacture a good product or that a general sporting-goods store doesn't sell good canoes, more than likely a specialty store is the place to shop. If this is your first canoe you'll need a specialty shop's expert advice in making your purchase. You'll also be able to try out a variety of canoes in the shop and that is absolutely crucial to getting the right fit—the proper model for *you*.

It used to be that canoes were sold in two colors—green and fake birch bark. Those colors are still produced but it's 1992, canoes are manufactured in every color of the rainbow, and specialty shops either carry those colors or know where to order them. You may see yourself paddling a pink, blue, white, or maybe even a custom-colored canoe—all available through a specialty shop. Not only will these shops help you choose the right canoe but they can fit you properly with a life jacket, a paddle, a car rack, and all the other necessary goodies.

Finding such a shop can be difficult in some areas of the country. Start by looking in the yellow pages under boats or sporting goods. Check your local newspaper for listings of canoe races; hang around the finish line after the race and ask the competitors where they shop. Or, if it's a large race, manufacturers and distributors may have booths, and boat demos may be in progress. I've been chased down on the highway by people who see the boat on top of my car and want to talk canoes—once by a state policeman with flashing lights and siren.

Another invaluable source of information is *Canoe Magazine* (see Periodicals in Resources). It's also on the newsstand—send for a copy of their *Buyer's Guide* (it can be worth the price of a subscription). After deciding which canoes interest you, write for catalogs, requesting the names of local dealers. Canoe factories are usually delighted to give information about demos and places to purchase their product.

Once you have located a shop, call and ask to speak with someone who knows about the type of canoeing that interests you. Sometimes white-water jocks or racers work in these shops and while they're great for information on racing, they usually have no idea about family paddling, camping, or canoe tripping. The first question a good salesman will ask is how you'll be using a canoe. Do your homework so you'll know the answer.

General recreation is a broad classification but one worth considering. It might include paddling local flat-water streams with two or more people in the canoe, taking short camping trips, or car-topping it to a paddling vacation. You may even want a canoe for fishing. Will you be doing any white water? Will you be racing? Answers to these questions will influence your choice. Many people say that they will only be doing "easy stuff," but a shallow easy stream with a rocky bed will do more bottom damage than a deeper, faster-moving one with fewer rocks near the surface. Trips that last a week or more in mixed conditions require a tough hull, but if you'll be doing long portages, a lighter-weight craft is best.

A canoe test-drive will probably occur on your second visit to the store. By then you've checked out various models and pored over catalog information and options. Don't be intimidated—even a complete novice can get a lot out of an on-water boat trial. As a beginner, ask the salesperson to paddle with you at first. A good salesperson is prepared to teach you the strokes needed to test-drive the canoe. Set your test-drive for a time when you will not be rushed; Saturday afternoons aren't good.

One of the biggest reasons why you haven't seen more women paddling their own canoes is that they can't get the darn things on and off the car! The *most important* prerequisite to choosing your own canoe is weight, so when shopping for a boat, pick it up and carry it around a bit. It's you who has to lift it on and off the car and over portage trails. A canoe that sits in the garage is less than useless.

Once out on the water, try paddling the canoe in a straight line. Eyeball an object on a far shore. Keeping it in view, paddle toward it. How much steering are you doing? Then gather some speed, stop paddling and lift the blade. A boat designed for flat water will go some distance before it starts to turn. A boat designed for white water will go no more than a boat length before it begins to spin on its own.

How easily does the canoe respond to paddle draw strokes? Can you pull it to the side? Will a slight lean away from the direction you want to turn make the boat spin easier? Can you make the hull move swiftly with little effort? To test tippiness, rock the boat gently from side to side. It should be easy to right once it's in the rocking motion. If you are lucky enough to test on a windy day, try paddling against the wind. The canoe should not seem hard to control.

One of my most memorable canoe experiences occurred years ago at the beginning of a week-long paddling trip. The outfitter sized up the group, issuing canoes, paddles, and life jackets. I was paddling solo and was given a 16-foot river canoe (which weighed a ton), and the first day out found me paddling across a lake into a stiff crosswind. I was blown all over the lake and spent the whole day struggling with compensating strokes, trying to make the canoe head in a straight line. It was a losing battle. To begin with, the canoe was not made for lake travel, and was too big (too long/too wide) for me to paddle solo. My hands were all banged up from trying to execute a decent stroke. (If you have to lean way out to place your paddle or if you have to angle the paddle, the boat is too wide. In that position the boat will automatically turn, necessitating constant correction strokes—an exhausting and nonproductive process.) By the end of the day I had charley horses as big as teacups on each shoulder and my back was killing me. The good part to this story is that the craft was wonderful for river travel, its depth and length great for poling, which is what I spent the rest of the week learning. So, it is important to determine the use of your canoe.

After trying and comparing several models, it will be fairly easy to make your decision. Remember, the salesperson knows that if you are happy with your choice you'll be back, seeking his/her advice on another canoe or to purchase more accessories. A proper first fit enhances that possibility.

PURCHASING YOUR CANOE

Now, let's get down to the business of buying your canoe. A good quality tandem canoe in fiberglass will cost between $600 and $900. At 16 feet, a perfect length for general tandem use, it will weigh 60 to 70 pounds. The same canoe made with Kevlar, at half the weight, will cost $1,200 to $1,500, but it weighs not much more than a sack of potatoes and is a lot easier to balance and carry.

Canoes are designed for specific uses and types of water conditions. If you will be paddling flat, protected water, you don't need a 15-inch deep hull, but for white water and tripping, that 15-depth will make things a lot dryer. If you want to do white water, a hull that turns easily is a lot more fun to paddle. For flat water or tripping, buying a hull that tracks so you don't always have to make correction strokes is a plus. The solo or tandem question is becoming easier to answer with hulls being designed to paddle both ways. Center seats allow paddling solo from that position and seats at the ends are used for tandem.

For your first purchase, consider the following specifications:

length: Tandem or solo: A 16- to 17-foot canoe is a good compromise between speed and weight.

width: A happy compromise is 35-inch to 36-inch width at the gunwale. Remember, however, that the width is measured in two spots—at the gunwale and at the 4-inch water line. The closer the two measures are, the more initial stability the hull will have. "The 4-inch water line," you ask, "What's that?" If you get into white-water paddling or long-distance paddling, you will need to know this information.

As an example: A pro-race boat is 33 inches at the gunwale and 27 inches at the 4-inch water line. A high-performance touring canoe is 33 inches at the gunwale and 31 inches at the 4-inch water line and a more casual craft is 35 inches at the gunwale and 33 inches at the 4-inch water line. The wider the boat at the 4-inch water line, the more stable the hull will be.

depth: Fifteen inches is as deep a hull as you will find in the 16-foot to 18-foot length. A deeper boat will give you greater carrying capacity but will also generate more windage.

keel line: The line along the center of the canoe from bow to stern is the keel line. The straighter the keel line, the less maneuverable the canoe will be. The only canoes that *need* an actual keel are aluminum—it holds the two halves together. Keels on all other canoes are purely cosmetic.

rocker: Rocker is the amount of distance between the flat surface and the up-turned ends of the boat. A canoe with a lot of rocker will look like a banana and turn on a dime. A hull without rocker requires more time and technique to turn.

bow and stern shape: Opt for a flare on the bow as well as on the stern. The flare causes the bow to lift when entering a wave and to lift in a following sea.

cross section: While a flat-bottom canoe may have greater initial stability, once the canoe starts to roll, caused by a wave, motorboat wake, or motion of a passenger, the canoe has very little secondary stability and rolls neatly over. In a quality canoe, the most common shapes are the shallow arch and the shallow or rounded V. Both of these shapes will return easily back into place even if it is rolled almost on edge.

shape above water: Tumblehome is a rolling-in of the gunwale. While it allows paddling closer to the canoe, it does hurt seaworthiness. Sides that go straight up are a good compromise. A flared side will keep more water out of the boat but makes paddling more difficult.

trim: Aluminum, plastic, vinyl, or wood is fine for trim, depending on how much time you are willing to spend on upkeep. If you choose a wood trim, opt for ash. It's durable and takes bangs and scuffs well and can be finished with varnish or treated with a penetrating oil.

Possible Choices

The Wenonah Solo Plus at 31 pounds makes a great triple-seat boat. The Mad River Malicite at 48 pounds has a bit more carrying capacity. The Jensen 17 can have a solo seat in the center and weighs in the 40-pound range.

The Mad River Explorer at 16 feet is designed for flat and white water. In its lightest lay-up it weighs 50 pounds. Old Town's 12-foot Pack weighs in at 33 pounds—ideal for solo paddling.

Materials

Royalex: Made by Uniroyal, Royalex is a sandwich of plastic layers. Once formed into a canoe hull it holds its shape during stress. The hull will tear under extreme force but that seldom happens. The main problem is weight at 65 pounds or more for a 16-footer.

Cross-linked Polyethylene: Old Town uses this material in its Discovery Series. It is less expensive but very heavy.

FRP (Fiber Reinforced Plastic): Fiberglass is a generic material that can be used in various ways. In its strongest and lightest state, it is a cloth. In its weakest and heaviest form it is chopped glass particles soaked with resin and shot into a mold.

Kevlar 49: The lightest canoes are made of this DuPont lightweight and strong fabric. The only drawback is price—the most expensive.

Spectra: An Allied Chemical product that is equal to Kevlar in strength, weight, and price.

If you are concerned about weight, consider Kevlar or Spectra. For price and durability, try Royalex and polyethylene. Fiberglass hulls fall somewhere in between in price, weight, and strength.

PADDLES

There is enough variety in canoe paddles to write another chapter, but we can cover the basics here. One of the mistakes paddlers frequently make is to buy a $1,500 canoe and try to paddle it with an $8 paddle. Outwardly it may not appear so, but there is a difference in paddle quality.

Paddles come in two styles, straight shaft and bent shaft. The straight-shaft paddle is the traditional style and made of everything from solid wood to carbon fiber and Kevlar. If a straight shaft is your choice, sizing it is relatively simple. Stand the paddle in front of you—it should reach from the floor to your chin. While this method of measurement is overly simplified, it gives you a pretty good idea of how long the paddle should be. There are often variables, i.e., shorter arms require a longer paddle to reach the water and paddling a high-sided boat may be more comfortable when using a longer paddle.

The theory is to get your blade buried in the water as soon as possible during the stroke—too short a paddle and you won't efficiently reach the water; too long and you are placed in a very inefficient paddling position, possibly straining your back and shoulders. With all the variables, you may well go through a number of paddles before arriving at the right one for you.

Bent-shaft paddles are a new phenomenon. Developed by Gene Jensen in the '70s for distance or marathon racing, they proved to be more efficient than the straight-shaft paddle for going in a straight line, but by the same token, not very efficient for maneuvering. Of course, the line you hear from paddlers is that since they don't race they don't need bent-shaft paddles. The fact is, bent shafts are easier on your body, your muscles, and your joints.

To determine the proper length of a bent-shaft paddle, stand the paddle in front of you. It should come up to your sternum.

Paddles come in many materials, the two extremes being wood and carbon fiber. Wood paddles are more flexible, possess natural beauty, and feel good in your hands, but they tend to be heavier than carbon-fiber paddles, which weigh as little as nine ounces. Carbon-fiber paddles tend to be very stiff and racers, in particular, find them tough on shoulders and arms if the going is hard. However, their light weight is great for touring since you don't have to push so hard on the shaft.

KAYAKS

Diversity is the name of the game in kayaks. You can find kayaks designed for white water, oceans, slow-moving rivers, and anywhere in between. Your use will dictate the kind of kayak you'll buy. Low volume, or high-performance kayaks are the sports cars of watercraft. They're designed to turn, spin on a dime, play in waves, and dance rapids with a flick of a well-placed paddle, but they carry no gear. On the other hand, while it has enjoyed wide popularity in Europe, the high-volume touring and sea kayak is a relatively new sight in North America. One reason why canoes have traditionally been used for touring in the U.S. is the kind of water in which we have chosen to paddle. For instance, the Boundary Waters in Minnesota or the canoe country of Northern Maine has many portages or carries, from lake to lake or around rapids or waterfalls. Kayaks are more difficult to portage and have less gear-storage space. However, now that we are starting to explore our coastlines, the touring or sea kayak is perfect.

Rotary molding revolutionized both the sea and white-water kayak industry, resulting in a more durable and affordable craft. The molding process is an interesting one. Originally kayaks were made by laying fiberglass cloth into two half molds. After the molds hardened, the two halves were fastened together. In the rotary molding process, the hull is made in one piece, creating a virtually indestructible craft.

The current flood of rotary-molded plastic kayaks come in various sizes, following no set of rules except that they paddle well. The kayak that has made white water accessible to so many paddlers is the Perception Dancer. The Dancer occupies the middle of the performance range in white-water kayaks. At one extreme is the squirt boat, a very low-volume craft designed to play in white water. In fact, squirt boats spend a lot of time under the water. Women are rarely seen squirt-boating, although since finesse and balance play such an important part in this relatively undiscovered variant, perhaps that will change. Risa Schmoda, a former U.S. World Kayak team member squirt-boats.

At the other end of this white-water spectrum is the steep creek boat, a very short (11 feet or less), blunt craft that is easily maneuverable and designed for very narrow and steep rivers and streams.

Now let's talk about open-water kayaks, commonly referred to as sea or ocean kayaks, that are appropiate for lakes as well as slow-moving rivers. But what makes a sea kayak different from a white-water kayak? Manufactured in the same diversity of materials, using the same manufacturing methods, white-water kayaks are designed to turn and spin while sea kayaks are designed to track, to go in a straight line.

Sea kayak models are available in solo or tandem models. Tandem kayaks are longer, up to 20 feet, and are perfect for carrying cargo. Another positive feature is that while paddling in separate boats one paddler might quickly outdistance the other, in a tandem, two paddlers of unequal strength can easily paddle together. Whether to paddle a solo or a tandem is a difficult choice because paddling solo, whether in a canoe or a kayak, is such a joyful experience. Once you step into your own little boat, even if you're paddling with a group, you have that self-contained feeling—it's just you and your boat and the water and you're off on a wonderful adventure, an adventure you can choose to share with fellow paddlers or one to keep as yours alone.

As with the canoe, there is no question that you must try different styles of kayaks in order to experience what a tippy or a stable hull feels like. When you shop for a kayak, adapt the canoe test-drive described earlier in this chapter, and whether you opt for a sleek and quick or a wide and slow boat, there are some things you should look for.

> *Deck lines:* You must have a place to tuck a pump, attach a compass, and carry a map or chart. Deck lines are also necessary for self-rescue in the event of capsize.
>
> *Cockpit:* Make sure you are comfortable getting in and out of the boat. Make sure that the seat is customized to fit you. There's a lot of difference in the way kayaks feel, both in paddling and in the way they fit your body. While seats can be padded to help with fit, it is important to get one as comfortable as possible to start with. The seats are plastic so you may need to add padding to seat bottoms and sides for comfort. This padding helps to keep you in the boat when you are being pushed around by waves and surf. Don't gulp, we know you'll try it sooner or later so you may as well get a proper seat.
>
> *Bulkheads or air bags:* Unlike canoes, kayaks won't float by themselves. You must add air in bags or behind bulkheads. In many sea kayaks, bulkheads are used to create watertight sections at the ends of the kayak. These are accessible using hatches in the decks that also accommodate gear.

In addition, a kayak requires a spray skirt, custom-designed for each individual boat. Manufactured of nylon or neoprene, the skirt fits very snugly over the cockpit, keeping out water and spray.

Kayaking Gear

For white-water paddling and playing in breaking ocean surf, a helmet is also a necessity and should be snug fitting and comfortable, protecting your temples.

You can use your regular outdoor rain gear (see What Am I Going to Wear?) for canoeing, but many kayakers choose specialized rain gear because of its neoprene neck and sleeve closures.

Dry suits have become standard gear for kayakers, particularly in cold-water areas. A dry suit is made of waterproof nylon or Gore-Tex, with tight latex cuffs and collar. The problem with dry suits is that you must add insulation underneath. Gauge that layer by how much heat you produce, how hard you work, and how cold the temperature is. Too little insulation and you will be cold; too much and you will perspire too much and be uncomfortable. The only way to determine what you should wear under a dry suit is practice—trying different combinations to determine what is right for you.

One of the best undergarments for a dry suit is a full-length pile suit with a front zipper. Separate tops and bottoms tend to split at the waist, leaving a cold gap as you paddle. The full suit alleviates that problem. For colder conditions you can add other insulation layers that we discussed in the What Am I Going to Wear? chapter. Dry suits by Kokatat and Stolquist have become standards in this sport, but there are many others from which to choose.

Wet suits made of neoprene are also used for cold weather and water protection. Several companies offer wet suits designed specifically for paddling. They include reinforced knees and are generally sleeveless, commonly referred to as Farmer Johns, for obvious reasons.

For hand covers we use the polypro glove liners and pogies for wind protection. Pogies deflect the spray and wind. When paddling in cold conditions you'll need a polypro or pile hat, balaclava, or neoprene helmet. The neoprene helmet will fit easily under a white-water helmet. Paddle jackets designed for sea kayaking usually have hoods. Some paddlers prefer a sou'easter hat.

Kayak paddles are "double-ended." The blades are turned at a 90-degree angle and are referred to as feathered blades. That angle allows you to push through wind and spray without resistance while pulling the other blade through the water. For sizing, stand the paddle up next to you and reach up. Your up-stretched fingers should just fit over the top of the blade. Sea-kayak paddles tend to be a little longer.

Paddle materials are wood or synthetic—fiberglass and carbon fiber. Sea-kayak and white-water paddles come in an array of blade shapes and styles. It is personal preference, but in sea kayaking the theory is that if you are paddling long distances, a thin blade is easier on your muscles.

Now, last but most important is—you're right—a life jacket! Don't leave home without it! Also known as PFDs (personal flotation devices), they come in zip-front and pullover styles. Both are category III and must be Coast Guard approved. Choose one that has flexible flotation panels that don't interfere with your paddle strokes. If possible, try paddling in your life jacket before you buy it; otherwise try some paddling movements in the store. Sit in a kayak to make sure the jacket doesn't hit the deck, rise up, and hit you in the chin. For fit, tighten the jacket and have someone stand behind you, grabbing the armholes and lifting. The jacket should not rise much at all. That test simulates what happens when you fall into the water. It is very difficult to swim with the life jacket up around your head.

OTHER SMALL BOATS

We've given you a lot of information about canoes and kayaks that are the "standard" for the industry but there are a couple of boats outside that realm that you may wish to check out. These boats are very accessible, relatively inexpensive, and are a great starting point—a way to launch yourself into paddling.

One alternative is the small, molded plastic kayak. Although many brands are available, including the Keowee from Aquaterra, we are familiar with the boat produced by Ann Dwyer, of Kiwi Kayak in Windsor, California. Back in the '70s while teaching paddling for the Red Cross in Marin County (she also founded the Canoe Sub-Committee for the Sierra Club National Outings), Ann found that the Kiwi was an easily manageable boat for beginning students, affording a perfect introduction to paddling. Impressed by the Kiwi's maneuverability, size, and weight, Ann refined the design and starting producing them herself. New models include the Kopapa, priced at $350, and the Q Star, slightly more expensive. When I met Ann in Buffalo, New York not too long ago she had a Kopapa tied to the roof of her rental car. Zipped into its own neat little traveling bag, the 8'8"-long, 33-pound kayak can be easily checked in as luggage on any airline. Ann says she never knows when she might want to paddle around in a little boat, so she never leaves home without it!

A friend recently purchased the Kopapa as her first boat. Now, after gaining paddling expertise, she's ready to move on to a more traditional kayak, but her Kopapa has maintained its value. On resale, she will not have lost a dime!

Another attractive feature of these small boats is their ease in storage. They are small enough to be stored in even the tiniest apartment. The folding kayak is perfect for the cramped apartment dweller who harbors visions of paddling off into the sunset. Originally designed in Germany, the Klepper Kayak has become a favorite throughout the world. It has been paddled on casual adventures as well as on major expeditions. The Klepper Aries II, a tandem model, has twice sailed across the Atlantic Ocean. That same model has also been paddled down raging white-water rapids in the Grand Canyon. Klepper also makes solo models. The glory of these folding boats is that they can be packed into several easy-to-carry bags, checked onto any airline, and upon arrival at your destination, can be easily assembled so you *can* paddle off into the sunset.

Feathercraft and Nautriaid also make folding models in both solo and tandem.

The inflatable boat offers another inexpensive way to enter paddle sports. Inflatables are relatively lightweight, inexpensive, and easily transportable on airlines, on horseback, and even by backpack. You will notice in the profile on Audrey Sutherland (in this chapter) that she is paddling an inflatable sea kayak. Audrey has logged 7,500 miles in 13 different inflatable boats but is pretty discouraged about the state of the inflatable market today. "There were more and better inflatable sea kayaks ten years ago," she says, "and there are more and better inflatable river kayaks now." Shopping for an inflatable can be a confusing, time-consuming process. We recommend that you read *The Inflatable Kayak Handbook* by Melinda Allan, a river guide from Oregon. This book will tell you what you need to know if your decision is to go the inflatable route.

TO BUY OR NOT TO BUY

With all this information you are now ready to shop for your very own boat. If you're still confused about what is the right boat for you, let us suggest that before opening your pocketbook you explore the following options. Renting affords the opportunity to try a few different styles, although rentals tend to be the lower-performance models. Another possibility is planning your vacation to include a commercial canoe or kayak trip or instructional program. Check the classifieds for used boats. Many people get excited about a sport, buy all the right equipment, and then end up storing their expensive gear in the garage after one season. Join an outdoor club—many include paddling programs. They almost always publish a newsletter that includes classifieds and frequently offer instruction. But, don't wait too long—no matter what boat and paddle you choose you'll become a better paddler, and most important, you'll have fun! Spending months trying to make up your mind is a waste of your valuable recreational time. As those ads say, *Just do it!*

Canoeing and kayaking are natural extensions to backpacking and camping. You can wear many of the same clothes and use the same camping gear. Boats can take you places that are inaccessible by foot—wild, remote places where few people go, places that you need to get to!

Profile: Audrey Sutherland

It isn't a question of can you or can't you, but of deciding what you really want to do, and then figuring how . . . and once you succeed, you know the true meaning of joy.

—Audrey Sutherland, "Profile,"
by Linda Daniel, published in
Sea Kayaker, *Spring 1988*

Take a close look at the boat in this photo. Neatly printed on the bow are the names of places Audrey Sutherland has paddled in this kayak, along with the mileage of each voyage: Hawaii, Alaska, and Norway. "I think the boat deserves its own log," she says.

Her motto: "Go simple, go solo, go now." Adhering to that motto, Audrey has logged over 7,000 miles, paddling in wild places around the world. But she didn't start out wanting to paddle; she started out wanting to explore.

Growing up in California with her parents and sisters, Audrey spent childhood summers in the backcountry building a cabin, exploring the forests and fields, and spending lots of time alone. Then, as a student at UCLA she learned to swim, "the most useful subject learned there," she wrote. "Water became my element. I delight in its color, its texture, the three-dimensional freedom of movement." Marrying a "seagoing man" she learned the fundamentals of sailing and seamanship, and together they ran their own commercial fishing boat.

Then happenstance found Audrey living in Hawaii in the '50s, working as a vocational counselor for the U.S. Army and raising four children alone. Feeling frazzled and frantic—two words with which we can all clearly identify—what she needed, she decided, was to "get to" some wild places, feed and soothe her soul. "I had learned as a child the joy of being alone, and I wanted that isolated country [back]," she wrote in *Paddling My Own Canoe*. It's interesting, isn't it, how in times of need, we can reach deep within, reconnect with and benefit from those experiences that gave us the most comfort and joy as a child.

The isolated country Audrey decided to get to was the northeast coast of Molokai. Like most of us committed to raising children and keeping home and hearth together, she was short on funds. Not owning a boat and with no money to charter one, her only means of access to Molokai, she decided, was swimming. By alternately hiking and swimming (towing her gear along in a jerry-rigged waterproof bag), Audrey would make her way along the coast. But it turned into a daunting experience. Repeatedly flung ashore by the breaking surf, she finally gave up and instead settled for exploring a small part of the island on foot, but not the part she so wanted to see.

In 1962 she tried again. More aware of what to expect, for this trip Audrey stiffened the jerry-rigged bag with a styrofoam shipping crate, rigged up a mast and simple sail, and planned to let the crate tow her around the coast. This swimming/sailing/towing technique was somewhat easier but still too slow and cumbersome. On the third trip she mail-ordered a six-foot inflatable boat to carry her gear but *she* was soon aboard, paddle in hand, the problem solved.

Molokai kept beckoning and Audrey kept going back. On each return she found new ways to make exploration easier, new ways to move in harmony with the ways of the sea and the land. "It was all trial and error," she said, "mostly error."

How did her children feel about her need to be alone? They understood "my wildcat need to go off alone for a while," Audrey wrote. Children deserve the right to be self-sufficient, she feels. They "need the opportunity now and then to be without [parents], to make their own decisions, to make their own mistakes and repair them."

A great believer in lists, Audrey keeps five-year lists and 25-year lists, of places to see, things to do. These lists are continually updated, prioritized, and costed out. Twenty years ago on a business trip, she flew over the isolated southeastern coast of Alaska, and, as with Molokai, decided it was a place she must "get to." She requested a two-month leave of absence from her job. It was denied. "I went home and looked at the list of things I wanted most to do, and at their priorities: paddle Alaska was number one. I walked into the bathroom and looked at the person in the mirror. "Getting older, aren't you, lady? Better do the physical things now, while you can."

The next day she handed in her resignation, and she spent that summer paddling 800 miles from Ketchikan to Skagway in Alaska. In her yet-to-be published book, *Paddling North,* Audrey wrote, "I would stand on shore and slowly turn around, trying to absorb the limitless distance. So much of my life had been limited by parameters of children, wifedom, jobs, cities, neighbors, friends, expectations. Now there were none, and the freedom was intense."

How does she afford this life of adventure? Audrey rents her house when away adventuring, receives small royalties on her books, collects a small pension, is paid transportation costs for symposia appearances, but most of all, she lives a life of spartan simplicity. Her time between trips is spent writing, carpentering on her house, drying and packaging gourmet meals for her next adventure, and haunting thrift shops for outdoor and camping gear. "Don't spend money on gear," she advises, "spend money on plane tickets to the places you want to see."

Does she ever feel lonely, going for weeks without seeing or speaking with others? Sometimes, but only briefly. "Daily we are on trial," she wrote in *Paddling My Own Canoe,* "to do a job, to make a marriage good, to find depth, serenity, and meaning in a complex, deteriorating world of politics, false values, and trivia. But rarely are we deeply challenged physically or alone. We rely on friends, on family,

Audrey Sutherland.

on a committee, on community agencies outside ourselves. To have actual survival, living or dying, depend upon our own ingenuity, skill or stamina—this is a core question we seldom face. We rarely find out if we like having only our own mind as company for days or weeks at a time. How many people have ever been totally isolated, ten miles from the nearest other human, for even two days?"

Does she ever get scared? "I go through all the what-ifs each day before launching, keep track of the wind and tide and always clip a shoulder harness onto the boat," Audrey says. "When you're alone you are more aware of surroundings, wary as an animal to danger. . . . Alone, you stand at night, alert, poised, hearing through ears and open mouth and fingertips."

What about animals? In Alaska, pods of killer whales approached her—one swam to within five feet to investigate her inflatable boat. "I dipped my paddle in the water so his sonar could determine where I was." In Hawaii she swam with a manta ray whose wingspan measured over ten feet, "He swam over and dove beneath me, so I dove down; then he turned on his back to look at me better, so I turned over too. It was a ballet," she wrote in *Paddling Hawai'i*. She has even come face to face with brown bears and wolves. "Animals that rely on scent seem to know I'm female, alone, no gun, no cubs—I'm not a threat. They regard me as another animal. We are wary, but we each go about our own business."

"Men and women are more alike than different," Audrey concludes. "Women, too, need to feel the coyote wildness, the pleasure of muscles moving in coordination, the sweat and the weariness, and the uncertainty of what the end to that effort will be."

Profile: Lynne Witte

Lynne Witte grew up on a Michigan farm. "We lived so far from town," says Lynne, "and always had after-school chores so my brothers and I didn't have a chance to participate in competitive sports in school. I have always loved to compete and feel that I probably missed out on a very positive experience. But there weren't many competitive sports available for girls at that time anyway," she adds.

As a kid, Lynne spent a lot of time with her family canoeing and camping, exploring Michigan's rivers and woods. That love of paddling, coupled with an intensely competitive spirit, makes her a real force in national-level canoe racing today.

During college in the '70s, Lynne started canoe racing with her brother. "I had seen the marathon and was fascinated by it," says Lynne. The marathon she is referring to is one of the longest and toughest canoe races in the country. Held in mid-July, the Ausable River Marathon starts at 9 P.M. and the fastest boats finish 14 or so hours later.

"In 1984, with friend Steve Landick, I entered that race and won the mixed class in record time—15 hours and 20 minutes." Lynne, who has been racing seriously since 1983, has broken that record four times since then, with 15 hours and four minutes being her fastest time.

"It is a difficult race," she adds. "During the night we paddle with headlights on our canoes. The Ausable has many twists and turns so it helps to really know the river. In that respect Michigan paddlers have a real advantage."

At 37, Lynne actually has two careers. She is an elementary school teacher, instructing first and second grades. She is also a committed outdoor woman. "I paddle all year round, which means in the winter, in the snow. We don't have a lot of freezing weather in southern Michigan so I try to get out and paddle at least three days a week." Weekends, she drives to local meets or gets together with other canoers.

"My goal is to paddle all the rivers in Michigan," Lynne says. "Off-season, when the rivers are empty—as long as it isn't sleeting—is a perfect time to explore."

Lynne and Steve Landick teamed up once again in 1991, but this time set their sights on the La Classique Race in Quebec, a professional canoe race that is a supreme test of endurance with 125 miles of racing over three days. The course includes long, windblown stretches of river with waves. In 1990 the wind was blowing so hard that some canoes sank at the starting line, before the gun went off.

This year's start was hardly less raucous. "The first day we did 90 miles on a very big river. The wind was behind us and became stronger as we paddled. It got to the point where we would surf on waves fast enough to bury the bow up to the bow paddler!"

In mixed boats (male and female paddlers), the woman paddles in the stern, assuming control of the canoe. Her partner sets the pace in the bow and does minor course corrections. The stern paddler calls the switches and handles most of the tactical decisions. Lynne and Steve won the mixed class and finished fifteenth overall out of 80 boats.

"Steve didn't feel like he was in top shape for a long race and we took it easy the first day. But as it turned out he was in great shape and we could have actually pushed harder and finished in a higher place." The race also includes several difficult portages (carries around unpaddlable obstacles). These portages are done at sprint speed, carrying the canoe on your shoulders. The best teams can run miles carrying the canoe at a five-minute-per-mile pace.

Lynne's season typically includes another long race, the General Clinton Regatta, a 70-mile, one-day event, held on the Susquehanna River each Memorial Day Weekend. Lynne has paddled it in both the pro-mixed and pro-women's division.

The Susquehanna River demands every paddle and boat handling skill. The race starts on a lake about a mile from the mouth of the river—60 or 70 canoes all start at once. You must sprint as hard as possible to be among the first into the river because a half mile farther on there is a portage with only a one-lane path around a dam and back to the river.

"We start off on a narrow stream with lots of current and difficult corners. After about four hours the river broadens and gradually becomes wider and more open. For added excitement there are two other portages and a broken dam to run. My partner and I won the pro-mixed race in 1991," she adds.

Lynne is multidimensional in her training, cross-training in the fall and winter. She loves cross-country skiing, so, you guessed it—she's

Lynne Witte (in the stern).

starting to race. Since her area doesn't get a consistent snow cover she uses roller skis and roller blades. "The cross-country stride gives you a great upper-body workout."

In the winter she also lifts weights. "It helps to keep and increase my strength. This year I intend to keep lifting during the racing season. I haven't done it before but after some experimentation this season I can see that it helps me maintain a high degree of strength."

What does she love most about canoeing? "What I really love about canoeing, besides being outdoors, is the fantastic competition and the camaraderie," she widely grins.

TAKING TO THE HILLS

I checked my watch. It was 2 A.M. Somewhere, in another world it seemed, two wolves howled their mournful pleas into the black night forest. My body tingled, every pore twitched alive. Tears cooled my face. I smiled, listened, waited breathlessly for the next howl, hoping the dialog would never end. I was blessed. Eavesdropping on this primal communication as it echoed through the misty old growth and floated into our lean-to on Russell Pond, there wasn't a more perfect spot on earth.

Ask ten people why they love backpacking and you'll get ten different answers. For me, backpacking is trekking out into the middle of the wilderness and living simply, quietly, and in harmony with earth for a week or more. It's the freedom of having everything I need on my back—of waking up with the sun, strapping on my pack, tramping till I'm tired, and resting with the rising moon. For some, a three-mile hike to a pond for a quiet overnight is sufficient. For others, nothing less than tramping the 2,000-mile Appalachian Trail, wandering over every major peak from Georgia to Maine, will do. But whether you go out for a weekend or a month, you'll carry essentially the same equipment— the only difference being the amount and weight of food you take. Whatever the length of your trek, equipment should be the lightest and best fitting possible.

Let's explore what you'll need to get out and onto your favorite trail. Whole books have been written on backpacking, many of which you'll find in the Bibliography. In this chapter we'll cover the two most important items you'll need—a backpack and hiking boots. Yet, probably more than any other outdoor equipment, backpacks and hiking boots are misfit. Why? One reason is that up until a few years ago, manufacturers did not make backpacks to fit women. They were sized to fit men. The frame was frequently too long, too wide, and too heavy for a woman's torso. The result: aching and burning shoulders and back problems. However, quality manufacturers now make backpacks sized for women, no matter what the salesperson tells you, there is no such thing as a unisex backpack. While many women can and do wear packs sized for men, the new gender-specific sizing has afforded more women the opportunity to take to the hills in comfort and safety.

SELECTING A PACK

So how do you select a pack? First of all, before you head for the store, determine what the pack will be used for. The season and the length of your trek will be a consideration. Packs used for a weekend camping trip would not be appropriate for a six-week jungle trek. Are you planning to summit McKinley? Then forget a pack suited for a week in the desert. "List all the features you are looking for, going from the general to the specific, and take it with you when you shop," suggests Jim Remza of CampTrails backpacks. You'll be surprised—this method culls out most of the packs before you're halfway through your list.

For day hikes you'll need a simple day pack. Just about any brand will do, there's no great mystery to choosing one—it's purely what strikes your fancy. Make sure the shoulder straps are comfortable and that the pack isn't too large for the job. There are very large packs sold as day packs but they are really weekend packs. Because winter hiking requires so much more gear (more clothes, water, ice axe, crampons, skis, ski poles, etc.) I use such a pack for winter hiking. But for the three other seasons of the year, carrying a larger pack is overkill. It's heavier to begin with and, as with my mother's purse, the larger the pack, the more *stuff* you load into it.

Backpacks are sold in two styles, internal frame and external frame. Both use framework of metal or plastic to help support the load. Kelty was the originator of the external-frame pack that remained the industry standard for years. For a while, in the '70s, external frames lost favor to the newer internal-frame packs, but they are regaining their status and lately are the pack of choice for many backpackers. You'll find that external-frame packs are perfect for trail hiking in open country, especially if you're carrying a heavy load. The external frame allows a variety of loading combinations, making it easier to rearrange cargo to correspond with your center of gravity. An exposed frame makes it easier to lash on odd-sized items such as tripods or fishing equipment. One of the things I find most appealing about this style pack is that it stands out, away from your back, allowing air to circulate between your pack and you. It may not seem like much but this feature makes a huge difference in comfort, summer or winter. Another attractive feature is that the pack stands up against rocks, lean-tos, etc., making it easier to find things.

On the other hand, if you'll be spending a lot of time bushwhacking through spruce stands or heavy undergrowth, rock climbing, skiing, or snowshoeing, internal-frame packs rate a second look. They don't get caught up on branches or other vegetation and allow arms and shoulders to move freely. The internal-frame pack travels close to your back and follows your moves in climbing, scrambling, and even skiing. For greater comfort, buy a breathable cover for the pad that rests on your back (sometimes called the lumbar pad). For proper fit, the stays that provide the upright pack support can be bent to your individual shape.

Both pack styles should have wide, adjustable, fully padded shoulder straps. On a woman's pack, the shoulder straps are placed closer together on the harness to allow for a narrow shoulder span (eliminating shoulder drag and back pain) but should curve out in the front for breast clearance.

A few years ago I bought a Lowe Regular "Backpacker." I'm 5'9" and weigh 135 pounds. After browsing through the selection of packs, the salesperson assured me that the "Backpacker" regular was my size, that I didn't need a small (he referred to a chart to determine that), and that through various strap adjustments the pack would fit perfectly. I tried the pack on in the store, packed it with a few items, and walked around a bit. It seemed all right. We loosened and tightened straps here and there, adjusted the Torso Trac Suspension System, and I was on my way. It took only one weekend trip to learn that facts are facts—the pack was too long and the shoulder straps were too far apart. It's a man's pack sized for a man's body length and shoulder width—a wonderful pack, but a man's pack. Consequently, after a few days on the trail my shoulders, back, and neck really suffered.

Mine is not an unusual experience. Some of us want to be on the trail so badly that we put up with the pain; others toss out the backpack and never venture out again. The fact is, packs are now made for women—we don't have to put up with poorly fitting packs anymore.

Look for a comfortable, well-padded, conical-cut hip belt that fits snugly around your pelvic area *without gaps.* I recently met a woman on the trail with an enormous pack hanging off her shoulders. She reminded me of Atlas holding up the world. She complained of pain and misery and damned her pack, but her problem was obvious to everyone but her. Her hip belt was just flapping in the breeze. A properly adjusted hip belt is crucial. That is the way your pack works— the frame moves the load from shoulders to hips, the stronger place to carry the load.

Most internal-frame packs have side straps, called compression straps, that enable you to condense the load, pulling it closer to your back for more stability. For easy gear access some packs have zippers, so you can open the bag lengthwise to get at gear in the bottom of the pack without taking everything else out through the top. You'll find this feature very handy. Side and top pockets put gear you need during the day—maps, water bottles, bug spray, or rainwear—within easy reach.

Pack carrying capacity is stated in cubic inches and women's packs generally range from 3,000 to 5,100 cubic inches. When fully packed it will probably weigh about 30 pounds. You can extend some packs with an internal cuff that adds almost 1,000 cubic inches to its carrying capacity.

External-frame packs list fewer cubic inches, but that's because the sleeping bag is carried on the outside of a external-frame pack and on the inside of an internal-frame pack. Sleeping bags fill quite a bit of space.

Whatever pack you decide upon, fit is extremely important. This is another area where the specialty shop shines. They will instruct you on how to adjust what may seem like a confusing array of straps, buckles, and snaps. If the shop offers rental packs, you might want to try out a couple on the trail before you make a purchase. Better yet, if you have friends who backpack, test their packs on short trips.

Many quality manufacturers make packs sized for women. Camp Trails produces Night Song, an ideal pack for women 5'4" and under. Mountain Systems markets their line in components, called Interlink System. You choose the frame, pack, and harness (shoulder pads and hip belt) that are best for you. The top pocket detaches to become a fanny pack—very useful for little side trips. Kelty's packs for women are called Radical Light, Track Pack, and Trekker. Lowe's sells the Women's Outback. A group of caretakers (men and women) at the Appalachian Mountain Club's backcountry shelters in the White Mountains in New Hampshire recently tested some packs for *Backpacker* magazine. Receiving good reviews as packs for women are: L.L. Bean's external-frame Expedition pack (one woman caretaker had carried this pack for 500 miles on the AT) and Vaude's internal-frame Leka. There are many manufacturers out there that make good packs, some well known, others not. Do your homework, take your time, and, most important, don't settle for something that doesn't fit.

Camp Trails' Skipper encourages the kids to get in on the fun. This small pack has a well-padded suspension system that protects a child's developing bones and muscles. There are even packs made to carry infants and toddlers on the trail. Long-distance hiker Cindy Ross recently hiked the 58-mile Loyalsock Trail in Pennsylvania toting four-month-old daughter Sierra on her back. If you're the parent of an infant or small child, *Backpacking with Babies and Small Children* by Goldie Silverman may be of interest (see Bibliography). The recent plethora of new technology enables the whole family to enjoy backpacking and hiking together.

WHAT TO PACK

Loading your pack is an art in itself. As you become more experienced you'll learn to think like a backpacker—less is best. In the extreme, backpackers cut the handles off toothbrushes and the little tags off tea bags. As a rule of thumb, aim for a weight limit of 25 to 30 pounds total. That includes your pack. Although it's tempting, you simply can't bring everything; you must decide what will do double and even triple duty on the trail. The first time I went backpacking I carefully loaded everything I thought I'd need into the pack, then couldn't lift the darn thing off the ground. It weighed a ton! Luckily, a friend who had trekking experience stopped in to say goodbye, spotted my dilemma, and gave me some good advice and instruction on packing. Only take what you *need.* Simplicity is why you're heading into the woods, remember?

The number-one reason for overweight packs is food. Food is

heavy and most of us take too much of it. Deciding what is light, nutritious, and delicious is a complicated process and there are books devoted to the subject. Don't get discouraged, it often takes more than a couple of pack trips to determine what you really need and want to eat, how to cook it quickly, and how to make cleanup efficient. Consult some good backpacking cookbooks such as *The Well-Fed Backpacker; Gorp, Glop & Glue Stew; Supermarket Backpacker; Cooking for Camp and Trail;* and *The Trekking Chef.* These books not only supply recipes but give interesting stories, nutrition information, and food drying and packaging techniques and menus. The *Supermarket Backpacker* even gives brand names with recipes. Although almost anything tastes great when you're outdoors, ending your trekking day with a delicious meal goes a long way towards keeping spirits high and your body functioning well.

To save weight in clothing, layering is the technique to perfect. Layering means using a combination of light layers so you can add or subtract a layer when the weather throws you a curve. Browse through the What Am I Going to Wear? chapter—it will give you the basics. Only through actual experience can you determine what layers you need to maintain your core heat and keep you comfortable. Let's look at clothing requirements for a weekend backpacking trip into the mountains. The following is a list of some things you might consider packing:

Rain jacket and pants: A rain jacket can double as a parka or a windbreaker. Some folks prefer a poncho to rain gear, and while it's true that a poncho is less expensive and it can cover you and your pack, if you're hiking through forested areas a flapping poncho only catches on branches and twigs. In the mountains especially, you must be prepared for all kinds of weather and widely varying temperatures, so consider a rain jacket and pants or rain chaps.

Hat: A brimmed hat to keep the sun off your face can do double duty by helping to keep you dry in the rain. It's amazing what a difference the brim makes in keeping driving rain off your face.

Warm knit hat: "If your feet are cold, put on a hat." A knit or Synchilla hat is the perfect heat regulator. Even in the summer, mountain weather can be extremely variable so a knit hat resides in my pack year round. Since I prefer to sleep outside rather than in a tent, I usually end up wearing a hat to bed. It looks pretty silly and you wake up in the morning with the worst "hat head" you ever saw, but if you're all zipped inside a tent, how can you hear a beaver tail slap the water or really appreciate the starry show nature puts on every night? Speaking of starry shows, I'd like to share this story with you: One night while camping on an Adirondack lake I woke up with a jolt. I thought someone was standing over me, shining a huge spotlight in my face. It was the moon. In all its late summer glory, a perfectly full August moon was shining directly on my face, as if saying, "Wake up. The night is for wonder." I sat up and looked around. There were millions of low-slung stars filling every inch of a perfectly clear night sky, all twinkling and reflecting off the glassy lake surface. I felt like the Little Prince or like I was sitting inside a Christmas tree, peeping out through the light-laden branches. I, a tiny little speck in the universe, sat at the center of this spectacle, in wonder, in grace.

Shorts: A pair of shorts that allow free leg movement for walking and climbing.

Pants: Many women hike in tights, but for colder conditions and for around camp, consider a pair of pile pants. They're really cozy and warm, especially if it's misty and damp, and they're great to sleep in. The only problem with pile is that it tends to be bulky and sometimes difficult to pack. If you prefer regular pants, a pair of rain pants with medium- to expedition-weight long johns underneath would work, doing double duty as pants and sleepwear, saving the weight of extra clothes.

Gloves: Warm hands are important for cold-weather comfort. A friend always wears leather gloves, which, by the way, are a great help for handling hot pots when cooking.

Camp shoes: Nothing feels better than getting out of your hiking boots at the end of the day. A lightweight pair of moccasins, down booties, or sandals and clean socks feel wonderful after a day of pounding the trails.

You'll also need two or three pair of socks (wool preferred), a T-shirt, a turtleneck (polypro or Capilene), a wool sweater, a change of underwear, and sunglasses. I always stuff my down vest in the pack. It is easy to pack and, believe it or not, the vest and a hat go a long way in keeping you warm. (Consult Packing List at the back of the book for other items you may need. Only through experience will you be able to put together a list that is tailor-made for you.)

Try very hard to keep one insulation layer for sleeping, in-tent, and camp wear. That sometimes means changing into slightly damp clothes in the morning to start hiking, but you'll have dry garments to put on at night when you are no longer generating heat. In a dry climate, attach wet gear to your backpack and they'll dry quickly in the sun. In wetter weather conditions you might consider taking your *slightly damp* clothes into your sleeping bag. If they aren't too wet they will be dry by morning.

HOW TO LOAD A PACK

Loading a pack takes practice, so if this is the first time for you, don't get discouraged. The first thing you do is lay out on the floor all the items you have gathered. See if there is anything you can discard. Then determine what you will use frequently—water bottles, Chapstick, toilet paper, rain gear, sweater, camera, maps, matches, flashlight— and put those items in outside pockets.

Next, line your backpack with a plastic garbage bag. Even the best backpacks are not entirely waterproof. If you have an internal-frame pack, the sleeping bag goes on the bottom. Then progressively pack light- to medium- to heavyweight items into the bag. Roll up your clothes and pack them tightly together. Make sure you pack heavy items high up and close to your back. That way the heavy items stay closest to your center of balance and won't pull you out of center. Distribute heavy items evenly so you'll be balanced. Pack your tent on top. The only way to know what we're talking about is to experiment and determine what is most comfortable for you. Once you hit on a comfortable load setup, use the same system each time—you'll always know right where everything is.

Carole Latimer of Outdoor Woman's School–Call of the Wild says she purposely uses a larger-than-usual stuff sack for her sleeping bag. At the beginning of the day she packs the clothes she will wear around camp that night—camp shoes, clean pair of socks, wool hat, and bedclothes—into the stuff sack along with her sleeping bag. When she arrives tired and hungry at the campsite at night no time is wasted in rummaging around in her pack. A helpful hint, don't you think?

HIKING BOOTS

Hiking boots are another major and necessary purchase if you intend to carry much weight on your back. They protect your feet from tough trail surfaces and keep your ankles from getting banged, twisted, and otherwise abused.

Boot fit is critical. Women's feet have a specific profile with narrower heel, wider ball, and a higher instep. Some boot companies build boots on women's lasts or forms; others expect you to fit into

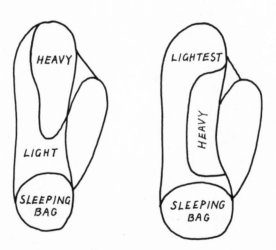

How to pack a pack: Always pack your sleeping bag in the bottom of the pack. Heavy items should be placed against your back—high if you're trail walking, low (for balance) if you're off-trail. Pack clothing around the rest of your items—that way they won't shift. Items you need during the day should be placed on top in the backpack itself or in the outside pockets. Odd-sized items can be lashed onto the outside of your pack with compression straps.

small men's or boy's sizes. Don't be talked into unisex boots—they seldom fit correctly. Contrary to what you're told, they will not break in! It's 1992 and manufacturers are cashing in on the women's market. Merrell, Vasque, Hi-Tec, Timberland, Dunham, Technica, Nike, and Raichle all make great boots for women. *Outside* and *Backpacker* magazines publish a footwear buyers guide once a year, reporting tests on just about every available outdoor shoe. Go to your local library and read those issues before you head for the store.

For short day hikes, athletic shoes or low hiking shoes work well. Although they cushion the bottom of the foot, they won't keep you from banging anklebones. These lightweight shoes are a pleasure to walk in, require little or no break-in time, and make good in-camp shoes. Ankle-high leather boots provide the most protection and cushioning and are most suitable for pack trips. They provide stability, comfort, and support when you're carrying a heavy pack and are the warmest and most practical for cooler weather. The new Gore-Tex and leather-top boots offer a good compromise. They are lightweight, supportive, and require little or no break-in period—perfect for day hikes or short weekend backpacking trips where you carry a lightweight backpack.

Look for a boot that holds your foot so it doesn't slide forward, causing your toes to bang against the end of the boot when going downhill. Lace the boot up in the store and tap the toe box lightly on the floor. Your toe should not hit the front of the boot. If it does, the boot is either too short or you haven't laced it properly. The boot must also hold your heel firmly so it won't lift, causing blisters as you climb. You need room to wiggle your toes, particularly in cold weather. That space allows for extra socks but also traps warm air, keeping your feet warm.

TENTS

I'm not going to talk a lot about tents. My advice is to buy the lightest-weight tent you can find. I bought a two-person, four-season Moss tent—you know, tents made by little old ladies in Maine. It's a wonderful tent for canoe camping, but a mistake for backpacking! I rarely need a tent and when I do, I only need a one-person tent. Unless you hike regularly with another person, buy a one-person tent. It is smaller and cozier and most of all *it's lighter.* The components of a two-person tent can be divided up and carried by two people, but if you are hiking alone or are tenting alone with a group, you simply don't need that extra space and weight. Before buying a tent (and they are very expensive), determine its use. Do you need a four-season tent? If you only backpack in the summer, a little pup tent with a rain fly might do. In any case, buy light.

OTHER NECESSITIES

One other item that is a worthwhile investment—not expensive and very handy—is a pack cover. It saves your pack and its contents in pouring rain. There are few things more discouraging than arriving at campsite with a soggy sleeping bag and wet clothes, especially when it could be avoided.

The most important item to take with you on the trail is a good attitude. You may possess the best and most perfect-fitting equipment in the world, but what will make your trip satisfying and memorable depends on you. The trick to backpacking is in your head. It's how you approach the outdoors. Or, more appropriately, it's how you attune to the outdoors. Just being outside, exposed to the weather, insects, and sometimes hard work, is often stressful and not always fun. But expect that. Do you know your physical self? Most women don't. How many of us know our strengths? Living outdoors will put you in touch with parts of yourself that you may not have known existed. I know it has me. You'll be amazed at how much you innately know. Sounds, smells, skills that you weren't aware of before. Ancient and long dormant genes come alive. Don't go outdoors expecting to be miserable or you will be. Conversely, if you expect to have a good time, you will.

If you've never been backpacking you may wonder how one begins. One of my favorite words comes to mind—networking. Learn the ropes with a friend or a group that has backpacking experience, or take a backpacking vacation (see Sporting Organizations in Resources). More often than not, hiking leads to backpacking, so go where the hikers are. Join a hiking or outdoor club. The nationwide Sierra Club may be a good place to start. There are hundreds of local and regional outdoor clubs around the country. Check the activities columns in your local newspaper. Hikers are a friendly bunch and you'll meet others on hikes who have the same interests as you. Don't be intimidated—we were all beginners once. Just follow the rule of low impact, walk softly, and have fun. You'll come home a new woman!

Profile: Cindy Ross

"It used to be that Todd and I would put in 25-mile days," says Cindy Ross, reflecting on her new role as parent. "But keeping that pace isn't that important to us anymore. Our friends warned us that a baby would change our lives. We expected changes but were determined not to give up hiking and our love of the outdoors. Taking Sierra on the trail is a lot of extra work, but as we watch her discover the texture of a pinecone or caw a response to ravens in the trees, we know that there is life after long-distance hiking."

Cindy was bitten a long time ago by the long-distance bug. Growing up along the Appalachian Trail in Pennsylvania, she often wondered "where it went." She was 15 and "hanging out along the trail with some friends" when they met a through-hiker. "He was tall and bearded," said Cindy, "and in a hurry. We asked him how far he'd come. Not slowing his pace one bit, he called back over his shoulder, 'Georgia,' and kept on walking, wet socks dangling from the back of his pack. That one word—Georgia—was all it took. I was hooked. It could be done—here was the proof. I started making plans."

It took only a few years for those plans to jell. After high school, Cindy enrolled in art school in Philadelphia, but the lure of the trail remained. Finally, unable to stand the city any longer, she left school and, with a friend, took off for Springer Mountain, Georgia to begin her quest. Their journey lasted all of two weeks. Cindy's friend quit, and as a self-described extrovert, Cindy found it difficult to hike alone. "I hiked fast, probably to get away from myself," she says in retrospect. That fast pace sent Cindy back home with a stress-fractured foot. But after a two-week recovery in the care of her family, she was back on the trail again, a little wiser in the process.

Cindy points out that although hiking alone can be difficult, even the company of a partner can be stressful. "You can't get away from each other," she says. "You depend on one another for support, companionship, entertainment, and help. It's difficult to be outdoors for

Cindy Ross: *Photo courtesy of Reading Eagle Company, R. Taylor Goetz.*

long periods of time and not see the people you care about." Many fail because they get bored and know little of what awaits them on the trail; others become lonely and depressed. Of the 1,000 that start the AT each year, probably fewer than 100 complete it.

Then what makes long-distance hiking so appealing? "It is a lifestyle," Cindy explains, "a different way of living. And once you've experienced it, you get hooked and want that experience again. It gets into your bones. There is a freedom you feel when you spend each night in a new and different place. It's like being a 12-year-old all over again. Simply put, you become addicted to walking."

After completing the AT, Cindy set her sights on the 2,600-mile Pacific Crest Trail, running the length of the West Coast. Taking a break from the PCT and returning to Pennsylvania for an Appalachian Long Distance Hikers conference, she met Todd Gladfelter, who had also done part of the PCT. After recovering from a broken foot he joined Cindy and they finished the trail together. Their adventure is recounted in her book, *Journey on the Crest.*

So is it any wonder that Cindy and Todd were itchy to introduce their four-month-old daughter to the joys of hiking? For their first hike they chose the 58-mile Loyalsock Trail in northern Pennsylvania. The Loyalsock crosses roads at various points so there were plenty of bailing-out points in case of emergency. Preparing for the trip, Cindy and Todd purchased a three-person tent and a baby backpack. They decided that Cindy would pack Sierra and a few other items, for a total weight of about 45 pounds. Todd was left with the brunt of the load, 65 pounds in all. Traveling with an infant, they determined the worst-case scenario and then planned for it. Interviewed in *Outdoor Woman,* Cindy said, "Our worst situation while hiking with Sierra would have been constant rain." Heavy rain would mean waiting it out in the tent and any rain would have meant setting up the tent every hour or so for Sierra to nurse. But they were lucky—it didn't rain at all.

Cindy and Todd planned the trip carefully. To make sure Sierra felt comfortable riding in the pack, they toted her around in it while doing household chores and mowing the lawn. She grew to love it. The next crucial aspect to the hike was making sure they had enough diapers. Before the trip they drove to the halfway point near the trail and buried three five-gallon buckets of diapers under some leaves, along with a sign saying, "These are for a couple backpacking with a baby—please don't touch." They allocated 15–20 diapers per day and packed a four-day supply. At night they would string up a line at campsite, rinse the soiled diapers, and hang them up to dry.

As it turns out, they completed the trail in five and a half days, rather than the eight they had planned, and had fun doing it! Cindy and Todd were surprised at how easily they fell into a routine and how quickly their priorities changed. Sierra was happy riding in the pack for an hour or so at a time, and they stopped every two hours to feed her. Instead of a fast pace, they were happy to keep Sierra warm and dry and happy. "If Sierra was happy for two hours straight, we were happy," Ross says in *Outdoor Woman.* "Everything was a gift!"

Cindy and Todd live in a log cabin they built near the AT and make their living on "spin-offs of [their] experiences." Cindy writes a regular column for *Backpacker* magazine and contributes to several others, and the two teach backpacking skills at a local college, give lectures on the outdoors, and are writing a book on "living simply." They are expecting their second child soon.

While Cindy is the first to say that long-distance hiking isn't for everyone, she firmly believes that it changed her life. "When I stood on top of Mount Katahdin and ran my finger in the routed wooden sign that read 'Springer Mountain, Georgia, 2,100 miles,' I realized that through hard work and belief in myself, I could make any dream come true. All it takes is a strong passion and a lot of perseverance. I had often wondered where my limits were or if I had any. Standing on top of that mountain made me think not."

Their plans for the future? As soon as Sierra can walk they plan to start hiking the Continental Divide, a section at a time—the whole family—every August till they finish.

WALKING

Better believe that it's a time for walkin—no time for talkin—
Grab the walking shoes that hang in the closet and go out for a
   walk in the air.
Breathe it all in and be glad to be there.
Smell the greenness—out goes the meanness—
Hey, look around, see the sun everywhere—just fly!
              —From "Walking Shoes," a song
                written by Gerry Mulligan,
                Bobby Troup, and Mel Tormé

Every time I hear Cleo Laine's sumptuous voice sing these lyrics I break into a silly grin, my spirits soar, and I feel like heading out of the house for a long brisk "walk in the air." That's just what happens when you walk. Walking lifts your spirits—somehow things look better after a brisk walk in the air—and walking puts a smile all over your face. Walking has been the most natural form of movement since human-kind rose up on two feet. Yes, even if you've spent the past 20 years glued to a chair, once you get out there and start moving along, arms swinging naturally, shoulders back, head held high, parts of you will come alive that you haven't been in touch with for years. After walking a while, it will almost seem as if your legs have a life of their own.

No fitness activity is more accessible than walking. It doesn't require a special room or place; you can walk just about anywhere at any time. Our favorite walking and running spot is a 3,000-acre wildlife refuge full of wild turkeys, flocks of ducks, geese, and whitetail deer. Walking is also a great time for talking. Unfortunately, we live in a hectic world and lead busy lives. Conversation is fast becoming a lost art. Walking with friends is a great time to catch up, to have a good talk.

WALKING AND TALKING

It is true, you know, that walking and talking go hand in hand. Following spinal surgery, a therapist we know had been concerned about sitting with patients for extended periods of time. So on her first day back at the office she asked her patient if he would mind walking during the session, explaining that it was difficult for her to sit for an hour at a time, but that walking for the hour was not a problem. "It opened a whole new realm of possibilities," says the therapist. "I discovered that my patients find it much easier to walk and talk at the same time. If you stop to think about it, sitting across from one person for a sustained period of time, seldom breaking eye contact, is a stressful situation. Walking, on the other hand," adds the therapist, "allows us to meet on a more even basis and encourages the patient to talk more freely. Now I meet with most of my patients on a walking basis. There is something about being outdoors and the easy, balanced, rotating movements of walking that frees one's mind."

GETTING IN SHAPE

You don't have to be athletic or even be in great shape to walk, but if you've been without an exercise routine for a while and have "gone to seed," a great place to start reclaiming your body is by walking. However, we cannot stress strongly enough that the number-one step to entering any exercise program, especially if you have led a sedentary life, is a visit to your physician for a thorough checkup. Walking in any form raises the heart rate and, depending on your physical condition, can possibly stress your body.

Even if you've never thought of yourself as an athlete, power walking is an easy entry into the world of athletics. While walking can be an excellent and thoroughly enjoyable sport in itself, there is no form of exercise that is more of a launching pad into self-propelled sports such as running, racewalking, hiking, backpacking, cycling, or cross-country and downhill skiing than walking. Although walking in any form is certainly better than not walking at all, in this chapter we'll focus on two types of walking—power walking and racewalking. The difference between power walking and racewalking is one of style. Racewalking is a particular stride, a learned technique that we will discuss later. Unlike leisure walking, power walking is a fitness-building tool, an aerobic exercise. The purpose of aerobic exercise is to increase heart and lung capacity and efficiency. To gain the maximum aerobic benefits from any exercise, adequate speed must be maintained to support an elevated heart rate over an extended period of time. Power walking is a perfect cardiovascular conditioning tool. While strengthening your heart (a muscle like any other), power walking also effectively reduces body fat; firms and tones muscles; lowers blood pressure; raises HDL cholesterol (the good kind), combating heart disease; increases circulation of oxygen to the brain; and releases endorphines (naturally occurring tranquilizers), providing overall positive feelings which help to eliminate stress.

A leisurely stroll is relaxing and certainly deserves a place in our lives, but leisure walking doesn't improve physical conditioning to any great extent. To achieve physical conditioning you must be aggressive while walking, swinging your arms as you hustle along. Interviewed in *USA Today,* Dr. James Rippe of the Rockport Walking Institute offered this advice: Walk "as if you are trying to catch a bus." One good test of whether you're achieving optimum speed is the ability to carry on a conversation while walking fast. Don't be so out of breath (anerobic) that you can't talk, but work hard enough so that you can *just* talk and walk—then you're walking at a good clip; you're doing it right!

Targeting Your Heart Rate

Another way to determine your most efficient training level is by calculating your target heart rate, that level of heart rate where the most effective and safest level of conditioning occurs. First find your resting heart rate. Before getting out of bed in the morning for the next three or four days, count the number of heartbeats by placing the fingertips against the inner wrist or on the side of your neck (the carotid artery) and count the pulse for 6 seconds. Average that number to find your resting heart rate. Now multiply that number by ten to determine your heart rate for one minute.

Use the chart on the next page to establish your target heart rate.

Research results from the Institute for Aerobics Research in Dallas showed that:

1. Walking a mile in 12 minutes provides the same healthy results as jogging a mile in nine minutes.

Nomogram for Target Heart Rate from Resting Pulse and Age

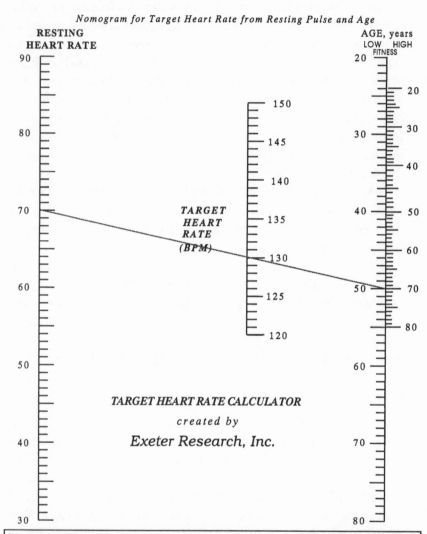

TARGET HEART RATE CALCULATOR

created by

Exeter Research, Inc.

This chart makes it simple for you to find your target heart rate. Just draw a line between your age on the right hand axis and your resting heart rate on the left hand axis. The point where that line crosses the middle axis is your target heart rate. You will notice that there are two sets of numbers on the age axis. One is for people who don't exercise regularly and have low fitness. The "HIGH" ages on the right side are for people who exercise regularly and would be considered fit. This chart allows you to compute target heart rate in the most accurate manner short of extensive laboratory measurements. E.G. a 50 yr old of "low" fitness and with a resting heart rate of 70 would have target heart rate of 130 BPM.

Establishing target heart rate.

2. Walking four m.p.h. to five m.p.h. increases cardiorespiratory fitness by more than 15 percent—the same rate as running or jogging but with less stress on joints and feet.
3. Walking at any speed increases HDL blood cholesterol (the so-called "good" cholesterol).

Make It a Habit

Embarking on an exercise program is similar to establishing healthy eating habits: once it becomes routine, it becomes part of your life. If weight loss is a concern, power walking can be a real enhancement to any dieting program—pounds fall off faster and stay off longer. One success builds on another and once physically fit, you'll become more aware of diet and how it effects your athletic performance. Women tell us that achieving even the slightest degree of athletic success inspires them to maintain or increase their potential, and for that reason it's not unusual to see a complete change in nutritional habits, as well as in life-style.

Regardless of what you're told, while it is easy to begin an exercise program, it is not easy to maintain it. Often we set goals for ourselves that are just too difficult to achieve. Just as often we overdo the routine, causing stress or pain to joints and muscles and, in agony, we give up. To begin any program, set realistic goals for yourself—not the goals of some famous athlete or those of your best friend or those that you have perhaps read in some magazine, but goals that fit you and your particular life-style. It's hard not to think of yourself as inadequate if you fail to maintain the exercise regimen that you set up for yourself, so start out small and increase to your goal in tiny increments. If your friends work out on Saturday morning and Saturday morning in your house means taxiing the kids to some place or other, unless you are part of a team, don't include Saturday in your routine—you'll feel bad if the kids have no chauffeur and you'll feel bad if you don't maintain your routine.

If you're a beginner it's hard, but after a few weeks of sticking to a simple routine you will gain self-assurance, increase strength, start to develop muscle tone, and begin to feel really great—quickly building confidence to go further. But be easy on yourself—don't expect miracles overnight.

Another way to enhance your chances of success is to walk with a partner. It's more difficult to skip a session when you're obligated to work out with someone else. Still another way is to keep a log book. Available through most sports catalogs or book stores, log books are fun and provide an opportunity to view your athletic progress over time—almost like your own sports journal. Looking back through them, at all you've gradually accomplished, will make you feel good. It is one thing to think back over your achievements but quite another to see them in black and white.

Kick off your fitness routine by finding a safe and enjoyable place to walk, preferably away from traffic. It's difficult to concentrate on walking and keep your eye on fast-moving vehicles at the same time.

Start training by walking *time,* not distance. For example, walk around the block as fast as you can for 20 minutes. If you haven't exercised in a long time and 20 minutes is too arduous, walk for ten minutes or however long you can walk in comfort. Increase the walking time gradually (over days or weeks) until you're doing 20 minutes, three days a week. Believe it or not, power walking for 20 minutes, three days a week will achieve a minimum level of fitness. We bet walking will make you feel so good that you won't stop at three days a week!

There are three ways to increase your fitness level: walk a longer distance, walk faster over the same distance, or walk more frequently. Whichever method you choose, after you've built a fitness base, try to plan one extended workout a week. For instance, a friend of ours power walks four miles every morning but one morning each week she walks five miles. It adds a little extra training time but not so much that she overdoes it. Extending workout time in this manner acts like building blocks—it destroys preconceived limitations of how far you can go and of what you can do, a little at a time.

At the same time, though, it's important to recognize when you are physically tired. There is a big difference between mental and physical exhaustion. Sometimes, after a particularly trying day, you may want to just go home, sit in a comfortable chair, put your feet up, and forget about the world—and about exercise. On those days, though, it may pay to push yourself. It has been proven that a brisk walk dissolves stress, replacing it with a sense of well-being. Occasionally, though, you may be physically tired and your body really does need to sit in a comfortable chair and just relax. The most important aspect to your training is to know when to take that time off, to not compare yourself to the condition or progress of others, but instead to follow and gain satisfaction from your own exercise program. Again, many well-intentioned exercise programs are scrapped because of unrealistic expectations—trying to do too much in too short a time.

Weather Or Not

Depending on weather conditions, the clothing required for walking is not technical, is inexpensive, and might include a pair of shorts and a T-shirt or, in colder weather, a sweatshirt and Lycra tights, or perhaps a wind suit. The current fitness craze allows you to dress with the flash that matches your personality. Serious walkers walk in any weather. Look through the What Am I Going to Wear? chapter for information about fabrics for keeping warm and dry, allowing you to get out on chilly as well as rainy days. There is nothing quite as invigorating as a brisk walk on a still, chilly morning with the sun glistening off frosty trees and listening to a downy woodpecker "Buddy Rich" its way through the neighborhood.

Toning Up

Walking is a great way to firm and tone leg muscles and buttocks but it is not as effective for arms, back, shoulders, and stomach. Light weights called Heavy Hands, when worked aggressively, can help tone upper arms and shoulders. Another possibility for a total workout is to use your cross-country ski poles in an activity called speed hiking. Cross-country skiers have used this method of training for years. You can use poles on any forest trail, swinging your arms the same way you would if you were skiing. It works particularly well on uphill sections where you can go at it with an aggressive style.

The glory of walking is that you can walk anywhere and the only gear you *really* need is a decent pair of shoes. Walking is the perfect exercise. A treadmill at the health club may give you a more controlled workout, but you won't find any of the little adventures that happen on your neighborhood street or on a path through the local park.

SELECTING SHOES

When woman first rose up on two feet, those feet walked on soft grass-covered trails and paths. Those feet were never meant to walk on hard surfaces, and therefore need proper cushioning and support. Pavement can damage joints, particularly knees, but good shoes help alleviate those problems. In a recent survey by the National Sporting Goods Association (NSGA), women comprised 63.9 percent of fitness walkers. As testimony to the number of women who participate in the sport there are at least a dozen brands of excellent quality walking shoes, built on a woman's last and available in countless styles and colors. *Walking Magazine* and *Runners World* magazine both publish outstanding buyers guides and are worth the price of a subscription.

Now, shopping for shoes. Don't shop in a department store for walking shoes—go to an athletic shoe store. There are scores of good athletic shoe stores around the country, among which are Fleet Feet (owned by a woman triathlete), Athlete's Foot, and Woman's Foot Locker. If you live in an area where athletic shoe stores are not available, try a catalog such as *Walk USA* or *Road Runner Sports, Women's Edition* (see Resources). Proper-fitting walking shoes grip your feet comfortably without pinching and hold the heel so it won't pull up, creating friction and causing blisters. Make sure you have ample room in the toe box, especially important on downhills when your feet want to slide forward and jam into the toe box. Is there a difference between walking shoes and running shoes? Well, the answer is yes and no. There are shoes designed specifically for walking, and some designed specifically for running.

The main difference between walking shoes and running shoes is heel cushioning. In power or racewalking the heel suffers the greatest impact and needs the most cushioning. Walking shoes are marketed with a particular emphasis on shock absorbing, beveled heels. However, I wouldn't get too hung up on whether to buy walking or running shoes. In actuality, good running shoes possess many of the same features as good walking shoes.

Shoes are constructed of various materials, including those with leather tops that are easily waterproofed for damp conditions or those with cloth uppers for breathability on steamy days, when your feet can become overpoweringly hot. Good walking shoes should feel practically weightless, possess good flexibility, and feel almost as if you were wearing slippers on your feet.

RACEWALKING

What often happens with power walkers is that after gaining confidence and speed they feel that there must be something more to the sport. And there is . . . running and racewalking. It's fun, after getting in shape, not only to test yourself against others, but to join with others in sharing athletic experiences—the real camaraderie of the sport. Now, since you already know the essentials of power walking, racewalking is just a step away and a heck of a lot of fun.

After building aerobic capacity and developing confidence in your athletic abilities, learning the racewalking style will be second nature. The most fantastic thing about racewalking is that you really do achieve an almost total body workout. The single most important element to speed is strike rate. Unlike running, the rules of racewalking require that instead of increasing your stride, you must take more steps to cover the same distance. If you've ever noticed Olympic racewalkers, their legs and feet move so fast they almost look like eggbeaters. Those increased muscular contractions burn more calories than running. Also, unlike running, in racewalking your upper body is swinging aggressively from side to side in cadence with your legs, burning even more calories and working those shoulder, chest, and arm muscles hard. If you suffer from premenstrual tension, including backaches, I have found that these circular hip movements relieve that tension, as well as water retention and pelvic cramps.

Last year, during a very stressful time in my life, I started running, but rather than relieving stress, running seemed to compound it—my body just didn't feel good. To make matters worse, while running in a local 5K race, someone eased past me—walking! Well, she was actually racewalking—sort of a combination of running and walking. What was fascinating was that her body movements seemed completely exaggerated: hips and arms seemed to be going in all directions, but unlike running, her feet barely left the ground. And unlike me, her face wasn't red and she wasn't even breathing hard!

After the race, I caught up with that woman and found out where to learn her style. Now racewalking has turned out to be one of the most pleasurable sports I know.

There are two rules to racewalking:

1. One foot must be in contact with the ground at all times, unlike running where both feet leave the ground. In an actual race, loss of contact with the ground is called "lifting" and is a cause of disqualification.

2. The leading or supporting leg must be momentarily straightened as your torso moves over it. If the leg is not straightened, this is called "bent knee" and also causes disqualification.

This all sounds confusing and it is until you catch on—then it isn't at all!

Recently, an article appeared in a woman's fitness magazine suggesting that one could learn to racewalk in an hour or so. Don't believe it! You may be able intellectually to grasp the fundamentals in an hour or so, but it takes weeks of practice to perfect the style. In fact, it took me six weeks to begin to really catch on to the particular stride—to get everything moving in the same direction at the same time. I was becoming very frustrated with my apparent lack of progression until a man I met on the track told me that even after racewalking for six years, some days it takes him a mile or so to really find the pace. A racewalking instructor told us that beginners shouldn't expect immediate results—that catching on to the racewalking technique takes time and plenty of patience. Lesson Number One: Go easy on yourself!

Videos are a great way to "see" what the technique looks like. Take a look at *Racewalking Technique* by Martin Rudow or *Racewalking: A Lifetime Sport* by Viisha Sedlak. Both are excellent and each presents the sport from a slightly different angle. Rudow focuses on imitating specific body movements as a way of learning the technique and Sedlak focuses on visualization as a training device. Both are worth watching. There are also a number of very good books available on the sport. Send a self-addressed, stamped envelope for a free bibliography of racewalking books and videos recommended by *Walking Magazine*. (Check Periodicals in Resources.)

To begin racewalking, stand erect but relaxed, and lean slightly forward from the feet—at more or less a 5-degree angle. When I started to racewalk I let my hips, instead of my shoulders, lead the way. This caused a slight slouching, depressing the diaphragm, which not only made it difficult to breathe deeply but restricted hip movement as well.

The peculiar stride that you see in racewalkers is caused by the combination of hip action, straight leg, and a rolling foot. As you step forward with a straightened leg, heel to ground, your weight will naturally transfer to that hip. As that leg passes under your body, it must remain straight. All the while you'll be rolling along the outer edge of that foot and finally pushing off with the ball of that foot and your toes, the big toe being the last part of you that leaves the ground.

In the meantime, the opposite leg (the bent leg) will be moving into the heel-down position, ready to straighten and take the body weight. That opposite hip will have dropped and moved forward. Only after visualizing my hip and leg functioning as one unit, moving as a whole, was I able to master this hip movement. The hips should not move from side to side (that's wasted movement) but instead should drop and move forward at the same time.

This sounds very confusing, we know, and is actually so unnatural to our normal stride that it does take practice but it will get easier, so don't give up!

Arms should be held at a 90-degree angle at all times with a relaxed fist, and swung aggressively more back than forward. A good rule of thumb is that at the full extension of your backward arm swing, your fist should be slightly behind you. The right arm swings forward to counterbalance the left leg, just as the left arm counterbalances the right leg. Howard Jacobson, author of *Racewalk to Fitness,* suggests that you envision a "T" drawn on the front of your shirt, one line at nipple height and one line straight down the sternum. As you move your arms forward they should not swing higher than the nipple line nor farther across than the center line. Also, don't allow your arms to flap from side to side. Rather, sweep them along the edge of your waist as they go forward and back. Correct arm movement is an important component of propulsion.

Another problem that I encountered at the beginning was sore shins. Ten minutes into a walk my shins would feel like they were strapped with hot steel bands. Luckily, a fellow racewalker assured me that this is not an unusual occurrence and that racewalking utilizes those muscles on the front of the shin that are rarely exercised. World

Masters Racewalk Champion Viisha Sedlak wrote that one cause for sore shins is tensed toes. "Make sure that you relax your foot after the push off," she says, "so that the toes drop downward to let the muscles in the shin rest. If your shins become sore as you walk, you are probably not letting those toes point toward the ground as the trailing leg moves forward in anticipation of your next step. The constant strain of holding your toes up will overstress those shin muscles."

7–DAY WALKABOUT
45 Minutes

10 minute warmup walk and stretching
10 minute cooldown walk and stretching

PLUS

Monday:	10 min. FOOT FOCUS: Lift toes each step and press ground with ball of foot as foot passes under you. 15 min. brisk walk
Tuesday:	10 min. ARM FOCUS: Bend elbows with forearm slightly above elbow. As you walk, arm swing is 8–10″ in front, straight back to line of buttocks. 15 min. brisk walk
Wednesday:	25 min. brisk walk
Thursday:	10 min. BREATHING FOCUS: Concentrate on exhaling quickly every fourth step; then every fifth step; then every sixth step. You will inhale automatically. 15 min. brisk walk
Friday:	10 min. FOOT FOCUS, as Monday
Sat. or Sun.:	25 min. brisk walk, raising arms and toes Relax. Have fun.

Walkabouts–North American Racewalking Foundation
P.O. Box 50312, Pasadena, CA 9115-0312 (815) 577-2264

The fact is that racewalking utilizes all the leg muscles. Running, on the other hand, works the hamstrings, the muscles on the back of the leg, and very little effort is placed on the quadriceps which are located on the front of the leg. For that reason, runners often have a muscular imbalance and are much more susceptible to injury than racewalkers. Also for that reason, racewalkers develop an all-around firmer leg than a runner. By the same token, those muscles surrounding your shin are rarely used, but in racewalking their constant exercise builds a well-defined leg. Because of muscle-contraction intensity in the racewalking process, the buttocks also tone and firm quickly and appreciably.

Perhaps the most important muscles to work (besides the heart muscles) are the abdominals. This is something you'll really have to concentrate on. Don't let your abdominals remain relaxed. Instead, use them for torso support. While maintaining the slightly forward lean, utilizing abdominals relieves strain on the lower back and allows your body to relax.

Howard Jacobson wrote in *Racewalk to Fitness,* "Don't look down to see if you are walking correctly. Instead, feel it from within. Concentrate on the muscular actions involved." Viisha Sedlak counsels the same thing and teaches the technique through visualization. In her video, Viisha presents the front shoulders of a trotting horse as a perfect example of the rolling and dropping forward motion necessary to racewalk. In yoga, we had been working on visualizing the function of our hips and how they operate as a perfect ball-and-socket joint. I was able to transfer that image to master the hip's forward thrust. If you are able to visualize the process, or visualize how your muscles move on the bones or how the bones and joints really work, rather than simply insisting that your body copy what you think it should be doing, after some practice those motions will become natural and free-flowing.

In any self-propelled sport good deep and even breathing is essential. Our muscles require oxygenated blood to function smoothly and continuously. The most efficient method of breathing for any aerobic sport is diaphragmatic (or belly) breathing. That means your belly expands on the inhale and flattens (closing the diaphragm) on the exhale. Believe it or not, if you learn this method of breathing, you will not suffer "stitches" in your side and will develop a steady breathing pattern enabling you to race along without appearing to be breathing hard at all.

If I had to do it all over again I would follow a training program similar to that proposed by the American Racewalk Association, espe-

Reprinted with permission, American Racewalk Association © 1988, Viisha Sedlak.

CORRECT RACEWALKING TECHNIQUE

1. Maintain good posture.
2. Reach out with straightened leading leg.
3. Arms move in a relaxed manner, elbows maintaining a right (90) angle.
4. Heel lands first as the leg strides forward.
5. By rule (in competition) weight-bearing leg must be straight at the knee as the leg moves under the hip.
6. By rule, one foot must have contact with the ground before the other foot loses contact.
7. Hip follows movement (forward) of the leg.
8. Head moves smoothly; no bouncing or bobbing.
9. Hips do not swing side-to-side.
10. Body weight "sinks" into supporting hip with each step.
11. Work on technique rather than speed.
12. Practice makes perfect.

cially in the beginning. A training program allows you to develop your conditioning and technique gradually with the least amount of stress and pain, making success almost inevitable.

Another alternative is to attend a camp. At larger athletic camps racewalking is often a part of the curriculum. The American Racewalk Association conducts clinics, lectures, and group walks around the country. Many running clubs have racewalking arms. Racewalking is becoming so popular around the country that very possibly there may be a racewalking group in your area. Check your local newspaper for clinics and seminars.

The only other advice we can give you regarding racewalking is, as a beginner, don't expect to perfect every aspect of the technique at once. Practicing one movement at a time is plenty. For instance, as a beginner, some days I worked on just the foot roll and some days just the arm swings, and on other days just the hips. To master the components of the racewalking technique takes time, practice, and most of all, *patience!*

While we haven't discussed running at all in this chapter, running is also a very natural and wonderful extension to walking. In fact, when you get into the groove in racewalking—when you hit your stride—and your body movements are flowing, you'll feel so strong and powerful and so good that it will be all you can do not to break into a run. And some of you may do just that!

It makes no difference what kind of foot exercise you do—power walking, racewalking, or running—a wise woman athlete will follow the rules suggested by the Road Runners Club of America:

1. Carry identification or write your name, phone number, and blood type on the inside sole of your running shoe. Include any medical information. Don't wear jewelry.
2. Carry a quarter for a phone call.
3. Run [or walk] with a partner.
4. Write down or leave word of the direction of your run [or walk]. Tell friends and family of your favorite running routes.
5. Run [or walk] in familiar areas. In unfamiliar areas contact a local RRCA club or running store. Know where the telephones are, or open businesses and stores. Alter your route pattern.
6. Always stay alert. The more aware you are, the less vulnerable you are.
7. Avoid unpopulated areas, deserted streets, and overgrown trails. Especially avoid unlit areas at night. Run [or walk] clear of parked cars or bushes.
8. Don't wear headsets. Use your ears to be aware of your surroundings.
9. Ignore verbal harassment. Use discretion in acknowledging strangers. Look directly at others and be observant, but keep your distance and keep moving.
10. Run [or walk] against traffic so you can observe approaching automobiles.

11. Wear reflective material if you must run [or walk] before dawn or after dark.
12. Use your intuition. React and avoid a person or an area if you feel unsure.
13. Carry a whistle or other noisemaker.
14. Call police immediately if something happens to you or someone else, or if you notice anything out of the ordinary.

And follow Cleo Laine's advice: "Grab the walking shoes that hang in the closet and go out for a walk in the air. Hey, look around, see the sun everywhere—just fly!"

Profile: Alice Thurau—Trail Runner

One might think that a champion ultra-runner with a background in biology and nutrition would have a secret to building a high-perform-ance body—that the strength and stamina she musters up to carry her through 100-mile races is the direct result of a special training schedule and diet. Not so. "I'm very unscientific in my training," claims Alice Thurau. "I don't have a schedule each week of what I plan to accom-plish. I just sort of run the way I feel. I really don't do speed work—like on a track."

A vegetarian, Alice doesn't eat meat, fish, or chicken, but she does occasionally eat eggs and cheese and drinks milk. "There are a handful of runners at the top who are vegetarians," she says. "A well-balanced vegetarian diet is, I think, the right way to go." Alice cautions, however, that while a balanced vegetarian diet can be high in carbohydrates, it can also be potentially low in iron so she says that women runners especially "should always supplement this kind of diet with iron." Her favorite cookbook: *Jane Brody's Good Food Book*.

Ultra-running is running distances longer than a marathon—dis-tances anywhere from 50 to 100 miles or more. The Leadville 100 is considered one of the ultimate challenges for the ultra-runner. Held in Colorado, this race covers 100 miles of roads and trails, climbing from 9,000 to 12,000 feet and back down again. In 1991 Alice Thurau came in seventh out of 300 people—the first woman to finish in the race.

Alice didn't grow up wanting to be a long-distance runner. It was by accident, actually, that she discovered she liked running at all. "Growing up surrounded by brothers," she said, "I developed a real

competitive spirit—I was a real tomboy. As it turns out, competing with
brothers was great training for ultra-running where most of the runners
are men." In college Alice wasn't attracted to any of the usual sports,
but to fulfill a requirement she signed up for a jogging class. "The class
turned out to be all women and when we ran laps I was the fastest. The
coach always pushed me the hardest and at one point she even suggested that I 'run with the men.' I guess, in a way, that extra attention
validated my talents, but at that time, my head just wasn't into sports."

Alice Thurau: *Photo courtesy of*
W. Keith Moore.

With the hectic pace of graduate school, Alice left running behind. But while living with a houseful of fellow students, she met two bikers who really "whetted [her] interest in biking." After graduation, burned out and needing to get away, she bought a bike and about a month later was on the road across country, by herself.

Alice started running again when she met her husband Keith Hileman, an ultra-runner. Beginning with some road running, she progressed through a 10K, then a marathon, and gradually over a period of two to three years worked up to long-distance running. What makes long-distance running and long-distance biking so attractive? "It is different, you might even say quirky," muses Alice. "I really love being self-propelled and don't mind doing things for several days or weeks on my own." Long-distance sports demand the same strengths—extra stamina and the ability to function for long periods of time outside the routine.

Alice and Keith have taken their running a step further—they run mountain trails. "Running trails requires total concentration on your footing. While some trails are smooth, pine needle-covered paths, on others you have to jump from rock to rock or over roots. It's a real challenge."

There are other benefits to trail running as well. "When racing on trails," says Alice, "if you're having a bad stretch you can just stop and catch your breath. With no audience, there's a sort of privacy . . . you can walk for a while and not feel the pressure from people around you. The diversity of terrain helps break up the race. Most of the races aren't pure trails anyway but a mixture of trails, dirt roads, and even some pavement. In road races you see packs of runners staying together for long distances. "In trail running," she points out, "even though we start in a group, that group quickly breaks up, so in some respects it is almost as if you are running alone."

Another reason for Thurau's and Hileman's attraction to trail running is where they live. In mountainous western Pennsylvania, surrounded by logging roads and trails, they've chosen a simple life-style that accommodates their sport. "Keith built a house with lots of windows and wood—just perfect for this forest setting. We can just step out of our house and disappear into the wilderness for six to ten miles. Trail running is sort of an extension of our home—it is peaceful and private."

Their life-style changed somewhat about three years ago with the birth of their first child. "I think parental responsibilities have helped me to put discipline into my running," said Alice. "I have much less time to run now, so when the opportunity presents itself I know I have to go and do it. I was just getting into ultra-running when I had Sarah, and I have to say she hasn't really stopped me from progressing in the sport at all. We include her in our racing schedule and she really enjoys being part of the scene. I think she thinks every parent runs."

Alice also thinks that what attracts her to running might attract other women as well. "You can run anywhere. Even if you have a busy schedule you can find time to do your sport. The Baby Jogger helps me. In fact, it has been the key to my getting back in shape after the birth of Sarah. I can run and Sarah can get her nap."

Most of the time Alice runs alone but once a week she gets together with a friend to do 18 to 24 miles. What makes this unusual is that her friend is a woman. "We started this routine when Sarah was an infant. Up until that time I hadn't had any close women friends in this area." Since ultra-running attracts mostly men, Alice finds this running relationship quite different. "It is funny, we can run for three hours together and it's nonstop talking. We don't pay attention to the running, we are talking—about our lives and our families and our relationships with our husbands and—it's almost therapy."

Ultra-runners are an especially friendly group, Alice says. "On the trail everyone is treated equally, male or female, but competition is definitely present. I'd venture to say that the majority of ultra-runners are running the distance to test their own endurance, to be with fellow runners, and to enjoy the scenery. The universe of ultra-runners is relatively small so there's a lot of socializing—pre-race dinner, often camping, a post-race awards get-together, and a general lounging around with new and old friends and acquaintances made on the trail. In contrast, at 10Ks and marathons you arrive, run the race, and go home."

Alice's advice to beginning runners: "Start off slowly—go easy on yourself—don't expect fast times . . . just give it a go and develop over the course of years. And go to some races! Experience the joy and camaraderie! Always remember, not everybody can win and even winners sometimes lose."

Profile: Valerie Meyer

"My mother always called me the 'bridesmaid' because it seemed that I was always a manager of some team or other and never a player," says Valerie Meyer. Although she played some intramural sports in high school and really enjoyed the team dynamics, "I was never what you'd call *athletic,*" she says.

But three years ago Valerie changed all that. She not only found a sport that she loves but lost 35 pounds as well. Valerie was 30 years old, overweight (5'8" and 190 pounds), had high blood pressure, and was asthmatic. "I had never been on a diet before," she says, "and actually couldn't stand the thought of it. Every woman talks about diets and I was afraid of slipping into that trap so I made a pact with myself that I would go on a diet only once—lose the weight and keep it off."

Valerie started a diet and started running at a local inside track. "Racewalkers in our area used that track to train. They would pass me on the track and their body movements seemed all funny but they seemed to be covering more ground than I did with far less stress. I decided to give it a try. Imitating their movements, I found that race-walking gave me the sense of speed without the stress of running. And the racers were great. They would pass me on the track and offer hints and encouragement. Now anytime I see anybody trying the sport I try to offer encouragement also."

Learning the technique was not easy, though, and Valerie, like many of us, suffered from painful shins. "I'm the biggest sissy in the world," she said, "but I was determined. I had found something that made me feel good and that I was good at." She attended clinics and joined a racewalking club and started participating in the races, first in 5 and then in 10Ks. In three years Valerie has progressed from being last in the pack to being first or second. "We have one nationally ranked runner in our area," she says, "and I usually come in behind her. In a race where national racers are invited, I usually come in around eleventh. I like the improvement.

"But it's pretty exciting to win even in small races," she adds. "I'd never experienced that before in sports. The consistency of going out and doing well—it gives me a real boost. And it's fun to talk about it with people at the office. They ask me about it and say that although they wouldn't do it they can relate to winning."

Valerie Meyer.

It took Valerie two years to really feel comfortable with the technique and now she trains five or six miles a day at an 11-minute a mile pace and does up to nine miles on the weekends. Sometimes she just goes to the track and does speed work—sprints and intervals. "I compete because it keeps me motivated to train," Valerie added. "I do about 20 races a year. In the process I have met a friendly group of people who accept you regardless of your abilities."

To Valerie, the camaraderie of the racers is the real prize. "But races also offer me the opportunity to see how much I've improved," she says. "In training you never do as good as you possibly can but racing stretches you closer to your potential."

Healthwise, not only has Valerie lost 35 pounds and a few dress sizes, but her blood pressure and cholesterol counts are lower, too. Her husband is the cook in the family and Valerie describes him as being "extremely cooperative." Eliminating items like butter and salt, they plan the menu together now and put a lot of thought into what's best for both of them.

Learning to breathe diaphragmatically has improved her asthma, too. "Through racewalking I have learned to breathe in an even rhythm. It's very important in racing to get steady, deep breaths. It was hard to learn in the beginning and I used to get terrible stitches, but now it just comes naturally."

Valerie feels that the psychological benefits of the sport are great. "Not only do I feel fitter physically but mentally as well," she says. "Because of the training, I have more energy to do other things. I may feel tired after a workout but it's a good physical tired and I still feel mentally able to tackle other projects in the evening—such as quilting. That gives me confidence and I feel good about myself."

Valerie's advice to others: "You can feel fit from doing a little or a lot. You don't have to be into racing to realize good results. Racewalking at any level is a good training and fitness routine."

"I really didn't have a major goal when I entered this sport. I just wanted to enjoy its many aspects, such as the camaraderie, meeting new people, and my constant improvement. From the beginning I thought, 'Oh, this is something I'm good at.' Even now, I don't have either short- or long-term goals. There may be some days that I can't get out at all and I don't want to have to worry about it—then the goal overtakes you. I like to be able to say at the end of the day, 'Today I've accomplished what I set out to do.' So I do one day at a time. I know it's a corny expression, but it works for me."

SAILING

At long last, women are taking the helm! Traditionally dominated by men, the blue-blood sport of sailing is slowly being altered by women who are claiming their place in this thrilling world of strategy and finesse. Despite what we have been led to believe, sailing rewards brains, balance, agility, and finesse, not just brute strength. Since the strength of women in sports lies in brains, balance, agility, and finesse, we're taking to sailing like ducks take to water!

Women's sailing events and competitions are springing up all across the United States and—guess what?—they're even beginning to draw corporate sponsors! Witness the Rolex International Women's Keelboat Championships, held each September in Newport, Rhode Island. In 1991 this race drew 48 skippers representing nine countries, all racing J/24 Class sloops. With a crew of ten women, Skipper Nance Frank has mounted a challenge in the corporate-sponsored 1993 Whitbread Round the World Race, a 33,000-mile event with stops in the United States, Australia, New Zealand, and South America.

Offshore sailing/racing, a thrilling extreme of the sport, is not new to women. In 1991, Frenchwoman Isabelle Austissier placed seventh overall in the BOC Singlehanded Round the World Race, becoming the first woman to race solo around the world. Tania Aebi recently completed a two-year solo circumnavigation, becoming the youngest woman ever to solo around the world.

Talking about extremes, read one of our favorite adventure books, *Alone Around the World,* by Naomi James, the first woman to single-hand around the world. Sailing a 53-foot boat and following the route of Sir Francis Chichester (the first solo nonstop circumnavigator), Naomi and her cat beat his time, even with two layovers for repairs. This inspiring account documents her journey and talks about the dangers and rewards of stretching one's limits and passing them.

Shrouded in masculine mystique, sailing is a sport that, until recently, attracted few women. Why? The reasons are quite simple actually, but the number-one reason is money. Sailboats are expensive. How many women do you know who can afford a boat of any size? Another reason is fear, an intimate acquaintance to many of us—fear of capsizing (one sailing instructor likened this to the fear of falling, as being almost an innate fear); fear of the boat heeling over and being unable to right it again; fear of "doing the wrong thing," being unable to perform as part of a crew; and fear of being out of control. Another reason is intimidation. The thing that has kept even the most adventurous of us (men and women) from sailing in all but the most menial positions has been the overpowering voice of the captain—that person who stands in the cockpit, hand confidently gripping the wheel, yelling confusing and sometimes contradictory commands in a language that's difficult to understand.

The captain is usually the owner of the boat and since typically men have owned the boats, men have been the captains. However, as women move into positions of greater power and achievement and earn higher salaries, they're buying boats and becoming captains too!

We'll talk more about being captain in a moment, but first, let's back up a bit and try to understand what it's like to sail as part of a crew, and why sailors are so passionate about their sport. Simply put, sailors who don't *love* sailing, don't sail. But of course, the real answer is as varied and complex as sailors themselves.

For a host of reasons, many of which have been thoroughly documented and discussed, women have had scant opportunity, and subsequently inclination, to perform as part of a team. But we're catching on! We're quickly understanding why the guys want to spend their Saturdays setting and storing sails and grinding winches, and why they prefer being drenched with ice-cold sea spray to staying home and mowing the lawn. To function as part of a synchronized team, where everyone works hard toward a mutual goal, is a real high, especially if you win. Each team or crew member is responsible for her job and the other team members count on her performance. No one can quit—a new experience for many of us. What's the reward for all this hard work and effort? Camaraderie! Man or woman, we all need camaraderie—it makes us feel good!

We've never met a sailor who doesn't wax eloquent about his or her time aboard, and "aboard" could mean on a dinghy or a yacht. Although the words sailors use to describe their experiences and feelings may vary, they all mean the same thing. "Sailing is the ultimate challenge; it's exhilarating; it's fun; all your senses burst alive." "Sailing is like flying. From the moment the wind hits the sail with a snap, the boat is off and you are flying across the sea." "The awesome beauty and power of nature could not be more profoundly apparent than at sea. Working with and using these natural forces you become one with the wind, the currents, and the tides." One sailor describes sailing as "being out there—a kind of communing with nature. Each time I go out it's almost like being with old friends . . . the stars, the sun, the water . . . the whole world is right there in your boat. It is so basic. It puts you right there. There is nothing between you and life. You don't have to sift through any peripheral 'things' to find it. It's powerful."

On the West Coast especially, but prevalent on the Great Lakes, East, and Gulf coasts as well, women's yacht-racing associations, women's sailing schools, women's arms of yacht clubs, and women's power squadrons are popping up in increasing numbers. For example, in February of each year, the Southern California Yachting Association, Women's Sailing Committee, holds a sailing convention and it's always immediately sold out! Women get together for the day, participate in hands-on clinics, demonstrations, racing strategy sessions, boat-maintenance seminars, and lots of sailing, networking, and fun. The West River Sailing Club in Galesville, Maryland sponsors a Women's Big Boat Regatta each June, drawing top women sailors from the Chesapeake Bay Area and Eastern seaboard. Men and women from the West River Sailing Club work together to provide the participants with social events, housing, and child care. Attending an event like this offers you a chance to find out what racing is all about, and presents an opportunity to network with skippers who may be looking for crew. It's also a great way to meet other beginners.

Why do women seek women-only sailing situations? There are many reasons, the most evident being that in a woman-only crew situation, you're sailing with peers (similar size, weight, and philosophy), and whether you pull galley duty or you're the skipper, *every* woman assumes a position of importance and responsibility. Captain Patti Moore of Sea Sense says that in women-only learning situations there is no opportunity for "gender role playing." In mixed-sex situations women are more likely to surrender their decision making to a man, rather than take a chance on making a mistake or being yelled at. On the other hand, in women-only situations there is no one to surrender your position to. You're sailing with peers and you must perform your role as a crew member. Sherry Jagerson of Women's Sailing Adventures said that on one sailing trip a woman threw up her hands and said she couldn't possibly do what was asked of her. "Then who will do it?" chorused the crew.

ASSUMING COMMAND

Now let's get back to the subject of captain—not an easy job. As captain you are in charge, you're in control, and control is synonymous with power—and we all know that the big "P" word gets a bad rap these days. In its exaggerated form, power is associated with political manipulation or the power of one person or group over another. In sailing, however, the captain is the focus of the boat, the power, the energy that helps the crew function as a single unit. When the crew captures that energy and works together as a skilled team, each member of the crew realizes not only her particular unique abilities and strengths, but can delight in the collective power of the crew as well. Tapping into your power enriches your life in every way.

Interestingly, what we hear time and again from women and men who teach sailing programs is that men and women have vastly different approaches to learning to sail and to taking command. Men come aboard "loaded for bear," sincerely believing that they already know how to sail and that, in fact, what they need is a "brush-up" course. Men assume that it's only a matter of time before they assume command. Women, on the other hand, come aboard with the idea that they know little if anything about sailing but are eager to learn. Being "empty and devoid of preconceived ideas," both male and female instructors agree, is a perfect place to start. Women want to know what to expect, don't want a lot of surprises, and, once told, perform their tasks well. Men, it seems, don't want to be told what they "should already know," which, many instructors agree, hinders their performance. Instructors agree that these two different responses are purely societal—they are role responses that originate in childhood.

Once a woman assumes command she tends to be less autocratic than a man and instead shares her power and decision-making responsibilities with crew mates, both male and female. Generally speaking, when men assume command, they perceive themselves as the boss and issue orders that they expect to be obeyed without question. Oftentimes, women crew members on male-dominated boats relinquish power rather than be berated, yelled at, or seen as doing something wrong in front of the rest of the crew. Many men on male-dominated boats feel the same way.

SAILING PROGRAMS

Women's sailing programs have demystified sailing. If you are a beginner, consider learning in a single-sex situation. Once you have acquired the basic sailing skills, you can sail with whomever you choose, confident in your knowledge and skills. You can hold your own whether setting a spinnaker, grinding a winch, or plotting a course. In single-sex learning situations crew positions are rotated frequently and sailing strategies are more likely to be discussed, with input from every crew member. You'll find that there are no secrets to sailing.

The most difficult aspect to sailing is learning the dynamics of wind-powered craft. Why does the boat move when the sail fills with wind and how do you use that wind to get to where you want to go? How does the design of the boat keep you afloat? These and other sailing topics fill countless books. Check the Bibliography for further reading.

There is a direct correlation between the boat you choose to learn on and how intimately you want to become acquainted with the water. We suggest that you begin by sailing the smallest craft possible, a dinghy, perhaps, or a Sunfish. Why? The glory of learning in a small boat is that it is immediately responsive to the wind and the currents, easily maneuverable, and relatively stable. You're close to the water; for each action you receive instant feedback. Things happen very fast on small boats, requiring your constant attention. For example, if you head the boat directly into the wind, the boat will stop. You know at that moment that you have done something wrong and you can immediately take corrective action, learning on the spot.

A dinghy is a very small boat (8 feet to 12 feet) and often comes rigged with a sail. The next level of involvement is the single-sail Sunfish or Laser-style boat, ranging from 12 to 14 feet. These boats are lightweight, easily car-topped, like the dinghy easy to sail, and are lots of fun. As with a dinghy, sailing a Sunfish or a Laser places you close to the water so getting wet is part of the fun. Sailed hard in gusty winds, these boats do capsize occasionally, but are easily righted.

The addition of a jib takes us into a whole new classification of small sloop-rigged sail craft that range in size from 14 to 16 feet, rarely capsize unless sailed hard on the wind, and are easily handled by one or two people. Cockpits in these boats are large enough to accommodate at least two people. Since this chapter addresses beginning sailors, discussions are limited to small boats.

Another style of boat that you'll no doubt see and perhaps become familiar with is the catamaran. Catamarans have two hulls, connected by a taut canvas deck called a trampoline. The two most popular brands of catamarans are Hobie and Nicra. With a moderate wind, catamarans are very fast and require a skilled crew to keep them upright, but they are lots of fun to sail. The most popular of these boats for women in the under-20-feet range is the Hobie 14. One problem with catamarans is that once capsized, they are not easily righted.

Once you have decided that sailing is a sport you'd like to know more about, attend a sailboat show and participate in the demonstrations or, better yet, take a lesson. One of the best ways to learn how to sail and to meet people to sail with is to join a club. Most major cities have a sailing club or a community-run sailing program. One of the better aspects of club programs is that as you progress in skill level you qualify to use larger and more sophisticated club boats, giving you experience at many levels, affording the opportunity to gain expertise in various styles of boats. Starting out on a Sunfish, you may graduate to a Laser, then perhaps to a Lightning, then up to larger cruising boats. While many clubs concentrate on racing, recreational sailing is encouraged. You're sure to find someone who has the same interests as you.

Another possibility is to take a learn-to-sail week. Offered all over the world, these programs include either hotel accommodations or the chance to live aboard the boat. If you can, try living aboard—it's different and fun. Sailing schools are usually held on boats 20 feet or longer and require a three- or four-person crew. Each sailor has a chance to try every job from navigation to sail handling, and shore time is filled with classroom discussion of various aspects of sailboat management.

DRESSING FOR SAILING

Sailing and bathing suits go together. If you learn to sail in the summer you don't have to worry about gear. Just about the only necessary items are a pair of nonslip shoes (Docksiders are really the best) and a PFD (personal flotation device) or life jacket.

When women approach me and ask how they can "get into" sailing, I always suggest that if they have little experience in boats of any kind that they learn in a dinghy, and set the following scene: You set out in your little boat, drifting along for a while, perhaps a little uncertain about these new floating sensations. You get brave and raise the sail. All at once the wind has you moving in directions you may not want to go. You react, you adjust the tiller, the sail. You try many things until you find out how to make the boat go in the direction you want it to go. You may panic, you may be scared, but you keep at it and eventually hit upon a strategy that will get you from here to there. You may even grab an oar and paddle a bit, but you will ultimately get to where you want to go. Don't you think that learning to sail is a perfect metaphor for life?

Profile: Gail Hine

Even on the telephone Gail Hine radiates energy and enthusiasm—especially when she talks about sailing. Gail's profession is advertising and public relations but her calling is sailing and she spends every spare moment spreading news of the joy of the sport to anyone who will listen.

When Gail and her husband moved to California in 1968 they didn't know anyone or have any idea where to begin to make friends. "We didn't have children so the PTA was out," she said, "but we did live near the water and noticed that a lot of people had sailboats. Hoping that sailing would put us in touch with some interesting people, we bought a Newport 20 and joined a local yacht club."

Usually when husbands and wives sail together, the husband assumes command and the wife is relegated to crew, but in this case the roles were reversed. "Since I knew more about sailing than Frank did I was skipper," she said, "and he was crew. He was great—this role reversal never bothered him at all. We had the Newport 20 for 14 years and not only did we get into class racing but became involved in setting up the Newport 20 Association as well."

Then, in 1972, Gail organized the first in a series of women's sailing seminars. "At that time there were very few women skippers or women who crewed, for that matter," says Gail. "The purpose of the series was to get more women out on the water." Open to women from all over Southern California, the series quickly grew from a three- to a six-seminar program. Starting in the morning, these one-day clinics offered a lecture session followed by two hours on the water. "After

Gail Hine onboard her
Newport 20 in 1980.

lunch we would go out on the water with a coach in each boat and work on whatever the subject was that day." Divided into beginning, intermediate, and advanced instruction, except for the last seminar in the series, the program did not focus on racing. "But a reasonable percentage of the women went on to race," said Gail. "Racing is great fun and one of the quickest ways to learn to sail." That program was in existence for almost 15 years.

In the 20 years Gail has spent promoting women's sailing in California, she has seen tremendous change. "Although there has been steady growth in women in the sport, that growth has really accelerated in the last three to five years. We now have four area women's sailing associations, and their membership is increasing by 20 to 30 percent a year." Economics, however, are changing the way people pursue the sport. Boating used to attract a lot of families, but with the current economic situation that just isn't possible.

"Now there are more and more partnerships in boating," said Gail. "Women have higher incomes and possess a heightened sense of assertiveness. They do things that women didn't think possible before." And the number of woman skippers has blossomed. "At this point we offer college courses for women in sailing. There are women racing teams. And the greatest thing is that junior programs are attracting more female participants."

By the late '70s and early '80s all the yacht clubs in the area started having at least one race a year for all-woman crews. Now some even have series races that attract anywhere from six to 25 boats and keelboats at a time, ranging from 25 to 40 feet long. "These boats are owned by women or are on loan or chartered, or in many instances are co-owned by husband and wife," says Gail.

Calling upon her inexhaustible energy once again, three years ago Gail, along with other notable yachtswomen like Peggy Slater, started what is now an annual event. The Women's Sailing Convention is in its third season. Convention day consists of both on-water and classroom instruction. On-water topics cover anything from "person overboard" or "running under power" to "advanced racing." Classroom topics vary from cruising information to chartering, skin care, beginning navigation, and piloting—all with female workshop leaders. The turnout averages 200 friendly sailors who get together and talk about sailing. One participant said, "It was an exhilarating experience—not only the sailing, but the opportunity to be with successful, confident, and bright women of all ages."

Since Gail has not only promoted women and sailing but has taught and raced for years as well, we asked her opinion about why women enter the sport and what the appeal of sailing with other women crew is. "For a lot of women the initial attraction to sailing is the guy they are dating, but once they find out how much fun it is, they are usually hooked. Then, of course, they learn that they can sail without a man. There is a certain comfort level and enjoyment in sailing with other women . . . I guess you could say we speak the same language. Women tend to network easily and help each other improve. You don't get that in many male-dominated boats. For instance, when a crew of women get ready to round a mark, they talk it out and decide who will do what, when, and how. What I've found is that once women learn to sail they can take that skill back to any co-ed crew situation and find themselves in a much better position than they had before. They have abilities and know how to assert themselves onboard—it's better than starting out by handing up the beer and sandwiches."

Gail's advice to other women when learning the sport: "The ideal way to learn to sail is in a small boat where you're closer to the elements—it's easier to understand the basics such as how to read the wind and the water and how to tack and maneuver. Although I learned in a keeled ocean boat, the best sailors began in small boats."

Gail's goal: "I love spreading the word to women about the joys of sailing and about being in command of one's own ship."

Profile: Betsy Alison

Growing up along a New Jersey river, Betsy Alison started sailing when she was seven—in a 12-foot Sunfish. In 1991, as skipper of *Playtime*—a J/24 (24-foot slooped rigged sailboat with a lead keel for ballast), she came from behind to win over 46 yachts from nine countries in the Rolex International Women's Keelboat Championship, held in Newport, Rhode Island.

Believing that sailing is a lifetime sport, Betsy's parents encouraged her competitive spirit as she learned to race—moving from the

Sunfish up through Blue Jays, M-Scows, and Lightnings. "I was really lucky," said Betsy, "my parents didn't care if I raced or not, they just wanted me to learn. It wasn't the Little League scenario."

Entering Tufts University in 1977, Betsy joined its sailing program and discovered aspects of the sport that she never knew existed. "I never really thought about sailing on a national or international level," she says. "But thanks to people like Dave Perry and coach Joe Duplin I got into single-handed sailing and loved it! Of course, then my goal became to make All-American during college. The coaches gave me a lot of extra attention—not only did they help me with personal training programs but one of the assistant coaches and I even weight-trained together. All that extra attention is why I was able to do as much as I did in the late seventies and eighties." (Betsy was identified in the "Faces in the Crowd" section in *Sports Illustrated* in 1978, made honor-

Betsy Alison.

able-mention All-American, and U.S. Amateur Athlete in Yachting in 1981 and 1982.)

That college experience was a fabulous arena in which to learn and improve. "Regattas took me to Italy, Mexico, and Canada, as well as around the United States." Many of the people Betsy races against today were those she raced against in college: Lynne Jewell Shore, crew member of the Olympic boat that won the gold in 1988; All American and Olympic contender J. J. Isler, whom Betsy sailed against at Yale, now ranked number-one on the U.S. Women's Sailing Team; and Jody Swanson from Buffalo, New York, who, although a few years behind Betsy in college, is one of the top-ranked U.S. women sailors today.

After their marriage, Betsy and her husband Mike (also a sailor) moved to Newport, where she added a whole new dimension to her sailing expertise. For five years now Betsy has worked as a sailmaker for Shore Sails. "I've been involved with sailing for what seems forever, but sailmaking was something new for me. It has given me more of a technical eye for the sport. A lot of sailing is done by the seat of the pants, but now I can look at a sail critically—at the way it's constructed—and can tell if it will trim right."

Newport is a town where sailing and breathing are synonymous. That, coupled with the fact that the J/24 is the largest one-design keelboat in the world, plus the fact that Betsy is the one-design production manager at Shore Sails, makes it logical that she would feel right at home on a J/24. "In our local fleet of J/24s there are 50 boats. In our summer series (from May to August) we get between 25 and 40 boats on Thursday nights. Of those boats there are seven women skippers and four or five all-female crews.

"One of the biggest problems for all female crews on a J/24 is the weight factor," she says. "According to the rules, the maximum weight you can sail with is 880 pounds and the boat goes better when sailed close to that limit. Because the crew averages 130 pounds each we sail with a crew of six instead of the usual five. Sure, it can get crowded onboard but that extra pair of eyes and hands comes in handy when doing things like rounding a mark, for instance, or watching for wind shifts and boat positions."

What is it like to sail with an all-woman crew? "With any team, male or female, you are going to have to deal with the various personalities on board," says Betsy. "Women tend to be more emotional than men, so keeping things on a even keel can sometimes be difficult, but on the other hand women also tend to work together as team units better. For instance, in this last Rolex Championship, we were behind going into the last leg of the race and it was astounding to see how the crew functioned as a team. It was tough—so tough that physically you begin to shake because you're so pumped to do the job.

"But every crew member rose to such a high level of perception and all were so supportive of one another. It wasn't that one or two people were doing the job—it was that six women were working together as a unit. In that case it was not you (the captain) against the world—it is you as team, working as a whole, against the world."

What is it like being the captain of an all-woman's crew? "Quite often men and women skippers do things similarly. In fact, I've learned many techniques from the guys I've sailed with and against. But, generally speaking, because women tend to be more social, I think they are more comfortable functioning as a group. We like to get together and try to figure things out as a whole. Women communicate more. I get a lot of the credit and glory because I'm the person who drives the boat, but the truth is, I couldn't do anything without the help of the whole crew.

"I have done a lot of crewing and really enjoy it so I know what to expect when you crew and I also know what the person who is driving expects. You know when you are appreciated and when you are not. An important aspect to sailing with women is encouragement. Whether setting up the team or learning new jobs, a little bit of encouragement goes a long way."

Rolex Awards are nominated by the U.S. Sailing Association (formerly USYRU) membership and voted on by a panel of journalists. Betsy won in 1981, 1982, and 1984 and was nominated in 1991. She feels that the greatest advantage to winning these awards is that "it gives a lot more credibility to women's sailing and to women in the sport. Men have dominated the sport, but that is gradually shifting. Women's abilities are quickly rising to a par with men."

Although Betsy sails at a level in the sport that few of us will ever achieve, she started in a Sunfish on a little river close to home. Her advice to you: "Don't be intimidated in the beginning by not knowing a whole lot. Get into a local community sailing program—learn the sport at a grass-roots level. Believe it or not, women tend to *learn* better when taught by women; maybe it's the style; maybe it's just perception, but generally speaking, it's true.

"Sailing is fun. It is also, as my father told me 25 years ago, a sport you can do forever—alone, as a mixed crew, or with whomever you wish."

SKIING

CROSS-COUNTRY SKIING

It's called cross-country skiing by some, Nordic or "skinny" skiing by others. It offers something for every personality and mood, and best of all, it gets the whole family outdoors and having fun! What else could you do with the kids in the winter that entertains, educates, and exhausts them; is inexpensive; and lets you have fun at the same time? Did you know that cross-country skiing is a complete body workout, uses every muscle group, and burns 600 to 900 calories per hour? Did you know that 52 percent of Nordic skiers are women? And psychologically—let's just say you'll rarely see a Nordic skier who isn't grinning from ear to ear. But anything that good must cost a fortune, you muse. Not so—a complete cross-country ski package, boots, poles, and skis sells for around $150, about half the cost of a pair of downhill ski boots.

Unless you live in a major city, with a few inches of snow on the ground you can ski right out your back door. One night I arrived home from work in a snowstorm, dreading the usual evening chores that we working women face. But the weather was on my side and chores turned into fun. I grabbed my backpack, snapped on my skis, and headed off through town to the supermarket. Of course, I was the only woman who skied to the supermarket, but hey, I was the only woman who looked like she was having any fun! Maybe that's why it's so popular—it's easy to learn, accessible, affordable, and fun.

The glory of cross-country skiing is in its wide diversity of style. Cross-country skiing is actually divided into several distinct sports, each requiring its own equipment and level of expertise. The three main areas of Nordic skiing are track skiing (diagonal and skating); touring (running the gamut from easy day trips to backcountry skiing—lasting from a day to a week or longer—to extreme descents); and lift-served skiing (telemarking and racing). Gone are the days when owning one pair of wood skis, boots, and poles totally fit the bill. Now, equipment depends on your level of involvement in the sport. Whether you prefer skating over fast packed trails at a ski area, making your own trail along backwoods roads, or strapping on a backpack to head off to the supermarket or to tackle long distances over extreme terrain, cross-country skiing may be the sport for you.

Think of a cross-country skier and what comes to mind? Probably the stereotype that pops into the minds of most people—noncompetitive, penny-pinching, granola-chomping, health-food freaks who wear gray wool knickers, gaiters, and Norwegian sweaters, right? But, with the advent of more technically sophisticated equipment and colorful and form-fitting clothes, that perception has changed. Surpassing downhill or Alpine skiing, cross-country skiing has become America's fastest-growing winter sport, and for good reason. You can cross-country ski on relatively little snow (as compared to Alpine); trail passes, if needed, seldom cost more than $6 to $8 (less than one fifth the price of a lift ticket); unlike downhill skiing, cross-country is relatively injury free; there are no lift lines; and a lesson or two gets you out and enjoying the sport right away.

Whatever your degree of involvement, there is equipment designed to handle specific conditions that you will encounter. Before you dash out to the ski shop, determine what kind of cross-country skiing you'll be doing. What is available to you? If the nearest ski area is two hours away, but you have easy access to a local park with ungroomed trails, you'll probably ski in the park. Do you live in the country where you can ski out your back door and onto a trail or woods road? Maybe you live in the mountains and prefer backcountry touring.

Let's look at the three types of cross-country skiing and decide what equipment is appropriate for you.

Track Skiing

Track skiing is actually divided into diagonal stride and skating. Done on groomed trails where you actually follow a track, diagonal stride looks like stretched-out walking and is the most commonly practiced style. Skating is done on smooth trails, groomed especially for the skating technique. Similar to an ice-skating movement, pushing off slightly to the side with one ski and gliding on the other, while at the same time using your poles to provide a strong additional push, skating is an aggressive and athletic technique resulting in great speed. It feels like you're flying!

To wax or not to wax, that is the question. Waxing takes practice and for diagonal stride, even old pros go waxless. We recommend waxless skis, especially for beginners. In fact, 80 percent of all cross-country skis sold today are waxless. But, even waxless skis need a good coat of glide wax from time to time. We'll discuss waxing later in this chapter.

Of the two track skis, diagonal stride waxless skis are the longer of the two. They have a pattern, called scales or steps, on the kick zone that grip the snow and allow the ski to glide forward. The ski has two sections: a kick zone (underfoot) and a glide zone (tip and tail). When you press down onto the snow, the kick-zone section provides traction. The opposite ski tip and tail (glide zone) glide forward along the snow. At the same time, poles are used to help propel you along. Arms are swinging as if you're walking fast, opposite arm with opposite leg. This natural motion quickly results in an easy cadence, kick, glide, kick, glide.

Skis enable you to stay on the surface of the snow and to glide along, but in order to do that they need to be sized to fit your body. Let's look at what makes a proper-fitting ski. Stand the ski next to you. Raise one hand above your head. The ski should be wrist high. Now stand on the center portion (the camber) of the ski. The function of the camber (curve of the ski) is to distribute the weight of the skier evenly along the entire ski. Can you slide a sheet of paper under your ski? If you can't, you need a longer or a stiffer ski. If the paper slides under too easily, without touching the ski, you need a shorter or softer ski.

As a general rule for diagonal skiing, pole length should be shoulder height and have small baskets. Inexpensive metal or fiberglass poles are adequate for all but serious racers.

Buy boots and bindings at the same time, making sure they are compatible. Despite what many well-meaning salespeople tell you, it's the boots, not the skis, that are the most important part of the ski package. Most skis are of decent quality; often, that is not the case with boots. Even with the best skis, you can't have much fun on two frozen feet. There are many good boot/binding systems available. The most popular styles are called NNN (for New Nordic Norm) and the Salomon System, both of which utilize a metal ring or bar at the boot toe, binding the boot to the ski. Both systems make good track bindings and both have rugged backcountry models available. In diagonal track skiing the tracks help keep skis from wandering so you don't need a lot of ankle support.

The three-pin binding system is still in use in lower-end ski packages and, although ten years out of date, the three-pin system still offers greater control in telemark and off-track situations. Boots for track skiing are the lowest, softest, and least supportive of the ski boots. They are ankle height, lightweight, moderately rigid to resist twisting (and thereby loss of control), and look similar to running shoes. After you have chosen a boot, take the boot by the heel and toe and twist it, as if you were wringing water out of clothes. If it twists easily, don't buy it.

Especially in unisex boots, women frequently encounter loose instep problems. The boot may fit in all other respects but the lace eyelets meet, with room to spare. If that is the case, try inserting a thicker insole, or if you regularly wear orthotics, remove the manufacturer's insole and insert the orthotic, and try it again. Many good boot companies such as Merrell are manufacturing ski boots on women's lasts, so don't give up if at first you can't find a good fit.

Try boots on over one light and one heavyweight pair of socks. For added insulation on really cold days don't add another pair of socks—that just restricts toe movement and circulation. Try overboots instead. Overboots are sometimes difficult to find but worth the effort and they're really just another aspect to the layering system. Above all, remember, beginner cross-country ski packages are designed for just that—beginners. Our guess is that once you experience the fun of cross-country you'll soon want to expand your horizons, so don't spend a lot of time worrying about whether or not you have purchased the *best* boot or the *best* ski. Finding a pair of boots that fit is a comparatively easy process.

Skating equipment, on the other hand, is designed strictly for speed. Skating boots are higher and stiffer than track boots, allowing you to kick off to the side while at the same time providing lateral stability and support to the inside of the ankle during the skating movement. Specialized boot-binding systems provide a solid boot-binding connection. Skating skis are shorter and stiffer than those designed for diagonal stride. Forward momentum is gained by pushing off on the edges of the skis—sort of like being on five-foot-long ice skates. Poles for skating are a little higher than those used for diagonal stride, usually reaching to your chin or slightly higher. While the salesperson will probably counsel you to buy high-tech, carbon-fiber poles, we recommend that you stick to the less expensive fiberglass pole, at least at the beginning. Although you won't need kick wax, apply glide wax over the entire length of your ski on a regular basis. It enhances the efficiency of the ski and protects it at the same time. Laurie Gullion has written an excellent book entitled *The Cross Country Primer*. It covers the care and maintenance of your skis, technique instruction diagrams, and practice runs—all written in an easy-to-read format (see Bibliography for further reading).

Touring Skis

These wonderful skinny skis can be your passport to winter adventure. Besides snowshoes, touring skis offer the easiest, cheapest, and most enjoyable way to get into the woods, whether on gentle trails or over extreme backcountry terrain. What more could you ask for?—your body working rhythmically, the earth covered with fresh deep snow; no people, just you and the sounds of winter; the sudden snap and creak of frozen trees echoing through the stillness; the lonely knocking of a far-off woodpecker; the sudden whump of falling clumps of snow; but best of all, each bend in the trail holding the possibility of new adventure.

Touring can be separated into distinct areas of expertise ranging from light touring (day trips over ungroomed trails or unplowed roads) to backcountry skiing (hut to hut or trips that cover long distances over extreme terrain while carrying a load). Light touring requires minimal expertise; you need only be properly dressed, possess the rudimentary cross-country kick-and-glide skills, and—most important of all—a desire to ski. Heavy touring, on the other hand, is the domain of the expert skier or the intermediate skier in the company of experts. Knowledge of map and compass is important. The ability to carry weight and to ski over extreme terrain is essential.

Equipment needed for light touring is very similar to that used in diagonal stride. Although touring boots are a little higher and have more insulation than track or skate boots, track gear can be easily adapted for lightweight touring. Wear gaiters to keep out the snow and, if it's a particularly cold day, use overboots for additional warmth. Though touring skis are wider and softer than track skis (to help you stay on top of ungroomed snow) and possess a more upward curved tip (so you can glide over the snow without submarining), with slight modification, track skis can serve double-duty for light touring. Most track skis, except the very cheapest, have NNN bindings, but if you spend more time doing light touring than diagonal stride, you may wish to substitute NNN bindings with 3-pin binding. These bindings are inexpensive, durable, and easily repaired with a piece of bailing wire in backcountry situations. Again, if you do more touring than track skiing, investing in poles with powder baskets is a good idea.

One other item that can make a world of difference in touring, especially if you live in the west where even light touring often includes mountainous terrain, is a pair of climbing skins that strap onto the base of your skis for uphill traction.

For heavy touring you must invest in backcountry gear—sort of a combination of Nordic and Alpine equipment, designed for carrying heavy loads, offering downhill control and added durability needed to negotiate extreme terrain.

Backcountry boots are higher and more insulated than track boots and are usually hinged to the ski with a heavy-duty three-pin binding. They range from leather boots with Vibram soles (similar to hiking boots with an extended toe) and designed for ease of forward flex while striding, to stiff double leather or plastic boots with cuffs and buckles for extreme terrain and demanding conditions.

Always longer than their Alpine counterparts, backcountry skis are varied in style but are usually designed with metal edges to handle icy or mixed conditions. Designed for stability, they are wider to keep you on the surface of deep powdery snow.

Telemarking

In the last five years we have heard more and more about telemarking. Telemarking is actually a graceful turning technique that was developed in Norway ages ago. It is used on downhill and steep backcountry trails and demands the ultimate in control. Telemark boots, similar to the heavy-duty backcountry boots, are the most structured of the Nordic ski boots. Calf-high, many have buckles and plastic cuffs. Telemark skiing is often lift-assisted.

Simply put, if you plan to backpack on skis and/or do terrain in tough conditions, you will be looking for metal-edged skis and boots that provide extraordinary support.

Adjustable aluminum poles that vary from waist to shoulder height are appropriate for backcountry or telemark skiing.

Dressing the Part

Nordic skiing produces a lot of body heat and moisture. A slow ski through the woods on an ungroomed trail at 15 degrees requires several layers of warm clothes and maybe a windbreaker. But, if you are flying down a packed track, working hard, you need no more than the lightest layers—a moisture-wicking underlayer, tights, and a pile jacket.

Double layers in the front help protect you from a cold wind. Often, a warm-up suit can be used to cover your tights and top until you have warmed up. When you are skiing hard you may need only to cover your ears with a pile or wool headband. While covering your head helps keep you warm, uncovering it will help to keep you cool. Dressing comfortably for cross-country, like any other sport, requires practice, and you probably won't get it right the first time.

Waxing

Waxing is a mysterious process, so one would be led to believe. But, in fact, taken a step at a time, waxing is simply a matter of a little practice and following directions. Most ski touring centers proudly display their choice for "wax of the day" and are more than happy to advise on its application. Wax is chosen for the air temperature and snow conditions, ranging from sub-zero to 60 degrees and from powder to slush. Although we have recommended that you buy waxless skis as a beginner, the glide of your waxless skis can be much improved with the addition of a glide wax on the tips and tails. That application also protects the bottoms of the skis. As you become a more advanced skier you may find yourself attracted to the additional speed of a well-waxed ski.

Renting Equipment

You've read all you need to know to get you started. Now let's get outdoors and have some fun! But, before you purchase equipment, consider renting a few times and try to choose different equipment each time. See if you like the sport and have a commitment to it before spending your hard-earned cash. As is the case with many sports, hastily purchased cross-country equipment can easily find a permanent home in the basement.

Your first skiing experience should be at a cross-country ski area where, for a few dollars, you can take a lesson from a certified ski instructor. Rental equipment is available, trails are groomed, tracked, and marked by their level of difficulty, and you'll get off to a good, safe, painless start. Many ski areas offer package deals with lessons, rentals, and trail passes included. Do not borrow equipment from a friend or let a friend teach you to ski. While well-intentioned, you don't want to learn someone else's bad skiing habits. Also, successful skiing depends on properly fitted equipment, and rarely does borrowed equipment fit. Ill-fitting equipment can make for a miserable skiing experience.

DOWNHILL SKIING

There is nothing that you can do in winter for greater thrills than downhill skiing. It is easy to learn if you start at the beginning and take lessons from a professional instructor. Well-meaning friends will try to convince you that they can teach you. Don't believe it! A professional instructor has trained for years to learn the easiest way to teach you to ski. Friends have great intentions but no teaching skills or technique. They can't show you the little tricks and exercises that make skiing skills easier to learn.

The National Ski Opinion Survey found that 57 percent of all first-time skiers are female. Yet, it remains that 55 percent of all skiers are male. Why? In 1975, Elissa Slanger recognized that women needed something more than the standard ski-school technique and that they could be taught more successfully in programs structured specifically for them. Women, it seems, are less competitive and less aggressive than men on the slopes. Quoted in *Snow Country* magazine, Kim Reichhelm of K2 Women's Ski Adventures says that "Men motivate themselves through competition, but women need a nurturing situation." Women seem to be more afraid of speed and loss of control; afraid of looking silly or embarrassing themselves, particularly in front of men (either instructors or other students); afraid of not being able to keep up; and afraid of hindering the learning process of others.

Consequently, schools like Woman's Way, founded by Elissa Slanger; K2 Women's Ski Adventures, run by Kim Reichhelm, Annie Vareille-Savath, Ski School Director at Telluride, and Toby Quinley of Breckenridge; and others across the United States have stepped in to fill the gap.

Through techniques as varied as visualization, Aikido breathing techniques, centering, and videotaping, programs like these provide supportive learning environments. So, as you can see, there are alternative methods to learning.

Traditional teaching methods work well for many. For instance, take a learn-to-ski week, offered by most major ski areas throughout the winter. These packages can include lift tickets, lodging, equipment rental, and lessons and provide a great way to learn the sport. You spend a week taking lessons in the morning and skiing on your own in the afternoon. If that isn't an option, take several lessons to get started. If you feel like you have reached a point where you're not progressing, take another lesson. Even the best skiers take catch-up lessons every once in a while.

An instructor will start you off on the gentlest of slopes. You will learn how to slow down, turn, fall, and get up again. Falling is something you should expect to do a lot of in the beginning. In fact, practice falling. It looks undignified and it's sometimes scary but it's something we all do and it really isn't as bad as it seems: just brush off the snow and keep on sliding.

Selecting Downhill Equipment

After you have decided you like skiing and want your own equipment, the next daunting process (even worse than falling) is going to the ski shop, where you will be confronted with walls of skis and racks of boots. How do you choose the proper equipment? First of all, don't feel pressured to buy in a hurry. Downhill ski equipment is expensive, and, contrary to popular belief, rental equipment is not always junk, so rental is a viable option. Good-quality rental equipment is available from downhill specialty shops, and they want you to have the best skiing experience so you'll return to purchase your own equipment. Renting is a smart alternative to get you through your first lessons, even your first season. Most instructors have a favorite brand of ski boots, skis, and bindings—ask her suggestions. Also, be aware that ski shops put together packages for different skill levels: beginner, intermediate, and advanced, thus eliminating a major confusion. The only requirement of you is that you accurately assess your skiing ability.

Some general rules for beginners include starting with shorter skis. When I bought my first pair of skis, I made a big mistake. I went to the ski shop with a boyfriend who was an expert skier. "Hold up your hand. That's it, the ski reaches the tip of your fingers. Okay, those are the skis for you," he said. I came away $500 lighter and with a pair of skis that can go 90 m.p.h. down the slightest hill. Even after gathering more experience, they still scare me. Needless to say, I made a bad choice. Shorter skis give you more control; they don't gain speed quite as quickly and are easier to turn.

Unlike cross-country skis, there is no hard-and-fast rule for determining the length of Alpine skis. Rather, it is your skiing style and ability that determines downhill ski size, pole length, and style of binding. We know that Kneissl, Rossignol, K2, and Blizzard design skis for women. Before making a purchasing decision, try the equipment or at least get suggestions from a skilled woman skier or instructor. Don't let an aggressive salesperson sell you something that doesn't fit.

"No boot is made to match the shape of a North American woman's foot," said Jackson Hogen in *Snow Country* magazine. Women's feet have narrower ankles, narrower heels, and higher insteps. Time and again we hear women complain about poorly fitting boots. This is probably the main concern of women downhillers. The problem with unisex boots is that the narrower general profile of a woman's foot doesn't fit a scaled-down men's boot. Heel and ankle fit is particularly important for control of the ski. That control is usually not possible in unisex boots. Mugsy Kolb of Foot Image Technology in Bend, Oregon says that "manufacturers seldom address the particular profile of a woman's foot; consequently, women end up buying many pairs of boots, hoping to find a proper fit. And women are becoming a greater force in the industry," she adds, "so manufacturers must start addressing their needs." In most ski shops around the country, for a $25 fee, Foot Image Technology makes a complete analysis of your foot via the Compufit System℠. Mugsy claims that this system saves you money right from the start by imaging your foot, enhancing the chances of a better fit. After a foot analysis the ski shop is able to access Foot Image Technology's data bank, which maintains a directory of boots that will fit your particular foot profile.

Expensive ski gear is an investment worth protecting. Most of us have to travel to downhill ski areas, and a major problem in car-topping is keeping the grit and grime off the skis while rushing up the interstate. Road grime gums up the bindings and sticks to the bottom, making your skis slow and sticky. Use binding covers, ski bags, or car roof-top boxes. There are special ice- and dirt-repellent sprays to keep bindings operating efficiently. Boot soles need to be flat and smooth to fit properly in the bindings, so don't walk long distances in your boots on rough ground.

Unlike cross-country skiing where you continually expend lots of energy, your downhill days include long lift lines, slow rides up the mountain, and stop-and-go skiing. The market is flooded with designer skiwear, all of which is expensive, colorful, and unnecessary, except to achieve "the look." Dressing appropriately includes layering, using wicking underwear, pile sweaters, down parkas, wind shells, and heavier hats, mittens, and gloves. For more information on dressing for cold weather, browse through the What Am I Going to Wear? chapter and leave your cotton jeans at home.

A great source for cross-country and downhill equipment and clothes is the ski swap. During October, November, and December, ski areas, clubs, and specialty shops offer this wonderful source for inexpensive, sometimes new, and sometimes barely used equipment. There is only one drawback—you have to know what you are looking for and how to get a proper fit. Check local ski shop bulletin boards, newspapers, and outdoor club newsletters for ski swaps and as a source for used equipment.

Skiing is a wonderful way to make friends, get some great exercise, test your limits, and explore the world at a time of year when most people choose to stay indoors. Our world has a different look in winter—a landscape of frost-covered trees, ice-filled brooks, and clear, crisp days.

Simply put, skiing makes you feel good all over, so we're looking forward to seeing you on the trail.

Profile: Laurie Gullion—
A Woman for All Seasons

In high school in the '60s, Laurie Gullion did some downhill skiing and gymnastics but had little understanding of her physical strengths until, as a student at the University of Massachusetts, she joined women's crew. "I was 5'6"—small for varsity, so I rowed in second, or JV boat. For some team members, including me, it was our first strong physical experience. We were continually being surprised, day-to-day, by what we accomplished physically."

An all-round outdoor woman, Laurie is a late arrival in the sport of cross-country skiing. In fact, she got into the sport "through the back door," you might say. In 1980 she and husband Bruce moved to Vermont where she took a job in the marketing department at Bolton Valley and Sugarbush, and Bruce worked for Tucker Hill Ski Touring Center. Through Bruce, Laurie met telemark skier Dick Hall. "I was an Alpine skier in search of new territory," wrote Laurie in her book, *The Cross Country Primer* (see Bibliography). Dick was one of the key people responsible for the growth of cross-country skiing in North America and for the rediscovery of telemark skiing in the world. Laurie got on cross-country skis only a few times before she fell in love with telemarking. "It was hard not to become a good tele-skier with Dick Hall always around egging me on," she laughs.

Then in 1983 Bruce accepted a teaching job in Massachusetts, so back they went. Looking for a job, Laurie called the director of skiing at Northfield Mountain and was invited to interview for a position as a cross-country ski instructor. "We had a common interest in white-water canoeing so we spent the entire time talking about paddling and never did get around to skiing," she says. "At the end of the interview he offered me a job teaching cross-country skiing. Although I had no cross-country experience, I had taught downhill and paddling and was a skilled tele-skier, so I figured, how hard could it be? Besides, I had three months until ski season and could easily learn. It didn't hurt that Bruce was a certified cross-country instructor, either. I knew I could study with my live-in coach!"

Laurie not only learned, but by 1985 had earned cross-country ski instructor certification, and has since published two books on the sport. She has been an instructor examiner—a teacher of teachers—for the last four years and is currently one of two female PSIA (Professional Ski Instructors of America) Nordic Examiners in the East.

Laurie's love of outdoor sports goes far beyond skiing. The outdoors has always been an intimate part of her life. "My father was head of the Fish and Wildlife Department in the State of Massachusetts," she says, "and my mother was an environmental activist in the small town where we lived. Our summer vacations consisted of camping in the White Mountains and canoeing."

But it seems that Laurie's proficiency in a sport nearly always stems from a chance meeting of someone while participating in some other sport. "Back in 1976 I was instructing at a small ski area in western Massachusetts," she adds. "A local college professor was also teaching there and he kept talking about white-water canoeing and how it started in March just after ski season ended. I know it sounds crazy but he offered to teach me canoeing with the idea that if I liked it he would train me as an instructor. I loved it."

That instructor was Tom Foster, currently in charge of all instructors and instructional programs for the American Canoe Association. Laurie went on to become an ACA canoeing instructor-trainer and, with input from instructors all over the country, she wrote the *Canoeing and Kayaking Instruction Manual,* published by the ACA.

"I like the mental game of canoeing. Picking my way through a highly technical rapid . . . putting my boat exactly where I want it. Paddling is like skiing; a timing and technique sport using powerful, aggressive moves. I like playing with the water, trying to outwit it. I think women especially are intrigued by a succession of very smooth moves; a series of strokes and maneuvers that flow together really well—like turning into an active eddy, for instance, then immediately turning out again—without interruption in the rhythm."

Laurie has paddled in national competition and won the Mixed and Women's National White Water National Championships in 1984 on the Indian River in New York, with partners Jill Runnion and Ray McLain. She has also made major expeditions in the Barren lands north of the Arctic Circle. "In 1980 I was working as a beat and environmental reporter for the *Greenfield Recorder* and desperately needed a change. I was sick of being on the sidelines . . . I wanted to be a participant.

Laurie Gullion.

At that time I was teaching recreational canoeing at a local community college and happened to meet physician Jim Abel. He served as trip physician for Arctic Barrens Expeditions and showed me some beautiful pictures of the north country—stunning sunsets and endless expanses of really wild country—a place I had never been. I signed up for one of the trips. It was the longest thing I had ever done—42 days on the Elk, Thelon, Dubawnt, and Kazan rivers. It was also the toughest and most rewarding thing I had ever done. There were 12 women and nine men on the trip. They were women like me, who accomplished far more physically than they had ever thought possible. I think women sometimes set their expectations too low. That trip showed me that I was able to handle adversity almost without knowing it. We ran rapids, carried packs on portages, lined boats down rapids we couldn't paddle—all without thinking about the harshness. I didn't realize how difficult it was until after the trip was over and we were back home." Laurie became co-leader on four more trips to the north country.

She has also been a beginning rock climber for more than ten years, not being able to spend much time with the sport, but liking the challenge nonetheless. "I enjoy putting together moves," she says, "for the same reason I like the moves in white water or handling different changes in terrain on tele- or cross-country skis. My boredom threshold is very low and I constantly change the sports I'm doing. Road biking and mountain biking help keep my legs in shape in the summer. I paddle white-water kayaks (a very fast, sleek, tippy style of racing kayak) in flat water to build both strength and fitness. Hiking with ski poles gives both an upper and lower body workout and is part of my off-season program. All the outdoor things I do get me to wild places, whether on rivers or ridges."

Laurie particularly likes working with women who have never been in the outdoors without their husbands, and who, in many cases, may for the first time be doing something on their own, just for themselves. "They seem to be willing to try things without the fear of looking foolish. They are willing to gamble. I like that."

Profile: Jean Thoren—
In Search of the Perfect Turn

Growing up in Northern Michigan, Jean Thoren was surrounded by snow. She was also surrounded by eight brothers and sisters. "Providing nine children with ski lessons and equipment was out of the question," she laughs, "so winter sports in the Thoren house consisted of ice skating and sledding. But we did have the essentials in life," she adds, "dancing and piano lessons." It wasn't until Jean was in the eighth grade and the family moved that Jean became involved with skiing at all. "In the new neighborhood all the kids skied. They gave me some old equipment, but I had no poles and the skis had no edges."

But Jean hung out at the ski hill with all the other kids anyway. Sepp Hoedlmoser, an instructor at the slope, quickly recognized Jean's talent for the sport. "Sepp would come over to me at lunchtime and say, 'Jeannie, come and give me a lesson,' and off we would go to ski for an hour. I, of course, thought we were skiing for fun. It wasn't until years later that I realized he was coaching me—Seep knew I had no money for lessons. We have remained good friends. Now he's in his seventies; I owe him a lot."

In 1964, four years after she first stepped into a pair of bindings, Jean made the Junior National Team. "It was the big turning point in my life," she said. But by the time she graduated from Northern Michigan University in 1968, it was obvious that "for a woman, there was just no place to go in skiing. There were no women's ski programs and no local competitions," she adds.

A season in Europe seemed like the way to get rid of the skiing bug. "I wanted to get skiing out of my system, so I went to Switzerland and got a job washing dishes in St. Moritz, figuring I could ski, work, and learn about another culture and language all at the same time." She did learn to speak German well, but she didn't get rid of the skiing bug—instead she ended up doing a lot more skiing and racing than she had ever dreamed possible, even winning some local women's championships. The result of all this skiing, however, reinforced Jean's realization that she had a technique problem—a problem that practice wouldn't eliminate.

Returning to the United States, Jean ended up in Jackson Hole,

Jean Thoren.

Wyoming. "Trying to perfect my turn, I decided that what stood in my way was that I skied knock-kneed—my knees rotated in." Christine Wells describes this common problem called "Q-angle" in her book, *Women, Sport & Performance: A Physiological Perspective.* "Women are more frequently seen with knock-knees than are men because of the way in which the head of the femur fits into the cup-shaped socket (acetabulum) of the pelvis. Because the pelvis in women is generally wider and the femur shorter, the angle between the neck of the femur and the shaft bone is less than 125 degrees. The smaller this angle, the more the shaft of the long bone will slope inward and the closer the knees will be. Consequently, women with average or wider pelvic widths may be predisposed to knee problems in sports that require jumping, running, or sudden shifts of direction."

"I have wide hips," says Jean, "so when I flex forward to set an edge to turn, I have to tuck one leg behind the other. If I bring my skis straight in line, then my knees rub together."

One day Jean was skiing a gently sloping and smooth track set between a steep upper face and a cliff below, with nothing but a rope in between. "I had skied it dozens of times," she says. "All of a sudden I caught an edge and the only thing that kept me from going over the cliff was the rope that I managed to catch hold of. It was sobering." Then Jean remembered a book she had read, *How the Racers Ski,* by Warren Witherall. In this book he mentioned "catching edges" as a symptom of needing cants (plastic wedges). "That's me, that's my problem," she thought.

Jean went to a local ski shop to discuss her conclusions with the pros. "They told me that canting was a bunch of bunk," she says, "that a skier of my caliber needs nothing but a slight change in technique and lots of practice." But she knew that wasn't true and had cants positioned on the inside of her bindings anyway. These cants repositioned Jean's foot on the ski to a flatter position. "I went up the mountain the next day and did the run from top to bottom. By the time I got to the bottom I was crying. That little piece of plastic made all the difference."

"If you have a canting problem," Jean says, "your ski edges are erratic and you are prone to catching without knowing what's going on. You can do all the right things and still fall. Cants are like glasses, she says—if you need them, you need them and if you don't you don't. Technology has changed since Jean's discovery. Now cants are placed inside the boot itself, not on the ski surface.

Jean's discoveries didn't happen overnight but occurred over many years. "Another breakthrough had to do with balance. I was aware that I always bent over at the waist rather than at the ankles and knees. The pros kept telling me not to bend over so far and I would try not to but then my skis would cross and the tips would wander. So I went back to my think tank—washing dishes in a restaurant. One night, standing at my usual spot before the sink, I got the idea to try lifting my heel inside the ski boot, allowing more forward lean. After trying several things, I finally hit on matchbooks and taped them in under the heels of the boot liners. The next day I took a run and once again ended the run crying. It was so simple. After that I used plastic wedges under my heels.

"Women can't flex as far forward at the knees and ankles as a man but are more flexible at the waist," Jean says, citing a Canadian study. "The shortness of the muscle at the back of the ankle prevents a deep bend and if a woman wears high heels consistently, that muscle becomes further shortened. Also, a woman's calf muscle is larger than a man's and attaches lower on the leg," she adds. "That makes it difficult to tighten the top of her boot. Heel lifts move that muscle up, allowing you to tighten the boot."

In 1979 Jean decided to attend the Women's Ski Expo at Stratton Mountain, Vermont. Not only did she get a chance to meet her two skiing heroes, Olympic Gold Medalist Andrea Mead Lawrence and Elissa Slanger, but she attended a lecture by Dr. Betty Coryliss addressing the physiological differences between men and women and how their bodies develop after puberty. "Betty said that the female adult carries her weight farther back through her heels, not on the balls of her feet as a male does," Jean said. "Consequently, women tend to ski back on their heels. Have you ever noticed women's figure skates? The skating world is aware. They realize that unless the female skater is up on the balls of her feet, she would be unable to do intricate leaps, twists, and turns. That's why the heel on a woman's skate is so much higher than that on a man's.

"Also, my turns seemed to happen a bit late—I couldn't get my skis to turn exactly when I wanted them to. I realized that this was caused by 'sitting back' on the ski. After hearing Dr. Coryliss, I moved the ski binding one inch forward and that, coupled with a built-up heel, enabled me for the first time to snap my turns just where I wanted them. I was finally able to put my weight on the ski properly—on the ball of my foot."

Now, with her vast accumulation of knowledge, Jean is helping other women find the key to fun on snow. After 25 years, she has perfected her turn and through Spirit Mountain Ski School in Duluth, Minnesota, passes her secrets—the Thoren Theory—on to other women. "We concentrate on finding the right ski—the right length and the right binding location. We have 25 pairs of skis at the school, all with movable bindings, all different lengths and different manufacturers."

Jean's favorite pupil is the intermediate woman skier—"the one with the husband and two kids, the woman who hasn't had the opportunity to stay in shape, the woman who rarely has time for herself and is usually using outdated, old equipment. Often she has been told it's her fault that she can't ski well, that she's too fearful or nonaggressive—the woman who has heard over and over again, 'Bend your knees, get forward, get your rear end down.' Well, you can't if you're nailed down in the wrong spot."

ROWING

I was five years old when I learned to row. It was a nice thick-o-fog Maine morning and Uncle Larry and his dog Smokey and I were on our way out to the *Millie Mae,* Uncle Larry's lobster boat. It was 5:30 in the morning and, carrying our gear for a day at sea, we three carefully made our way down the rocky bank to the fish house and down the ramp to the little skiff tied up to the dock. "I'll tell you what, Patti, Smokey and I'll be the passengers this mornin' and you can row us out." I quickly claimed the center seat in the skiff, Smokey taking the bow and Uncle Larry the stern. Dropping the long oars into the oar locks, Uncle Larry passed the handles to me and said, "Now just grab ahold of them oars, drop 'em in the water a bit, and pull hard." Arms barely reaching the oars, feet bracing the ribs of the boat, I did as I was told. The boat moved. Sighting the *Millie Mae,* Smokey led the way by his nose.

I will never forget those first powerful feelings—the overwhelming pride of supplying the power that moved the boat. At that moment I probably could have turned inside out. But, perhaps most important, it was the first time I experienced being free of the restrictions of land. To this day, every time I step into a small boat and shove off, I am free. You'll hear those sentiments echoed time and again by rowers of small boats as well as those of racing shells.

The feeling of buoyancy, of bobbing along with the currents, and the sensation of powering yourself by oar are magical. For those short moments on the water you're the master of your own destiny. In an article published in the *New York Times* a few years ago, one rower said, "I can't think of anything more relaxing, more enjoyable, than just getting into a boat and getting out on the water under my own power. I'm fascinated by how easily the boat moves over the water."

If you live near any body of flat water, with some initial investment (no more than the purchase cost of downhill ski equipment),
rowing is an accessible sport. There are many styles of recreational
rowing craft. At one end of the spectrum is the rowing shell—the
sleekest and fastest of boats but one that requires the most skill to
row. Shells don't forgive mistakes easily. At the other end of the spectrum is the standard rowboat, and, depending in which part of the
country you live, could be known as a wherry, pram, punt, dingy, or
skiff. Not offering much in the way of performance, these traditional
boats will give you some exercise; they're great for exploring; and, to
quote Rat from *The Wind in the Willows,* "Believe me . . . there is
nothing—absolutely nothing—half so much worth doing as simply
messing about in boats." And an oar-powered boat of any kind is just
about perfect for "messing about in."

Traditional rowboats outfitted with fixed-bench seats are very
seaworthy and were developed as work boats, to be used in all kinds
of sea conditions. Recreational or racing shells, on the other hand, have
sliding seats and were developed specifically for competition, speed,
and exercise. Defining a boat as "recreational" can be confusing to
many people because even the most traditional rowboat used to poke
around in inlets and coves can certainly be classified as recreational.
However, since the creation of the sliding seat, "recreational" has
become sort of a generic term used to describe any rowing craft with
a sliding seat that is not specifically a racing shell.

Oar-powered boats claim a long and colorful history. The first
recorded craft propelled by oar dates back to 3000 B.C. For thousands
of years after that, Egyptians, Greeks, Romans, and Phoenicians uti-
lized oarsmen to propel ships of trade, transportation, and war. With
the increased sophistication of sailing craft, oar power became relegated to propelling small work boats, such as whaling boats, White-
halls, pea pods, and dories—all craft used for transportation and
fishing, and all designs that are still in use today. It was only after the
Industrial Revolution, in the late 1700s, that common folk had time for
recreation—and many headed for the nearest body of water to play in
small boats.

Given the nature of humankind, when offered the slightest opportunity, we love to compete. The first informal rowing competitions that
we know of took place in England among the watermen who lived and

worked along the rivers. Competing in the boats of their trade—boats not at all like the sleek racing shells that we know today—they merely turned the skills by which they earned a living into skills on which serious wagers were placed. The first recorded formal rowing event on the now-famous English racing venues took place in 1828 at the Cambridge Rowing Club and the following year saw the beginning of the Oxford-Cambridge Races, a competition that is still one of the most important rowing events in the world.

Sliding seats and outriggers are two devices that revolutionized the sport. In 1846, Oxford University Boat Club developed the outrigger. The oars were mounted not on, but outboard of the gunwales. This led to a narrower and lighter hull design and, consequently, increased speed. In 1870, the Yale crew started greasing the seats of their pants so they could slide forward and back, adding leg power to their strokes. A year later the sliding seat was born.

With the arrival of these two innovations, the sport of rowing really took hold, particularly in colleges and universities where competition was enthusiastically embraced. The main reason why rowing was the sport of colleges, universities, and the elite was and still is, to a great extent, the price of the rowing shell. Designed and built for speed, not durability, these delicate boats require large monetary investments and constant maintenance and tuning, keeping them financially out of reach for most people.

If anyone could be described as the father of modern recreational rowing, it is Arthur Martin. In 1971, Martin, a naval architect, decided to build a seaworthy boat that could be rowed by anyone and still possess the performance features of a single scull. The result was the Alden Ocean Shell. This recreational shell maintains some of the quickness of the single scull, but is comparatively inexpensive. Designed with outriggers, a sliding seat, and fiberglass hull, the Alden is "stable, seaworthy, and adjusts to fit any rower." Today, an Alden Ocean Shell costs approximately $2000 complete, as opposed, for example, to a Maas Aero that costs $2500 plus $350 for a pair of oars. The Alden Shell, in some ways resembling a kayak with outriggers, opened the door to recreational rowing, made the sport more accessible to the masses, and introduced performance rowing in open water. For the first time, rowers could explore offshore areas and larger bodies of water in a responsive, high-performance, and stable boat.

WOMEN AND ROWING

In 1903, in *Athletics and Out-door Sports for Women,* Lucille Eaton Hill, then Director of Physical Education at Wellesley College, wrote:

Rowing, for girls . . . may be divided into skiff or pleasure rowing, pure and simple, and crew rowing, which is, indeed, also a pleasure for those who delight in constantly being found fault with because they cannot do 26 things at the same time, although it is not by any means simple or a recreation in the same sense with skiff rowing.

Perhaps the choice between skiff and crew rowing must be decided by one's love of scenery, as the skiff oarswoman can happily gaze on the face of Nature while the crew oarswoman fixes her eye on the neck of the girl in front. . . .

The physical benefits which women derive from rowing cannot be exaggerated, provided they are willing to master the rudiments of the sport—for one must strive for good form, deep breathing, strength of back and chest, and wear no tight or stiff clothing about the waist. Correct rowing induces an erect carriage and finely poised head, a full chest, and well-placed shoulders. Incorrect rowing disturbs all harmony of the figure. One can row one's self round-shouldered as easily as erect!

This passage could be enough to discourage any potential oarswoman, but the fact is that rowing for pleasure and rowing in competition, while very different, are both extremely enjoyable aspects of the sport. However, rowing as part of a crew was and is a skill learned primarily in school. Up until the 1960s, with the passing of Title IX, there was scant opportunity for women to row, so the sport was dominated by men.

We are beginning to see women just coming into their own in rowing. According to the United States Rowing Association, in 1991, 29 percent of master rowers (those over the age of 27), were women—an increase of almost 224 percent in ten years. Those are just masters' rowing statistics and do not include school-age girl rowers. Considering the fact that in 1938 Ernestine Bayer and her partner Jeanette Hoover were the first women to race on the Schuykill River (and perhaps in America), and given the fact that there was no women's

Olympic rowing participation until 1976, and considering that in the 1988 Olympics the American women's eight was the only American crew to win the gold—in a little over 50 years, I think it's safe to say, "We've come a long way, baby!"

BOATS

Racing shells come in four types—singles, pairs, fours, and eights (as well as variations on pairs and fours), and are designed for speed. They are long, narrow, and built with the lightest-weight materials; their purpose being not just durability but to win races.

There are two types of recreational shells—singles and doubles. The most noticeable difference between racing and recreational shells are length and width. Recreational shells are wider, built for stability. The narrow racing shell is more difficult to balance, but something you will probably work up to after rowing a while.

Rowing a single racing or recreational shell is called sculling—one rower using two oars (called sculls) to propel the boat. Rowing a double is also called sculling because two rowers each use two oars to propel the boat. Once you get to fours and eights, though, each rower uses one oar to propel the boat.

Every rowing craft needs oars. Sometimes oars come with the boat but often they do not. Sculls come in two types—those made of wood and those made of a composite material. Although oars made of wood are available, they are dated. The modern, carbon-fiber oars are much preferable. They are lighter in weight, maintenance free, and extremely durable.

ROWING TECHNIQUE

Rowing is a graceful, rhythmic activity. The elements of the stroke are catch, drive, follow through, finish, and recovery. These elements flow together in a circular movement and it's that repeated movement that becomes so addictive to the rower. There are eight steps to the stroke. Writer and rower Rebecca Busselle so perfectly describes the routine: "I lift the oars and slide forward until my knees are almost to my chest, my body crouched like a frog ready to spring, arms straight in front; I drop the oar blades square into the water. As I pull back, power moves through my arms and shoulders, then through my thighs, and finally into my back and stomach at the finish of the stroke. When my hands hit my sternum, I push the oar handles away from me and the blades feather the waterline to begin another stroke. I am rowing."

RECREATIONAL ROWING

What attracts women to recreational rowing? The same things that attract men. Rowers tend to talk about their sport in almost Zen-like terms but what it boils down to is this: It's a fantastic aerobic exercise, pumping huge amounts of oxygenated blood through your veins with every pull of the oar. It promotes psychological as well as physiological well being; perched close to the water in a tiny little boat, rhythmic body movements coupled with the movement of the water put you right there, in tune with the elements. Rowing is a perfect time to be alone with yourself in an otherwise hectic world. Rowing is total concentration—to row successfully you must think rowing and nothing else. You can row at your own pace, going full tilt or perhaps just gliding leisurely along or maybe even stopping to watch the gulls.

Let's start with the exercise connection. Rowing offers a total body workout, working muscles that women often find difficult to keep in tone. Using proper technique, rowing not only builds aerobic capacity, but works the arms, shoulders, chest, legs, back, and abdomen as well—all while sitting, so joints are not stressed. Rowing is a high-intensity aerobic sport and burns as many calories as cross-country skiing. During a good row, lungs are pushed to capacity, building cardiovascular systems superior to those of long-distance runners.

Rowing is a nonstress sport and is practically "ageless." Forty-two-year-old Vicki Scott started rowing a few years ago to "try to get in the best shape I could by the time I was 40," she said in an interview in *USA Today*. After shedding two clothing sizes and 20 pounds, and having a lot of fun doing it, Vicki decided to find a coach to see just how far she would actually go in the sport. She qualified for the 1991 Pan Am Games!

Picking up an oar for the first time in her 40s, Ernestine Bayer (profiled in this chapter) now 81, still competes regularly against men and women in their 60s, 70s, and 80s, and often wins! Rowing several times a week in a recreational single, she recently encouraged a friend to start rowing. Her friend is 57.

Ernestine suffers from arthritis in her back but is quick to point out that rowing doesn't aggravate that condition in the least because "legs—not your back—give you power," she says. But to row effectively, there is a part of your anatomy that must be able to function without problem—your knees. You must be able to get in and out of the boat, you must bend your knees at a 90-degree angle in the catch-and-drive phase of the stroke, *plus* healthy knees are necessary to lift the boat on and off the car.

What special equipment do you need to enter the sport? It's simple—a boat (called a shell) and two oars (called sculls). Are you longing to buy a boat and get onto the water? We don't blame you, but let's talk about it. The first order of the day is to determine where you will row. Will you be rowing in protected or open water? Unlike in the East Coast, open-water rowing is very popular in the West. For most of us, car-topping is a necessity. But perhaps the most important question to answer is: Can you carry the boat you have chosen by yourself? For example, the Alden Ocean Shell is 16 feet long, 25 inches wide, and weighs 63 pounds with the rowing rig. It's only fair to mention here that the Alden rig detaches from the hull for transportation. But the hull alone weighs 40 pounds. Compare that to another popular single, the Maas Aero, at 21 feet long, 25 inches wide, and weighing 40 pounds, complete with rowing rig. Whether you live on the water or not, you will have to carry the boat from the boathouse to the water or from the garage to the cartop. Like a canoe or a kayak, a boat that you can't transport to the water is worse than no boat at all!

Have you had any rowing experience? If the answer is yes, then test-drive as many boats as you can before buying. Builders often attend large regattas and bring along extra shells that they encourage rowers to try. Dealers usually carry more than one brand and style, often give lessons, and will always encourage you to try out and compare their boats. Take one out for a half hour or so—shopping for boats can be fun! But it can also be time-consuming and sometimes a daunting process. While we can give you some very bare-bones buying guidelines in this chapter, books have been written on the subject. We urge you to talk with other women rowers and find out what their experience has been. A boat that is good for a 200-pound man is not good for a 120-pound woman, so don't take the advice of just anyone. Gain as much knowledge as you can before you head out to the store. The chart below will give you a comparison of rowing boats by speed and stability. As you look over this chart you will see that between the Alden and the Maas lie a wide range of shells of all weights, prices, designs, and styles. Check the Bibliography for books that will help in your pursuit of the boat for you.

Boats are expensive, so consider alternatives to purchase. One of the glories of joining a rowing club is to access the club's boat inventory. Try their singles and, believe me, once you find the craft you like, other members will be eager to steer you in the direction of a distributor. Then again, you may find that you won't need to purchase a boat of your own at all—that the club boats are just fine. But, if you live in an area where clubs are not an alternative, take your time in shopping. Boats are very personal items and what's a perfect boat for one person may in no way be perfect for another. In the end, it's the boat that you see yourself as rowing that will close the deal. Although used boats are available all the time, recreational shells are virtually maintenance-free and maintain their value, so don't expect any bargains.

If you already own a small boat or canoe, consider a device like the Oarmaster. Martin Marine makes this rowing rig that comes com-

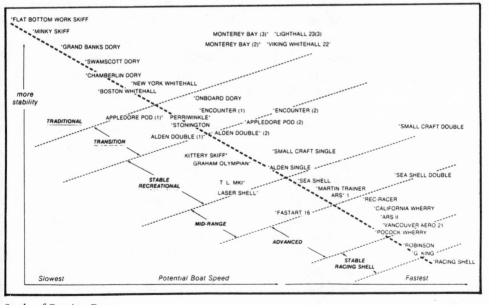

Study of Rowing Boats.

plete with outriggers and sliding seat and can be installed easily in most small boats. Mad River Canoe Company also makes a rowing insert for canoes. Because they are sleek, with finely tapered ends, canoes make good rowing craft and they are reasonably seaworthy.

Other attractive features to joining a club (and there are hundreds of clubs across the country. See Rowing Clubs in Resources) include: Instruction is always available, whether on a formal or informal basis; if you own a boat, storage is available; and clubs usually have specially designed launching docks. Most clubs hire coaches, schedule clinics and races, and sponsor social events. But one prerequisite to choosing a club is knowing what kind of rowing you will be doing. Some of the more traditional clubs concentrate almost solely on competition while newer clubs tend to focus on recreational and open-water rowing— their activities include cruising as well as racing.

While learning the technique of any sport from a spouse, friend, or lover can be fun, it's really ill advised. For starters, you don't need to pick up anyone else's bad habits, and in those learning situations patience often wears thin and tempers flare; then everyone's experience is ruined. Rowing is a technique that takes time and patience to perfect and it is better to learn from a professional. That way you'll get off to a good start and develop a style of your own. After you learn the basics, *then* row with your friends. The United States Rowing Association in Indianapolis maintains an updated list of schools and clubs nationwide. Another alternative is to attend a rowing camp. Larger camps such as the Craftsbury Center in Craftsbury Common, Vermont, for instance, offer weekends as well as week-long sessions that include not just rowing instruction but emphasize weight training, cross training, video coaching, and diet, as well as an all-around assessment of you as an athlete, helping you get the most from your athletic experience.

Although rowing is an easy-entry sport that quickly produces huge and very rewarding dividends, we cannot stress strongly enough that because of its aerobic intensity, rowing does require some degree of physical conditioning to get started. Don't expect to just jump into a boat and go. In fact, many rowing clubs, including the Moms (profiled in this chapter), require a doctor's certificate to join.

COMPETITIVE ROWING

We've talked a lot about recreational rowing which is usually done in a single. Now let's talk a little about rowing as part of a crew.

As mentioned before, until the passage of Title IX, money for women's crew was scarce. Historically, women's teams were not plentiful and since crew is primarily learned in a school situation, few women have had the opportunity to participate. One oarswoman in her 50s said, "I think one reason women have so much fun with crew and feel so committed to it is because when we were in school we didn't have the opportunity to perform as part of a team, to become part of a whole."

Perhaps more than any other sport, crew requires intense commitment, concentration, and synchronization. On the water, each crew member must think and move in unison to make the boat run smoothly. International competitor Vicki Scott described team coordination, "Everybody putting their blades in the water and taking them out at the same time. Your head, your little finger, your butt—everything moving at the same time as seven other women."

When boating a crew, the coach spends hours of practice time determining the strength and stamina of the individual rowers in order to seat them properly. Each seat in an eight (or a four or a pair), has a particular function in the speed and the balance of the boat. Then through practice the boat rows as a whole unit, a smooth-running machine. Although some crew members may be moved around within the boat, a rower from outside that crew is not easily substituted. For while that new crew member knows how to row as part of a team, she will have to find the rhythm and style of the new team before she can become effective. For that reason, commitment to crew is vital. If, for instance, one of the rowers decides not to show up for a practice or a race, the whole team suffers. Many women who join clubs and compete are young mothers, so it's not unusual for Dad and the kids, or a babysitter, or the next-door neighbor to pitch in and help Mom meet her obligations to the team. One Mom said, "It makes it very special when you finally figure out a way to have someone else assume those responsibilities [of parenthood] temporarily."

In talking to various oarswomen, one subject that always comes up is the intensity of concentration it takes to row. Martha Beattie, coach of Martha's Moms, calls this process "tunneling in," or total concentration on the moment. The greatest benefit derived from that period of total concentration is that it cleanses your mind. One of the Moms describes it this way, "You think only of moving in sync with the woman in front of you; of lifting your oar; sliding forward; crouching; dropping your blade squarely into the water; pulling hard; pushing oar handle away from you; sliding back; catch, pull, release, feather in cadence with seven other women in the boat."

So why do women row? Because it's so much fun! Because it's hard work that pays off. Because it pushes you beyond your limits. Because you make a variety of friends—women of all ages and life-styles wherever regattas are held, women you probably wouldn't know otherwise. Because physically it's such a great outlet. Because it makes you feel good all over. The team experience shouldn't be missed. One rower compared rowing recreationally to rowing with a team. "It is different and something very special. It's like driving a Pontiac as compared to driving a Mercedes. Once you learn to drive well, you want to drive the best."

Camaraderie among oarswomen is special. Gretchen Hull of Martha's Moms in Seattle says that the friendships forged among the members of their club are long lasting and supportive. "Women share many common experiences," she says. "We are a very support-ive group and even if our crew is not racing on a particular day, we show up to cheer the others on. Members who have had difficulties either in their marital, work, or family life have found a lot of under-standing among the Moms."

Through rowing, you catch power and freedom while propelling yourself along, gliding back and forth on a sliding seat, nestled in a fragile shell perched lightly on the surface of the water, feeling the rhythm, feeling the synergy of every muscle in your body as you push and pull. You're the boat. You're the water. You're a graceful dragonfly skimming the surface. You're free.

The more we support and encourage young women in sports, the more women's masters' sports will continue to grow. That means an even greater demand for crew programs for older women. What a nice prospect!

Profile: Ernestine Bayer—
The Mother of American Rowing

"I never set out to make history," Ernie Bayer said. "One thing followed naturally on another, and everything I did, I did simply because I love rowing." When Ernestine Steppacher-Bayer got hooked on rowing, she had little notion that 50 years later she would be called the "mother of American women's rowing." She is still a little incredulous that her love of rowing and her joy of teaching other women to row has been taken so seriously.

Ernestine, who had never rowed a stroke in her life, married Olympic oarsman Ernest Bayer in 1928 and used to accompany him on his daily walk to a Schuylkill River boathouse where she sat and watched as he and his crew mates rowed their piece. One day she asked Ernest why there were no women rowing on the river. "They don't have any place to row *from*," he said, "and women don't row!" Well, if that was the only reason, thought Ernie, then women would indeed be seen on the river.

Ernestine Bayer.

Now, if there's anything Ernie really loves, it's a challenge, and once she decides to do something, it's done. In May of 1938, gathering a group of 14 interested women, she rented a boathouse and established the Philadelphia Girls Rowing Club (which is still in existence today). The women gracefully accepted cast-off shells from boat clubs up and down the river and were soon out on the water rowing. Ernie's husband and another well-known oarsman coached the group in a borrowed training barge.

Ernestine and her partner Jeanette Waetgen-Hoover (who still maintain close contact) competed in the Fourth of July Regatta that year, becoming the first women ever to race on the Schuylkill (and maybe in America)—and they won! Of course, "all hell broke loose" along male-dominated Boathouse Row. Some longtime friends shunned the women for competing. One man pulled Ernie's husband aside and wanted to know why he permitted his wife to row. "Aren't you afraid your wife will contract tuberculosis from rowing?" he asked.

But Ernie had experienced her first taste of competition and was hooked on the sport. She rowed every day for an hour or more, May through October. Leisure time in the life of the two Bayers focused on rowing. Their daughter Tina, born in 1945, has early memories of her parents at the boathouse and on the river. She took her first step and celebrated her first birthday in the boathouse. As Ernie became more proficient at the sport, she hankered for stiffer competition, and entered her first out-of-state race in Florida at age 47, rowing seven seat in an eight.

As they say, the rest is history. Ernie has spread her joy of rowing through teaching the sport to literally hundreds of other women. In a recent *Yankee* magazine profile, Liz O'Leary, an Ernie Bayer protégée and sculling coach of the 1988 U.S. Women's Olympic rowing team, said, "It's unusual, perhaps unprecedented, for 90 percent of current participants to know their sport's founder the way American oarswomen know Ernie Bayer."

But that's not all. Ernie single-handedly raised the funds to take the first group of American girls to European competition in 1967. With daughter Tina, in 1973 she organized and coached women's rowing at the University of New Hampshire. In 1972 she formed the first recreational rowing association in the United States (now the largest amateur rowing group) and achieved recreational club status within the U.S.

Rowing Association. In 1984, she was inducted into the U.S. Rowing Association's Hall of Fame. Then 75, Ernie was asked by the women's Olympic eight, the first American women's eight to win Olympic gold and also Hall of Fame inductees, to row with them the next day. "I was humbled by the power of that row," she said. "Those strong beautiful oarswomen, my beloved Schuylkill like glass, the feel of that boat . . . we were airborne." They similarly were honored to row with her.

In February 1991 Ernie raced in the C.R.A.S.H.-B Sprints in Boston (indoor competition using ergometers). Of course, officials had to create a new division to accommodate her—women 80–89. "I'll always love a good race," she grins. She bested women in younger age categories to make the age-60-and-over finals.

At 82, Ernie Bayer (a.k.a. Mamma Bayer) lives along the Squamscott River in New Hampshire and rows four times a week in a racing single with a friend (who at 57 just started rowing a year ago). "When I go out for a row," she says, "I might be upset about something, but I row until I'm tired . . . then I can only think of that tiredness . . . it's soothing . . . it's soothing and just plain lovely."

Profile: Martha's Moms

"As Pat Nevler and I were putting the shell into the water the other day we were joking around and saying that at some point we may have to get down to our boats using walkers," laughs Gretchen Hull. Pat is 65, Gretchen 59. Both started rowing just a few years ago. Both are members of Martha's Moms, a women's rowing team in Seattle, Washington.

Three days a week, the Moms gather at 6 A.M. at the Lakeside School boathouse on Lake Washington to begin their workout—four or five days a week if they're training for a regatta. The workout starts before they reach the boathouse, though. Before lifting the 60-foot-long shells over their heads, down the ramp, and into the water, the Moms have stretched out muscles well, left their various daily family routines behind, and are "psyched," as their kids say, for an hour and a half of working together as a team. Few women have had the good fortune to experience team discipline previously and for this reason, women's masters' rowing clubs are springing up around the country.

Martha's Moms was started by Gretchen Hull and Penny Lewis, parents of students who rowed at Lakeside High School in Seattle. At an annual Parents' Day, the two women experienced rowing in an eight and quickly understood why their kids were having so much fun. They enlisted the expertise of Martha Beattie, head crew coach at Lakeside, and began learning the skills necessary to make a shell move through the water. The program started with eight women, then the word spread about the great workout and the opportunity to learn to row. Seven years later the Moms have 43 members (ranging in age from 27 to 65), two (and sometimes three) coaches, and an official T-shirt—crossed oars over an apple pie. They named themselves Martha's Moms because many of the women in the club were truly old enough to be Martha Beattie's Mom.

A few of these women had rowed long ago in college, though not competitively, and a few were familiar with row boats or wherries, but none had real rowing experience. Through a lot of hard work, dedication, and mutual support, this team now competes in regattas around the country and has won the Master's Nationals in their age category three out of the last five years. Although proud of their success, the Moms don't talk much about national-champion status. Instead, they emphasize how great rowing makes them feel as individuals and how much they enjoy building on and sharing that experience with their teammates. "I never thought I was competitive until I saw another boat creeping up on me," one Mom said.

The Moms are quick to stress that rowing competitively is not a prerequisite to joining the Moms. Some rowers prefer rowing for exercise and recreation and the team is supportive of that. As young women, many of the Moms felt that they lacked athletic opportunities, and through the years many have been busy supporting husbands and children in their athletic pursuits. "But now it's their turn, as the Mom's enter their middle and later years and discover an unknown side to themselves," wrote Bev Wessel in an article about the Moms that appeared in an edition of *Outdoor Woman* newsletter.

Winning isn't everything, though. The Moms are also committed to promoting rowing as a lifetime sport for women. A newcomer need only possess a commitment to learn and dedication to working hard to earn the support, friendship, and skills given freely by her teammates and coaches. "I used to think of myself as clumsy," said Darleen Bunker, who has been with the Moms for a short time. "Now I feel powerful." One of the Moms went beyond talking about how rowing

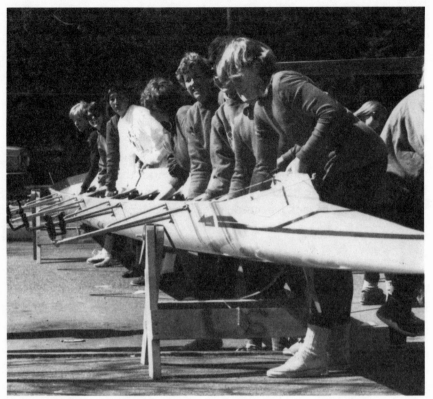

Martha's Moms: *Photo by E.A. Cicotte.*

has improved her physical being. Counseling? Who needs it? She exchanged mood swings and therapist bills for an oar, a shell, and a terrific group of "gung-ho ladies."

The best part, however, is being part of an all-women crew and listening to the voices of their coaches shouting instructions from megaphones in the launch boat traveling alongside them. "Arms, hips, back should be one solid piece," coach Karen Lewis calls out. A slight change in hand position is instructed; a challenge to catch the leading boat is cast out across the water.

A very important aspect that a team like the Moms offers is the diversity of rowing partners in terms of age and rowing abilities. The Moms say that this diversity enables the older women to challenge themselves through the strength of the younger women and that the younger women, in turn, learn a lot from them. "If you are 59 and rowing with women who are in their 30s and 40s, you are really challenged and have to work a heck of a lot harder," says one Mom, and adds, "On the other hand, some younger women are immature and I think they have learned a lot from us. Everyone ends up learning and feeling good."

What is it like when every woman in the boat is pulling together, rowing as one whole, as a team? "When the team is perfectly synchronized," Gretchen says, "the boat makes a sound and you have a sense of gliding . . . the sound of water rushing under the boat is like wind blowing through the trees . . . it's powerful. You know you're doing it right when you hear that sound."

BIKING

The bicycle . . . has been responsible for more movement in manners and morals than anything since Charles the Second. Under its influence, wholly or in part, have wilted chaperones, long and narrow skirts, tight corsets, hair that would come down, black stockings, thick ankles, large hats, prudery, and fear of the dark; under its influence, wholly or in part, have blossomed weekends, strong nerves, strong legs, strong language, knickers, knowledge of make and shape, knowledge of woods and pastures, equality of sex, good digestion, and professional occupation—in four words, the emancipation of women.

—John Galsworthy (1867–1933),
English novelist and playwright

A bike is the personification of the freedom and joy of childhood, and few of us grew up without one. Jumping on a bike as an adult, those childhood memories will come flooding back as you remaster the magical balancing and pedaling technique. Learning to pedal and balance at the same time is a step in learned coordination, part of the process of skills development. But, more than that, as a youngster a bike was your ticket to freedom, your first step away from home. Learning to ride was probably the first time you experienced the glory of being self-propelled, the first time you experienced unrestricted speed—the feeling of flying. It may have been the first time you were in total control of a mechanical "thing."

Somewhere along the way, along with the innocence and simplicity of childhood, we left our bikes behind. As teenagers we quickly acquired the trappings of adulthood. It was cool to cruise around with friends in a shiny one-ton steel box. But in the process, we lost touch with our active selves, becoming not participants but passengers. Well, the great news is, you haven't really lost that active self, but have simply forgotten it was there.

Quoted in the *New York Times,* Olympic Gold Medal cyclist Connie Carpenter Phinney said, "Bicycling is pure fun. You feel like a kid again." While some of us may not have had the chance to ride as kids, it has become increasingly apparent that even as grownups we shelter a child within, and, like any child, she needs time to play. And play, translated into grownup language, means sport. Readily accessible, the sport of cycling is easily learned if you've never tried, quickly remembered if you biked as a kid, a fantastic total body workout, and, best of all, as Phinney says, just "pure fun."

Believe it or not, around the turn of the century, before Henry Ford put a car in every garage, the bicycle market was huge and women comprised one third of that market! At that time the Starley Brothers mass-produced the first woman's bicycle, strangely called Psycho Ladies Bicycle. A rather peculiar name, to say the least, but perhaps it had something to do with the running debate over whether or not a woman should even be sitting astride a wheel. In an essay, "Women and Cycling: The Early Years," published in the book *How I Learned to Ride the Bicycle,* Lisa Larrabee describes the attitudes of the day. Doctors prescribed that "women should practice moderation in their efforts," and went on to say that "one Parisian claimed that bicycling ruined the 'feminine organs of matrimonial necessity,' thus bringing about the end of womanhood." In 1895, *The Cosmopolitan* argued that by riding a bicycle, a woman would "become mistress of herself." On the other hand, Lisa contends, bicycles freed young women from the bonds of chaperones—most chaperones being elderly and unable to "keep up with speedy young cyclists." Lisa's essay also recounts the daring solo cross-country bicycle trip by Margaret Valentine Le Long in 1896! Following "railroad tracks through Nebraska, Wyoming, Utah, Nevada, and California . . . she carried a light load—a shirt, change of underwear, clean hanky, toilet articles, and a pistol. She only had to use her gun once, and that was to scatter a herd of unmoving cattle in Wyoming." Famed mountaineer Fanny Bullock Workman rode over much of Europe, North Africa, Palestine, Syria, and Turkey. Between 1897 and 1899, she covered a total of 14,000 miles—the length and breadth of India—including 1,800 miles in Ceylon and 500 miles in Java.

In the survey, "Sports Participation in 1990," conducted by the National Sporting Goods Association, it was found that women comprise almost 53 percent of recreational bikers. I guess there is something about biking that we really love.

Biking is actually divided into two sports: road biking and off-road or mountain biking, and although the market is seeing a lot of crossovers recently, mainly from road to mountain biking, both sports have their zealots and rightly so. Fat, knobby-tire mountain bikes are built for off-road travel and can handle the roughest terrain. With their sturdy frame, straight handlebars, and up to 21 gears, these bikes are great for climbing the steepest trails and for bouncing over woods roads and trails, but they're sluggish and heavy on paved roads. Imagine, the first bicycles featured substantial frames and fat tires, and although the phrase hadn't as yet been coined, those first bikes were actually all-terrain or mountain bikes. It wasn't until Mr. McAdam mixed up his gooey composite called tarmac that sleek, narrow road bikes were even the remotest possibility. Lightweight, skinny, smooth-tire road bikes are built to ride on smooth pavement. Holding onto drop handlebars, the rider is placed in an aerodynamic, 45-degree angle, perfectly positioned for speed. Both are great fun, and each has its definite place.

ROAD BIKING

Road biking can mean a variety of things, one of which is racing. Competition spurs a lot of us on and many feel that there's nothing like meeting up with a bunch of buddies on Sunday mornings to pedal as fast as you can over any number of miles, testing both your endurance and biking skills. Besides, after the racing is over, it's great fun to get together to compare techniques, equipment, and catch up on the latest news about kids, family, and friends. Famous racer "Alice B. Toeclips" aptly sums it up: "After a race, women love to greet each other and, well, gossip about how it all went down."

Road biking can also mean touring, and touring can mean anything from day trips on local roads or bike trails to pedaling around the neighborhood or even across the country. We spent the '80s working out at the gym, getting in shape, discovering our physical selves, and fitness is no longer limited to three times a week at the gym—it has become a way of life. It makes sense that an active vacation is a natural next step. In 1989, over one million people (almost 50 percent of them women) took part in bike tours in the United States alone and many had such a great time that they bought bikes of their own.

Bike tours are an easy entry into the sport. Rides are set up in a variety of ways so whether you're a beginner or an advanced rider there is a route to match your ability. The pleasure of this type of vacation comes from riding with a group of like-minded individuals who have the same goal—to ride, to see the countryside, and to have fun. One rider said, "You don't think about the distance of the ride or the difficulty of the terrain when you're riding with a group. I was surprised, the miles just roll by." Another seductive feature to bike touring is the "sag wagon," a van that accompanies the group, carries all the gear, provides assistance in case of breakdown, and carries you if you get tired.

MOUNTAIN BIKES

On the flip side of the biking coin is the off-road or mountain bike. Originating on the miles of California dirt roads in the mid-'70s, wide-tired bombers replaced the skinny-tire road bike that just couldn't cut it in the dirt. The only bike that stood up to dirt-road abuse was the Schwinn Excelsior, manufactured from 1933 to 1941. To this bike, an enterprising Marin County tinkerer added a derailleur and some gears and a revolution started. With continued development, that revolution produced the very stable, easy-to-ride 18- to 21-speed mountain bike. This bike offers increased stability, it's easier to turn, and, because of the upright position of the rider, she can see better and sit more comfortably, making the mountain bike an ideal first choice for women.

On an off-road bike you can ride worry-free over potholes, steep terrain, sand, and gravel or any of the other vagaries of road and trail. So, no matter what you call it—off-road, all-terrain, or mountain biking—it all means the same thing: Pure biking fun!

HYBRIDS

A bike that you'll be hearing more about, an offshoot of the mountain bike, but actually a cross between a mountain and a road bike, is what's called a "hybrid." A hybrid frame is heavier than a road bike but not as heavy as a mountain bike. Its handlebars are straight across like a mountain bike, rather than drop. The tires are wider and have more tread than a road bike but are not as fat and knobby as a mountain bike. Most hybrids have 21 gears like a mountain bike and can climb the steepest hills. However, overall, the hybrid isn't as strong as a mountain bike and can't take the same abuse. It falls in the middle of the biking spectrum, and for beginners is a very good choice.

WOMEN BICYCLISTS

Women's interests in biking seem to run the gamut from racing to touring, from the smoothest road surfaces to the toughest mountain trail. For instance, Debbie Breaud (profiled in this chapter) rode in RAAM (the Race Across America) in 1991, a grueling cross-country road race that takes years of preparation and training. Gail Koepf of Fairbanks, Alaska won the Women's Iditasport race in 1990. The Iditasport, a 200-mile off-road bike race across frigid, windblown and snow-covered trails, is a test of mental stamina as well as physical strength. "As a 40-year old mother of two strong-willed daughters," she said, "who are only beginning to face the challenges of life, I believe in role models."

Jacquie Phelan of Fairfax, California (alias Alice B. Toeclips) is founder of the Women's Mountain Bike and Tea Society (WOMBATS), a nationwide organization of "uppity fat-tire women." She is also a founder of NORBA (National Off Road Bicycle Association) and a three-time NORBA champion who spends every waking moment riding her bike or writing about and promoting biking. An environmentalist, Jacquie tries to pry people out of their cars and onto bikes. "One of the great things about riding a bicycle, whether in Madagascar, Midland, or Marin, is the fact that every errand has the potential to unfold into an adventure," Jacquie said in *California Bicyclist*. Virginia Urrutia—a 70-year-old grandmother—cycles around the world. Every time she feels an adventure coming on she not only buys a plane ticket but digs out one of her many bikes as well. In her book *Two Wheels & A Taxi*, Virginia describes her ride across the Andes. "The bike is primarily for me a way to observe and to know people. All bicycling does not need to be done with head down and legs straining—much can be seen and learned by poking and prowling, by taking advantage of the curiosity of the people you visit."

CHOOSING A BIKE

We bet you're itching to head out to the bike store to get yourself a set of wheels. Stop! A good bike is a very expensive investment so let's ask a few questions before you go. Do you want a mountain bike, a road bike, or something in between? Where will you do most of your riding? Decide whether you will be riding on the road exclusively or on some dirt roads and trails as well. How much can you afford to spend? How much biking do you think you'll do? What about "women's bikes"? Only after determining your biking needs can you start to shop around.

When we were kids, the only prerequisite to choosing a bike was the color, but like everything else in life, choosing a bike these days has become increasingly complicated. So a specialty bike shop is the best place to start. Stay away from discount houses and even sport shops that carry bikes as a sideline. Discount-house bikes are heavy and clunky and usually poorly made. Your bike will need an occasional tune-up and discount houses won't provide that service.

Walking into a bike shop you'll be confronted by dozens of bikes—a potentially confusing situation. *Bicycling* and *Bicycle Guide* magazines publish annual buying guides. Also check *Consumer Reports*. Talk to other women who ride. Listen to their stories—we all have some. If you don't know any women bikers, contact a local bike club. Bike club information can be found in the outdoor-activities column of your local newspaper or on library or local cycle-shop bulletin boards. Most outdoor clubs, such as the Sierra Club or the Appalachian Mountain Club, have entire biking sections. Riders love to talk equipment and you'll probably get more information than you know what to do with.

Even after determining the type of bike you want, perhaps the greatest dilemma you'll face is finding a bike that fits. Despite the fact that in the late 1800s the Starley Brothers designed the Psycho Ladies Bicycle, women have been essentially ignored by the industry ever since. Faced with the choice of riding a bike that's too big or not riding at all, women have spent years coping with aching backs, legs, and bottoms. The worst part is, many thought they were supposed to suffer.

The facts are, the average woman has longer legs and a shorter torso than a man. She is also narrower in the shoulders, has a wider pelvis and smaller hands. Traditionally, bikes have been designed to accommodate a man's body.

The biking industry had all but ignored the growing women's market until engineer and biker Georgena Terry stepped in. Georgena, who had logged as many as 8,000 miles a year, knew intimately the unique problems women faced in finding a bike to fit. She determined that because women have a shorter torso length they needed a bike with a shorter top tube—the connecting piece on a bike between the seat and handlebars. Otherwise, when seated, they have to stretch out to more than a 45-degree angle to reach the handlebars, causing back, shoulder, and neck pain. Her Terry Precision Bicycle (see Catalogs and Mail Order in Resources) is built with a shorter-length top tube. Added features include narrower handlebars to accommodate a woman's narrower shoulder width, smaller crank arms, and smaller brake levers to fit a woman's grip.

Recognizing that short women face an even more difficult task in finding a proper fit, Terry proceeded to design a bike for women 5'4" and under. However, in the smaller frame sizes she found that the front wheel hit the pedals when turning. To alleviate this problem she replaced the front wheel with a smaller 24-inch wheel for clearance. These small bikes tend to look a little strange at first, because the back and front wheels are different sizes, but they are extremely comfortable to ride. Mike Levy noted in an article appearing in *Outdoor Woman*, "Susan Notrangelo, for example, the founder of the Women's Cycling Network and a noted 'ultra-marathon' racer who has broken the women's record three times in the Race Across America, in 1989 finished the 3,000-mile coast-to-coast run in nine days, nine hours, nine minutes . . . on her Terry." Quintana Roo makes an ATB bike for women, utilizing a shorter top tube and two 26-inch wheels. Other manufacturers, including Bianchi, Cannondale, and Nishiki, manufacture some off-road models that feature sloped top tubes. But then again, you may choose to go the custom-built route, in which case, contact Zinn Cycles (check Resources) in Boulder, Colorado. Specializing in custom bikes for women, Zinn has a particular interest since Zinn-Alfalfa not only sponsor a woman's racing team but Leonard Zinn's wife is a road racer, so they're really tuned in to the unique needs of women and what it takes to achieve a comfortable ride. They recently built a mountain bike for a woman who is 4'5". Although expensive (starting at $1250 for a frame and $1800 for a complete bike), if you have trouble finding a bike that fits, a custom bike may be the answer.

Now that you've found some bikes that interest you, it's time for a test drive. You'll want to try several different models before you decide what's best for you. A good shop will let you take the bike for a little ride, but before you take off, make sure you understand how to shift the gears. Although the new Index or click shifters give a clear indication of when you've shifted correctly, they still take a little time to get used to. The great thing about Index shifting is that the gears audibly snap into place, unlike the old friction-type shifting systems.

EQUIPMENT

The number-one item that you'll need besides a bike is a helmet. Don't leave home without it. There is always the danger of falling while biking. A helmet should be made of a hard shell material and fit snugly enough that it won't fall off. The new models are very lightweight and well ventilated. If you're one of those people who thinks helmets are stupid-looking, take heart—you can jazz yours up with a bright Lycra helmet cover to match your shorts, jersey, or your mood of the day.

Another necessary item, if you do more than ride outside the neighborhood, is a frame pump. Depending upon how much riding you do, you may want to invest in a stand-up pump, easier to operate than a frame pump and much more efficient. An item I have found to be of great value is a small compressor that runs off a car cigarette lighter. It has a gauge that indicates air pressure to prevent over-inflation, fills the tire slowly so there is no chance of blowing the tire off the rim, and saves a lot of guesswork and manual labor.

When you purchase a bike, seriously consider buying a small tool kit in its own carrying case. In the tool kit you'll find a tire patch kit, tire-removal tools, and instructions. It's really easy to change your tire and tube, but before you get stuck on the road, practice at home. Many bike clubs and bike shops host seminars on bike maintenance—a fun and rewarding way to spend an evening. Another must-have item for your kit is a spare inner tube. Changing is easier than patching.

The better frames have brazed-on (welded) connections for a water-bottle holder. Some bikes have room for two bottles and that isn't a bad idea, especially for lengthy rides.

Handlebar and seat bags are handy for carrying tools, your lunch, rain gear, and other necessities. There is a variety of different styles that attach to various parts of a bike. These choices are purely personal.

If you're a "gear head" you may want to invest in a new toy called a cycle computer. This fun little item can be programmed to tell you how far you've gone and at what speed, pedal rotations per minute, duration of the ride, average speed, and distance to your destination. Some computers even monitor your heartbeat.

A real problem, even if you find a bike that fits, is finding the right seat. Women's saddles need to be slightly wider in the back to support a wider pelvic structure. The front, or the nose of the saddle, on the other hand, should be shorter than a man's. There is no need to ride a bike with an uncomfortable seat. Seats are relatively inexpensive, easy to change, and easier still to adjust. For years I resisted changing saddles, even though the saddle that came with my bike was uncomfortable no matter what adjustments were made. I recently purchased an Avocet Touring W II and love it. Now that I've ridden on the wider gel saddle, I can see that a comfortable seat really does make all the difference in the world. Womyn's Wheel (see Catalogs and Mail Order in Resources), a mail-order catalog, sells Vetta Gel Shock Absorber saddles and Waveflo's Flolite, both made especially for women.

CYCLING CLOTHING

For years, cycling clothing was extremely limited in style and color. Everyone wore black wool shorts and plain wool jerseys. Things sure have changed. Bike wear is all the rage these days and not just bikers wear the colorful Lycra/Spandex bike shorts, now available in every color imaginable—in fact, in every style imaginable from skin-tight one-piece bibs to briefs to loose and baggy shorts. They all have one thing in common—a comfortable, well-padded crotch. Stylish synthetic fiber jerseys made of Ultra-Max, Coolmax, or lightweight Lycra/cotton blends not only make fashion statements but political and environmental statements as well. The great thing about all this is that these clothes are designed for women—something unheard of in the past.

Pearl Izumi makes the designer look in bike clothes. Hind created a line called For Women Only. Marti Stephen notes in *California Bicyclist* that Hind's "T-back . . . provides support across the lats and shoulders. The tail of the T-back is cut slightly longer than the front. The neck and arms are cut deep enough only to reveal a serious cyclist." Other brands to check out are Descente and Specialized. Womyn's Wheel catalog has a fantastic and lively selection of what's available on the market today, not only in women's biking attire but in biking equipment as well. Schnaubelt Shorts (see Catalogs and Mail Order in Resources) is another possibility. Biker Cathy Schnaubelt designs high-fashion bike wear in sizes ranging from very small to very large. "There are women who weigh 175 to 200 pounds who are serious riders and we try to make our larger sizes proportionate to their bodies," Cathy says. "Women have arrived in cycling and they have much more freedom to express their femininity in the clothing that they wear. Now it's okay to wear florals if you want to wear florals."

Not only are bike shorts and jerseys more comfortable and easier to ride in than jeans or sweats, but they make a statement—they're fun. The two other pieces of equipment we recommend you eventually invest in are bike shoes and gloves. There are shoes for women, but like everything else, you may have to search a little longer to find them. Shop in a specialty store for shoes, where more than likely you'll find someone who understands their purpose and how to fit them. Gloves typically feature leather palms and Lycra uppers and should fit comfortably and snugly. Gloves insulate you from road shock, cold, and blisters, as well as absorb perspiration.

We'd like to leave you with a little story about a grand, feisty woman who advocated that by mastering the techniques of riding a bike one could, in the process, learn the lessons of life.

Hailed as the "foremost woman in public life," in 1893, world-famous educator and suffragist Frances Willard, then 53, was presented with a bike. She promptly named it Gladys. In a delightful little book called *A Wheel Within a Wheel,* published in 1895, Willard, one who loved to teach by parable, encouraged women to step up to the challenge, to develop their physical selves, and to see that through that process they could realize their own unique potential. "When the wheel of the mind went well," she wrote, "then the rubber wheel hummed merrily." She told women that "it was the hardihood of Spirit that led me to begin, the persistence of will that held me to the task, and the patience that was willing to begin again when the last stroke had failed." Willard went on to say that "she who succeeds in gaining the mastery of such an animal as Gladys will gain the mastery of life, and by exactly the same methods and characteristics."

Profile: Debbie Breaud

"I've always been a quiet, withdrawn person and I wanted to do something that stood out—that not a lot of people could do, something that would sparkle and totally set me apart from the rest," Debbie Breaud says. "I guess RAAM was it for me." RAAM is the 2,930-mile

Debbie Breaud.

bicycle Race Across AMerica that starts in Irvine, California and ends in Savannah, Georgia, and includes riding over high mountain passes, across searing deserts and plains, and through cities and towns stretching from the Pacific to the Atlantic. In 1991, 34 bikers entered the race, four of whom were women. Debbie Breaud of Fort Worth, Texas finished 16th overall, the second women.

But Debbie wasn't always a biker—in fact, it wasn't until she was 25 years old and going through a divorce that she began exploring her athletic self at all. "My family life was bad," says Debbie. "I was raised by an alcoholic mother, and spent my growing-up years withdrawn, overweight, and rebellious. Sports just didn't interest me."

Breaud started running, entered a race, and won. "I found out I was good," she says. "And if you do well at any sport, it becomes sort of an addiction and you want to do it again and again." But stress injuries sidelined Debbie's efforts. Then a friend encouraged her to join him and the Fort Worth Bicycling Association on a club ride, and that 40-mile ride opened the door to a world in which Debbie Breaud would thrive. Her first ride was on a Sears Free Spirit. "Everyone laughed," she smiles, "but I did just fine." After a couple more rides Breaud fell in with some ultra-marathon people, traded up to a Centurion (a lighter, faster bike), moved on to a Klein and then to a Kestrel.

Gradually increasing her mileage, Breaud awakened a drive within herself that she never knew existed. "I wanted to prove myself," she says, "and that's what competition is all about." Before long she was riding in local and regional road races, then happened to hear about RAAM. "I thought it might be something I could do," she says. But there were complications—Breaud is the single mother of a pre-teen daughter, and putting in the time and mileage necessary to train for a race like RAAM would cut into her time spent with Autumn.

There were also finances to consider. Breaud, a secretary at a Fort Worth consulting engineering firm, was in no position to support an expensive bike-racing effort. Participants will tell you that it takes at least $10,000 to $15,000 to train and compete in RAAM. And according to *Texas Bicyclist,* some of the more extravagant competitors raise $20,000 and up. So obtaining sponsorship is imperative.

Further, consider the planning involved in such an effort—the time it takes not only to care for your child but to hold down a full-time job, plus compete in qualifying races and train up to 700 miles a week.

But once Breaud made the commitment to RAAM, the pieces started falling into place. Breaud's friends, many of them members of the Fort Worth Bicycling Association, held rides, fund-raising dinners, swap meets, and bake sales. Debbie's daughter Autumn was included in those efforts. Members of the group with daughters Autumn's age volunteered for overnights and weekends when Breaud had to travel. They were also the support crew that followed Breaud across country—driving a van at an agonizing 18 m.p.h. Jim and Rhonda Hoyt of Richardson Bike Mart in Fort Worth became Breaud's official sponsor, not only supplying a top-of-the-line bike but product and financial support as well. Breaud's boss supported her efforts with flexible hours and extra time off—with pay. "Everyone was just great," Debbie says. "I couldn't have done it without them."

Finishing the race after 13 days, 7 hours, and 49 minutes, Breaud said, "It was a wonderful adventure. I don't think there was any time during the race that I wanted to quit." Recognizing that it is a success in itself just to finish the race, and although she had planned to do RAAM only once, Debbie now has her sights set on '93. "We were rookies," she says, "and made a lot of mistakes. I want to do it one more time—and finish in ten days. By '93 I should be ready!"

However, Debbie is quick to point out that biking is not just training for long-distance races. "It's about building self-confidence," she says, "and about fitness and camaraderie. It's fun to watch yourself improve. You get an overall good feeling about yourself when you're in shape—a feeling that carries over into every aspect of your life. I may not race forever, but I will never, never give up my bike."

Profile: Joan McGuffin

Canada is a big country—bordered by three oceans and extending over ten provinces. Its topography is diverse, its cultures even more so. Born and raised in Thornhill, a little town north of Toronto, Joanie McGuffin yearned to see what the rest of Canada looked like. She decided to see it on a bike.

Biking was not new to McGuffin. In fact, she comes from "a biking family," and learned to ride as a youngster, not so much for sport as a mode of transportation. In Thornhill, her mother was known as "the lady who rides the bicycle."

Joan McGuffin near Beaver Mountain, British Columbia: *Photo by Gary McGuffin.*

On April Fool's Day in 1986, McGuffin and husband Gary set off to explore Canada. Their plan was to touch each of the three oceans that bordered Canada and ride through each of the ten provinces. The route they chose took them over parts of the Arctic ice cap, through the rugged mountain ranges of the west and the flat plains and northern forests of central and eastern Canada, and finally into the lush provinces along the Atlantic. They started off from Tuktoyaktuk, Northwest Territories, a town situated on the Beaufort Sea, 100 miles south of the polar ice cap. "The first 120 miles were rough," McGuffin says, describing her ride on black ice. "It was polar bear country, and every time I looked up from the road, I would wipe out. Studded tires are available now," she adds, "but in '86 they didn't exist."

Riding 100 to 150 miles a day, their trip lasted seven months, covered 7,500 miles, and afforded them the education of a lifetime. "We weren't burning up the pavement," McGuffin says, "nor did we feel the need to. We just stuck to back roads and enjoyed making our own pathways." Unable to find bikes to suit their needs, McGuffin and her husband built their own. "We worked on the bikes for about three months," she says, "and combined the best of both mountain and touring bikes."

The trip proved not only a great lesson in how to approach a journey—with maps, food, camera, packing and carrying gear—but a lesson in self-sufficiency as well. "I've always been a big scope kind of person," McGuffin says. "But the bike made me focus on something small, nit-picky, mechanical, that had to be tuned to run perfectly. It took a while, but now I can take my bike apart, clean up the pieces, and put it back together. If it makes the tiniest little sound that is out of the ordinary, I have to fix it, and learning that was good for me. Read *Zen and the Art of Motorcycle Maintenance*—you'll see what I mean."

Coping with the elements was also a test. To cover a country the size of Canada is to ride over all kinds of landscape in every season. "We rode through rain and freezing cold and blistering heat. We had hail the size of small ice cubes in southern Saskatchewan. Gary and I just huddled under our bikes laughing—it was too unbelievable to be true! And riding, you create your own wind chill," she adds. "Sometimes I wore two layers of long underwear, plus fleece, a balaclava, and anything else I could find."

Financing their trip was yet another challenge. One method was to document their journey for CBC Radio. Riding through the provinces, they would call in and describe the trip—the landscape, the people, and the culture. Through "Morningside," a nationally broadcast morning show, homes across Canada shared their journey. "Experiencing the trip through us," McGuffin said, "people could see that it was a route they could travel," pointing out that their broadcasts opened doors to meeting people in every small town along the way. When no phone booth was available, they would knock on a farmer's door and ask to use the phone. "People across the country were curious, helpful, and friendly. You come in the back door of people's lives when you're self-propelled," she adds. "On a bike you are open and people like that. They respond."

McGuffin feels that we live in an insular, visually stimulated world.

"On a bike, you have the feel of the land, the road beneath you, every bump. I can feel and hear Canada," she adds. "It's not just a visual impression. It's wonderful to ride into a small town in the early morning, smell the bakery, go in for coffee, and meet the locals."

Now living near the Apostle Islands in Wisconsin and working on a book about the Lake Superior Basin, Joanie looks back on the expedition as the turning point in her life. "Up until that time," she says, "Gary and I were a couple journeying together. When we did the Appalachian Trail, we hiked at the same pace; and when canoeing, we paddled in tandem. But the bike trip was different—we were together, yet separate. I was my own transportation and it felt good. For the first time I had the opportunity to examine parts of my self that I never knew existed.

"That biking expedition was living a process," she continues, "sort of a metaphor for life. You have to travel through a storm before you know what you're made of. That trip took me to my limits and allowed me to look at my physical and mental capacity to overcome fear. I lacked the self-confidence to cause change before that. That trip helped me to feel strong in myself—I'm on my way."

Where will McGuffin's journeys take her next? "I have a dream of some day circumnavigating Newfoundland in a sea kayak—alone," she grins.

FISHING

Sometimes, in early spring, in the deep of the night, when the moon was full and the tide was right, Dad would wake us with the news—the smelt were running. We'd quickly dress in high boots and warm clothes. Armed with buckets and our trusty Ray-O-Vacs, on these special nights we would pile in the car and head for Moxie Stream.

The banks of the stream would be lined mostly with men, standing around on thin, hard crusts of snow, winter's last vestige, talking and laughing, catching up on news of local politics, family, and friends. I loved being part of that group. After staking out our position on the stream bank, Dad would position us in a nice fast-running, shallow spot, someplace in midstream, with strict instructions not to wander around, possibly stepping into a deeper spot or into someone else's "territory." And there we would stand, bucket and flashlight in hand, waiting for the first excited yelp from somewhere downstream, signaling the start of the run.

Smelts, in the '50s in Maine, were caught only by hand—a great conservation method, a great way to fish, actually. The equipment necessary to participate in this annual springtime ritual was, like the times, simple: a left hand and a right hand, a pair of boots, a bucket, and a flashlight. My brothers and I would form a team and one would hold the bucket and two would reach down into the icy-cold stream and try to grab the slippery fish as they swam upstream on their annual pilgrimage. Then we'd switch off to give our freezing hands a rest. The holder of the bucket was also in charge of directing the beam of light into the swollen stream. When the light hit the water it came alive with countless reflecting silvery scales. The pressure of an ice-cold spring runoff swirling about your legs, the hoots and hollers of fellow fishermen, the smell of a streamside wood fire mixed with the cold, foggy

Maine night air was a joyful experience—one I'll never forget.

But as much fun as smelt fishing was, I have to admit that from adolescence on, my interests turned to speedboats and boys, and more important, I wanted to be like everyone else . . . I didn't see many women fishing at all. Each year there was much ado as my father and brothers planned their annual backcountry fishing trip in search of the "one that got away." Actually, my mother did most of the "planning" (sewing, cooking, ironing, packing), but neither she nor I were invited. In fact, I don't think it even dawned on us or on them that we might like to go along. That trip was just for the guys.

Last spring, while rushing along a back road on some errand or other, I happened to travel along a river swollen with snow melt and dotted with anglers at every bend. Memories of spring fishing in Maine came flooding back. So I started poking around a few fly shops, checked out some waders, bought a vest and a hat, read a few books on the sport, then signed up for a fly-casting class. Maybe it's my age, I thought. After instruction on a pond next to the school, we graduated to a pool on a nearby river. Stepping into the river, feeling the pressure of the currents weaving around my legs, was soothing and real. It was like coming home.

I was lucky to take my first fly-casting lesson with Joan Wulff, a guru in the world of fly casting. Linking arms and wading across a wide shallow spot in the river, Joan pointed to what looked like tiny twigs but were in fact insect egg cases, stuck to the rocks in the streambed. She described how those insects hatch, how they then rise to the surface, dry their wings, then fly away, and how the fish rise to feed on them. The purpose of choosing the right fly, she said, was to imitate that hatch—to seduce the fish with a make-believe bug called a fly. Joan spent the afternoon talking about how the fish react to the weather, to light, to shadow and water temperature. She talked about "reading the water," about watching how the stream flows around boulders and rocks, about how to gauge depth. Fish like depth. Then the fun began. She started to cast, whipping the line out in long graceful movements and plopping the fly exactly where she wanted it, on the opposite streambank, beneath an overhanging tree. "Think like a trout," she yelled above the noise of the stream. "Where would you be in this stream if you were a trout? What looks good from a trout's point of view?"

Fishing with a fly, she said, is a mental sport—"You must think like the fish that you're after." Before I had time to absorb any of this, Joan passed me the rod and proceeded to open a small metal tackle box that hung from her neck and from which she chose a brown furry fly with long black whiskers. Then she chose a tiny, compact, light brown, short-haired fly. Without missing a beat, she launched into the difference between dry flies and wet flies, about how dry flies can imitate tasty bugs that have just hatched, or they can imitate bugs that skim over the surface of the water, or perhaps a bug that can stand on top of it, and that wet flies imitate bugs or nymphs that live beneath the surface. We scanned the stream looking for insects and watched to see if any fish were feeding, and if so what they were feeding on. That is how the afternoon went. I didn't catch a fish, but then, I didn't need to. Just standing in the stream and swaying with the water, listening to Joan's gentle instruction, concentrating on the cast—cock the elbow just right and keep the arm relaxed—watching the line roll off the reel and struggling to lay it flat on the water, hoping to hear the tiny "plop" as the fly hit the water, was enough. It completely filled the day.

That is what fishing is all about. It really doesn't matter whether you fish for panfish or bonefish or trout. It's all about being outdoors, physical exertion, using all your mental skills to try to outsmart the fish, and, most of all, camaraderie with friends.

While the type of fishing you do depends a great deal on where you live, angling is a great excuse to get outside and poke around in just about any body of water. Fishing can be defined in a dozen different ways. It can mean spending an afternoon lying near a stream-bank, binoculars or book in hand, glancing now and then at a bobber with a baited hook, waiting for some hungry fish to happen by. To a bass angler it can mean poking around on a lake in a canoe or a flat-bottom boat or zooming across the water in front of a 175-horse-power outboard, in search of the perfect spot. To a fly fisher it can mean spending hours in one pool or perhaps walking two miles up-stream only to fish her way back to the start.

According to the National Sporting Goods Association (NSGA), 15 million women sportfish in this country and make up one third of the fishing population. They also spend over $128 million annually for fishing tackle and related merchandise, and those numbers are grow-ing by the day.

Although bass fishers and fly fishers consider themselves worlds apart in ideology, technique, and style, and while they are generally perceived as representing opposite ends of the fishing spectrum, both groups must use similar tactics to catch fish, both practice catch-and-release, and both attract more than a few women.

All fishing has to do with fooling the fish, which isn't always easy. You are presenting them with something that looks like food or behaves in a way that makes a fish crazy enough to want to catch it. Your lure might represent something in the food chain—a minnow, a junebug, mayfly, or other insect. But that isn't enough. It must be presented in a way that the fish can see, and for that you need to understand where fish spend time and how they feed, and that each fish species is different.

BASS FISHING

Bass of one kind or another are found in every state except Alaska and in just about every body of water, making bass fishing an extremely popular sport. Well, that's great news, you say, but how do I catch one? The good news for the beginning bass angler is that the initial outlay for equipment and clothing is minimal. Once you've decided that bass fishing is a sport that you'd like to try, go to your local tackle shop and talk with the owner. (Be aware that many old-timers still consider women intruders in the traditional male world of fishing, and while it depends in which part of the country you live, there's a good chance that you may encounter an attitude that's just a tad shy of patronizing. Not all tackle shop owners are bad mannered, so don't be put off. Just close your purse and move on. Remember, there are plenty of places to shop.) Make sure you're honest and tell him that you're not an experienced angler but want to learn. Ask his opinion about rods and reels and tackle. Ask about local fishing rules and regulations and find out which local clubs offer instruction.

One excellent starting place is Bass'n Gal (check Sporting Organizations in Resources) in Arlington, Texas. Started by Sugar Ferris in 1976, this organization has built a nationwide network of women anglers. With 26,000 members and 82 chapters scattered across the country, you'll find it a place to meet other anglers, to learn angling skills such as tying knots, outboard-motor maintenance, how to read the water, fish and habitat conservation, the philosophy of catch-and-release, etc. Most of all, you'll find a place to swap fish stories and have a lot of fun.

A $15 annual membership includes six issues of their magazine, *Bass'n Gal,* membership patch and decal, fishing information services, instructional clinics, and the opportunity to participate in the women's bass fishing tournament circuit. A similar organization is Lady Bass, located in West Monroe, Louisiana (check Resources).

Bass-Fishing Gear

The gear you'll need to get started is quite simple—a fishing license first of all, and a five- or six-foot graphite rod with a closed-face spin-cast reel will do. Rods come in three basic actions—light, medium, and heavy—and the action you choose will depend on the species of bass you're going after and the water you plan to fish in. If you're thinking of small-mouth bass only, opt for a light-action rod. However, if you're looking for larger bass such as striped bass, which can weigh up to 30 pounds, you'll need a heavy-action rod. With a medium-action rod you can catch small or large-mouth bass, and a good rod and reel shouldn't cost more than $40. One other suggestion: If you're a beginner, stick with a closed-face reel—it prevents backlash. There's nothing more discouraging than spending valuable fishing time sorting through clumps of tangled line. Companies such as Shimano, Zebco, and Daiwa manufacture reliable products.

You'll also want a small tackle box. Don't get too hung up on filling the tackle box with all sorts of fishing paraphernalia—that will happen slowly as you become more involved in the sport, fish different areas, and decide what tools/accessories will make fishing successful for you.

There are millions of lures on the market, available in the greatest array of mind-boggling colors and styles. The choice and effectiveness of the lures depend on where you fish. Every lure isn't effective on every body of water. On my way to Thousand Islands, New York (in western New York, on Lake Ontario), I stopped at a tackle shop in Lake George, New York (in eastern New York near Vermont) and bought a few lures. The tackle-shop owner assured me that those lures were guaranteed bass-catchers. Well, they may have been bass-catchers on

Lake George, but the bass in Lake Ontario were not impressed.

You won't need a tackle box full of lures, but you will need more than one or two. Sugar Ferris suggests that you start off with a few small spinner baits. "Smaller baits catch more fish," she says. "But don't give up if after a few casts with that sparkling new spinner bait you don't catch a fish. Fish are wily critters and may have been caught before. If the bait is presented enough times, the fish will probably strike." Another way to get started is to hire a guide for the day. If you decide on a guide, it's important to let him/her know at the beginning of the conversation that you're a beginner and may need instruction. The glory of a guide is that he/she knows where the fish are and what bait they are attracted to in that particular body of water. Although a guide's services can cost up to $125 a day, split between two people, a successful day of fishing is not that expensive.

For bass fishing you need no special clothing. In fact, the older and more comfortable the clothes, the better, but you should always take along rain gear, sunglasses, and a hat. Also, never leave shore wearing just a bathing suit and shorts. Not only can the weather change quickly, but the sun is very intense on the water and you'll need clothing to cover yourself before the day is through. Refer to the What Am I Going to Wear? chapter for clothing selection. As in any sport and depending on the weather, layering is important.

Bass fishing is tantamount to tournament fishing. In fact, some argue that it was fishing tournaments that built the $50-billion-a-year bass-fishing industry, not the other way around. Founded over 20 years ago, B.A.S.S. Inc. is the company that all but owns bass fishing, and until 1991 had successfully barred women from competition.

Bass fishing is a sport that requires neither much muscle nor that you be in the prime of your life to participate. But it does require large doses of intuition, coordination, and finesse—traits that women possess. The B.A.S.S. Bassmasters tournament trail is a high-stakes contest, with annual prize money approaching $3 million. Now that's a lot of lures and tackle boxes!

One of the principles on which Bass'n Gal was founded was to end discrimination against women's participation in outdoor sports, especially angling. Although Sugar Ferris stepped into this void and has done a fine job of providing a nationwide professional showcase for women to display their fishing expertise, earn valuable prize money, acquire sponsorship dollars, and have lots of fun, there is still a gap. That gap is the astronomical difference in prize money available between the men's tournaments and the women's tournaments. Angler Linda England talked about this difference in dollars. "On the Bassmasters circuit invitational tournaments, the top 40 winners share $175,000. There is a $600 entry fee—no qualifying rounds. On the women's circuit, i.e., Bass'n Gal, $40,000 is split between the top 20 winners and there is a $150 fee."

What is equally important to the winner is money earned in fees paid for product endorsements. Because the men's tournaments receive such expanded media coverage, Linda said, "the fees paid for endorsements and appearances [are] top-level business. Men are also able, through their high exposure, to gain top-level sponsors. The women don't have a chance to compete for these remunerations." It will take a few years to break down those barriers but the wheels are in motion. In 1991, the U.S. Army Corps of Engineers said it would prohibit B.A.S.S. tournaments in their jurisdiction if B.A.S.S. persisted in their discrimination against women. Shortly after that announcement B.A.S.S. received similar responses from state officials in proposed tournament sites. Interviewed in *USA Today,* Bass'n Gal champion Fredda Lee said, "There may be a little flak at first, but it will settle down. I think it will help the sport develop more of a family image."

That one layer of discrimination has dissolved, but how should women react to similar blatant discrimination in sports in the future? "We women should make ourselves known," Linda England says. "Traditionally, we have taken whatever [men] dish out. Women could do so much more if [they] recognized the fact that we have to work together, we have to speak out. We are a very powerful element of society, yet we don't exercise our power. For instance, I sell my boat each year at the end of the season. Last year I could have sold it four times! The first three guys who came to look at it came with their wives. Their wives didn't like it so they didn't buy it. The fourth guy came and didn't really like it too much but his wife loved it. He bought it. That says something, doesn't it?"

FISHING WITH A FLY

In spin fishing and bait casting you are casting the lure. The weight is at the end of the line and the rod propels it with a snap of the wrist. When you cast a fly, on the other hand, you are actually casting the line, the casting action stemming from your forearm rather than your wrist. The fly is almost weightless; the line is weighted.

Because of its diversity, I think fly fishing is the most interesting of all fishing techniques. No matter what kind of fish you catch on a fly, from a 6-inch brook trout to a 30-pound tarpon, while the rod and line weight will differ, the casting technique remains the same. Casting is the heart of fly fishing, and once you have learned to cast properly you can fish for anything—even bass. I cannot stress strongly enough that the best way to learn to cast is to take a few lessons. Videos are available, some very good ones in fact, produced by Scientific Angler/3M (800–525–6290). Joan Wulff has also produced a video called "The Wulff School of Fly-casting," and has written a book as well, *Joan Wulff's Fly Fishing: Expert Advice From a Woman's Perspective,* available from Stackpole Books. While a video helps to visualize the proper technique, there is truly no substitute for good professional instruction.

Check your local fly-fishing shops for instruction, guides, clubs, and organizations. For instance, we know that Trout Unlimited, a stream-conservation organization, has 400 chapters nationwide and often gives clinics and instruction. The number of women who participate in Trout Unlimited instructional clinics increases annually. In fact, more than a few chapters have recognized this growth area and offer special women-only classes. Trout Unlimited is located at 800 Follin Lane SE, Suite 250, Vienna, VA 22180-4959, (703) 281–1100. Another excellent source is the Federation of Flyfishers, P.O. Box 1088, West Yellowstone, Montana, an international educational organization that gives clinics and instruction all over the world. They have chapters nationwide. Women's fly-fishing clubs are starting to appear also. Try Golden West Women Flyfishers, 317 Vista De Valle, Mill Valley, CA 94941 or Northwest Women Flyfishers, 2474 Dexter Avenue North, Seattle, WA 98109. Consider a fly-fishing school as a vacation. The following are excellent choices:

Joan & Lee Wulff Fishing School
Lew Beach, New York
(800) 328–3638
Weekend classes cost $450.

Bud Lilly's Trout Shop
P.O. Box 698
West Yellowstone, MT 59758
(406) 646–7801
Classes range from half-day for $65 to five days for $530.

Maggie Merriman Fly Fishing School
West Yellowstone, MT 59758
(406) 646–7824
Maggie holds half-day classes costing $100 and three-day classes
    that run $300.

Cathy & Barry Beck's Fishing Creek Outfitters
RD 1, Box 310-1
Benton, PA 17814
(717) 925–2225
One-day classes start at $135. They also conduct two-day pro-
    grams.

Dorothy Bergmann
2744 Saint Albans North
Roseville, MN 55113
(612) 484–0053
Dorothy holds three- and four-day clinics in Northern Wisconsin,
    fishing for trout, and in Michigan fishing for steelhead. The
    Wisconsin trip includes lodge stay and costs about $500.

Johnson's Pere Marquette Lodge
Phyllis and Jim Johnson
Rt. 1, Box 1290
Baldwin, MI 49304
These weekend trips cost around $325, including classroom ses-
    sions and float trips.

The Sporting Gentlemen
306 East Baltimore Pike
Media, PA 19063
(215) 565–6140
Ask for Mary Kuss, who teaches fly casting and fly tying. Her fees run around $75 for a half-day.

Gloria Jordan's Fly Rod Shop
P.O. Box 667
Manchester Center, VT 05255
(802) 362–3186
Guiding on the famous Battenkill and Mettawee rivers for groups or individuals at $150 a day.

Kaufman's Streamborn Fly Shop in Portland, Oregon (503–639–7004) reports that up to 20 percent of his fly-fishing classes are women. Orvis, located in Manchester Center, Vermont, was one of the first to offer fly-fishing instruction. Call (800) 548–9548 for a list of Orvis schools around the country.

Learning to cast takes practice and it takes time, so be patient. Echoing the words of angler Margot Page, editor of the *American Fly Fisher,* "Take a few lessons from a professional, and then practice until you've conquered the frustrating but [if you stay with it] eminently satisfying and exquisitely beautiful art of casting."

Joan Wulff has perfected a tool for teaching casting called the "Fly-O." It is a cut-off rod tip, driven into a cork grip and threaded with a piece of fat orange yarn. For $25, the Fly-O is a great way to acquire the casting rhythms and movements without fear of either breaking up the house or hooking yourself, your neighbor, or your cat. The beauty of practicing with the Fly-O is that you can cast anywhere. I walk around my house casting at every picture and plant in sight. I love it when, after casting at a particular leaf on a plant, the yarn tip actually touches it. Once you feel at ease with the basics, then take out the fly rod—you'll feel more secure and you'll do less damage.

Flyfishing Gear

Now that you're hooked on casting, the next logical step is to buy your own equipment. The first thing Sugar Ferris tells women who attend her fishing seminars is, "For goodness' sake, stop accepting hand-me-down fishing equipment. It is well to note that you get what you pay for and a good rod and reel combination will last you for years or even a lifetime!" We agree. While it is all well and good to borrow equipment, you need your own gear. As in any other sport, you'll develop your own style, one that's truly you and not a reflection of someone else.

Before heading out to the fly shop, gain some knowledge of what equipment is available and, most important, determine what you need. Buying equipment is an investment and can be a daunting process, and it's easy to overspend if you don't know what you want. If you're lucky enough to have had a female instructor, ask what her recommendations would be. If you know other female anglers, ask their advice. If you're a beginner, we recommend that you start out with an 8½- or 9-foot graphite rod for a 6-weight line. This recommendation is truly middle-of-the road. After getting into the sport you may wish to invest further and go lighter or heavier, depending on what you fish for the most. Don't be afraid of rod length. Writer Carolyn Shelton says, "I'm 5'2" and learned on a 10-foot, 7-weight rod. Women in Great Britain cast great 16-foot spey rods regularly. Casting is technique, not brute strength."

Rods are measured by the weight of the line being cast (i.e., 7-weight, 6-weight, etc.) and not the length of the rod itself. The heavier the fly you want to cast and generally the larger the fish you expect to catch, the heavier weight line and hence rod you will use. You can use a tiny 2-weight rod and line for those little trout but will need a 12-weight saltwater fly rod for tarpon. There are rods, reels, and lines for everything in between.

Recently, manufacturers have begun to notice the growing women's market, designing equipment specifically to address that need. Orvis markets the Mary Orvis Marbury rod, designed especially for women. You might also consider a starter kit, consisting of matched rod, reel, line, cloth rod bag, and carrying tube. G. Loomis markets one for $190 that includes a fly and an instruction booklet that says, "The only thing you need is time to go fishing." Sage makes the Discovery Series that includes eight models, from 6- to 8-weight rods, retailing from $215 to $275. If you find the cork grip on any rod too large, angler Carolyn Shelton recommends that you "simply spend an evening or two sanding it down with fine-grit sandpaper until it's comfortable."

If you're still having trouble locating a rod that fits, call a rod maker such as Gloria Jordan at Gloria Jordan's Fly Rod Shop, P.O. Box 667, Manchester Center, Vermont 05255, (802) 362–3186 or Dorothy Bergmann, owner of Rodsmith at 2744 Saint Albans North, Roseville, Minnesota 55113, (612) 484–0053. They both build rods and restore old tackle and bamboo rods.

Now, don't forget a reel. Reels can be very fancy and complicated but, in fact, in fly fishing their only purpose is as a place to store the line. You can get a good reel for $50. The fly shop will match a reel to the rod that you purchase.

There are a couple of other items that you will want to invest in—gear that will make your fishing life easier and more comfortable. Let's start off with waders. Until recently, poorly fitting waders were the bane of the woman angler. Historically, women have had to settle for waders sized for men, but thanks to the growing population of women anglers, manufacturers have begun to adjust their thinking and with a little determination a woman can now find a pair of waders that fit. Waders come in two styles, bootfoot or stockingfoot. Bootfoot waders are made in one piece. Stockingfoot waders are worn with a separate boot. Stockingfoot waders come in two materials, neoprene and waterproof nylon. Neoprene fits snugly over your body, making movement much freer and easier and the material itself is thicker, providing extra warmth, especially important in cold water/weather conditions. Waterproof nylon waders are lightweight, easy to pack, and really good for warm-water fishing. They are also baggy, making it easy to add extra layers of insulation. Cabela's (800–237–4444) carries a woman's neoprene bib-style wader in navy blue that costs $79.95. Simms waders for women cost $210. Red Ball and L.L. Bean sell lightweights for women.

Wading shoes in women's sizes are available from:

Simms
P.O. Box 2913
Jackson Hole, WY 83001
(307) 733–2266

Gary Borger Ultimate Wading Shoe
108 South Polk Street
Merrill, WI 54452
(715) 536–5521

L.L. Bean
Freeport, ME 04023
(800) 221–4221—ask for their Flyfishing Specialties Catalog.

There are two other items that will make your on-water time more enjoyable—a fishing vest and a wading staff. Maggie Merriman makes a vest for women that carries her name. Columbia, Stream Designs, and Patagonia also make fishing vests. A vest is a great way to keep your hands free to fish, but try on a couple before you buy. A wading staff is a necessity in fast-moving water, and provides the extra support needed to pick your way across rocky streambeds in fast-moving water. Folstaff makes a folding wading staff that is shock-corded like a tent pole. When not in use, it can be collapsed and attached to your fishing vest, ready to go when you are. They run about $50 and, some say, are worth every dime.

CATCH-AND-RELEASE

Conservation is everyone's responsibility. Native, or nonstocked, fish are becoming scarce in every part of the world. For that reason, concerned anglers everywhere practice catch-and-release, a method of catching the fish quickly and returning it unharmed to its environment. Catch-and-release takes practice but, as the famous fly angler and conservationist Lee Wulff wrote in 1937, "A good game fish is too valuable to be caught only once. It is the finest gift one angler can give another and, who knows, that trout you just caught may have been some other angler's gift to you."

FISHING WOMEN

Fishing is a natural sport for women, and fishing history—believe it or not—is peppered with impressive women with whom we can all be proud to identify. The earliest-known writing on fishing with a fly is *The Treatise of Fishing with an Angle,* written by Dame Juliana Berners around 1421, and it remains one of the finest pieces of writing on sport fishing. In 1892, Mary Orvis Marbury wrote *Favorite Flies and Their Histories,* a landmark book. For a real treat read *Uncommon Waters: Women Write About Fishing,* edited by Holly Morris and published by Seal Press. This anthology is about modern-day women who fish and why they do. In the book's preface Margot Page writes, "These women speak of our desire for temporary freedom from sobering human foibles, weighty professional and domestic responsibilities; they describe our struggle to find our way; and they are testimony to our wish for communion with the majestic natural world, of which we are, after all, just another species."

One of my fishing heros is Cornelia Crosby, also known as Fly Rod. She was a writer, a passionate conservationist, a friend of Annie Oakley, a holder of the first Maine Guide's license, in 1895 the first woman exhibitor at the famous Sportsmen's Show at Madison Square Garden, and the State of Maine's first paid publicity agent.

This all happened because of a fly rod. Counseled by her doctor to take "large doses of the outdoors," Fly Rod moved to the country near Rangeley, Maine where she learned to "cast a fly rod, shoot a gun, and read the ways of the woods." By chance, a male friend gave her a gift that would change her life—a five-ounce bamboo fly rod that he had made—with advice that if she didn't like the "darn fool thing to just break it up and throw it out."

On long solitary walks, Cornelia practiced her cast, becoming so adept that anyone who saw her was startled. Inspired by her success, and wanting to share her joy of the outdoors with others, she wrote about an outdoor adventure and sent it to a local newspaper under the pen name "Fly Rod," sure it wouldn't be published if she used the name Cornelia. The editor replied, "Send some more right away." That launched "Fly Rod's Notebook," which grew into a regular syndicated outdoor column published in major newspapers around the country for years.

Guiding was a rough business in the Maine woods in the early 1900s and although Cornelia relished her job she never lost touch with her feminine side. On her backwoods trips she would often take a satin-lined wicker basket filled with delicately hand-painted cups and a teapot. Can you imagine the look on a woodsman's face when he happened to come upon her sitting by a trout pool, daintily sipping tea between strikes?

Before her death at 92, Fly Rod wrote, "The time is past, I thank kind Providence, when it was thought unladylike for a woman to be a skillful angler or a good shot . . . there is no more graceful, healthful, and fascinating accomplishment for a lady than fly fishing, and there is no reason why a lady should not in every respect rival a gentleman in the gentle art."

I always smile when I look up from my desk and see one of my favorite photos, a picture of Fly Rod poised serenely in her canoe, dressed in the latest fashion—sassy little hat perched just so on her head, fly rod in hand . . . reeling in a big one! Every inch a woman. Every inch an angler.

Profile: Linda England—Bass Champion

Linda England has always been a competitor and has always fished. "When I was little we had some friends who had a farm with a creek on it and a gang of us would go there every chance we got. There was one particular boy—about my age—who lived nearby and we spent a lot of time playing by the creek. The man who owned the farm was an invalid and it was our job to catch him some catfish or bass whenever we visited. That boy and I always competed to see who could catch the most and the biggest fish for our host. I just loved it! That's my first fishing memory—going down to the creek with a steel rod and level-wind reel with braided Dacron line. One cast and you would spend the next three hours sorting out the backlash."

Born and raised in Nashville, Tennessee, Linda excelled in competitive sports like basketball and tennis. "We were the basketball league champions in my senior year and I made the all-Nashville team which was a very distinguished honor," she says with a laugh. "I was very proud of that."

Married right after high school, Linda stayed home with her two daughters until they were seven and nine. "That was when I started tournament fishing," she says. "I enjoyed fishing with my husband and friends of ours as a weekend pastime, but I hadn't competed at all before then." That was back in 1977 and Linda competed in the first Bass'n Gal event ever held. "I was attracted to tournament fishing for three reasons: number one, for the fishing and number two, for the competition. The third attraction was that, having just turned 30, I had reached a point in my life where I needed to make some kind of move. I was tired of making beds and doing dishes and was sure that there must be something more to life than housekeeping and child rearing.

So I fished that first tournament mainly to get away and see what it was all about and I got hooked."

Qualifying every year since then for the Women's World Championships, and attaining Classic World Champion twice, Linda is one of the superstars of the women's professional bass-fishing circuit and is the all-time money winner. In 1989 she was not only Lady Bass Angler of the Year but was inducted into the National Fishing Hall of Fame as well. In 1990 she was the Lady Bass and Bass'n Gal Angler of the Year. Linda has made a business of fishing. Between tournaments she and partner Fredda Lee (also a professional angler) tour the country as seminar speakers and lecturers. She writes a regular column, "Fishing with Linda England," appearing in several regional publications, and until recently hosted a nationally syndicated radio show. Besides being a photographer, she and Fredda wrote a book, *Bass on the Line.* As if that weren't enough to keep her busy, she has promotional obligations as well. You're apt to meet Linda in your local sporting-goods store or at a regional outdoor show promoting her sponsors, Stratos Boats, Daiwa, DuPont Stren Lines, Johnson Outboards, or Lowrance Electronics, to name a few. "Everyday we do something related to fishing," she says.

The bass-fishing industry is a $50-billion-a-year industry and the tournament scene represents big money if you are successful. Linda spends between 16 and 18 weeks a year on the bass circuit. Interviewed in *Lady Bass,* she said, "I find that I'm happy spending 150 to 200 days a year fishing. Fishing for fishing's sake is fun, but fishing for money requires 100 percent. You have to have top skills and the determination to win. I measure my success by two things: how well did I fish, and how well did I take advantage of whatever opportunities I had?"

It would be hard to find a sport that requires a longer daily schedule. "We rise by 3:30 A.M. on tournament days and have the boat in the water an hour before daylight. There is a lot of preparation—getting the rods and reels ready, choosing and tying on lures and baits, and arranging everything in the boat. But what we are actually doing is getting ourselves psyched. Your mental approach needs to be right. You go over where you're going to fish, what lures you will use, and how long you will spend at each spot. Fishing is a game of strategy—a mental more than a physical game."

On competition days a blind draw is held and two names are drawn from a hat. Those two people fish together for the day. "We discuss our strategy for the day—where and how we are going to fish. Each person gets to fish where she wants to for half the day. She also controls the boat.

"The hardest decision to make is deciding when to move. Fishing isn't like running track or playing tennis—sports that can be practiced. Fishing is battling unpredictable obstacles, weather being the major one. You must decide whether to stay in the spot you're working on or look for something else. The right decision can make the difference between a poor finish and a major victory."

What really makes a professional angler successful? The most important ingredient to successful fishing, Linda says, "is to really open up—use all your senses. You have to be totally focused and concentrate on what is happening at the moment. People who are not as

Linda England: *Photo courtesy of DuPont.*

intense might miss those important little details—a small change in wind direction, or maybe the tiniest fraction of light filtering through the water, indicating a color change in your lure, or perhaps a change in current velocity. All those things play an important role in your success and you must be open to absorb it all. I guess you might say that the mark of a really successful fisherman is being able to completely adapt."

Bass pro Rick Clunn totally agrees but takes it one step further. Interviewed in *USA Today,* Rick said, "If you want more than just what flows through you as you sit fishing in a sort of contemplative way, then you've got to demand more. Competition can do that. It can force you to an awareness level you can't get any other way." Rick has developed his concentration and intuitive powers to the point where, he told us, "I can almost envision the fish I am going to catch."

If Linda hadn't been attracted to fishing, she said, "I really don't know what else I would have done. I would have missed a lot." To other women she confides, "Any time you get outdoors, open up to it, just let it happen, experience it. I get into the boat, fire up that Johnson engine, and take off up river—all the cares of the world just blow away in the wind."

Profile: Joan Wulff

Joan Salvato Wulff tells the story of being six years old and fishing with her parents. "Father fished," she says, "and Mother rowed the boat." Joan remembers those idyllic moments in sounds such as "the whir of the line and the plop of Dad's favorite bug as it landed on the water." But she remembers other sounds as well. "Every so often that silence was broken by Dad's critical comments about the boat's being too close or too far from the bass cover." In an article in the *New York Times* (April 3, 1988), Joan wrote, "I had never heard him speak to mother like that before." Joan was smarter than many of us. She was only six when she learned Fly Fishing Lesson Number One: It's better to be the fisherman than the rower.

Joan's father, Jimmy Salvato, owned the Paterson Rod and Gun Store in Paterson, New Jersey. Despite long hours at the store and writing a regular outdoor column for a local publication, he took every opportune moment to fish—on summer evenings after work and on

Joan Wulff—1953, Peoria, Illinois, National Casting Tournament.

Saturdays and Sundays. It didn't take Joan long to realize that if she wanted any attention from him at all, she had better learn to fish. And of one thing she was sure—she wouldn't be rowing the boat.

When Joan's father invited her younger brother Jimmy, age eight, to attend a casting practice session at a local casting club, another fact became clear. Joan, the older child, age 10, was bypassed. Message: Girls don't fish!

Not one to be ignored, Joan set out to learn fishing on her own. With mother's approval she assembled her dad's bamboo fly rod and headed for the casting club dock. As luck would have it, in her efforts to cast, the rod separated, sending the tip hurtling into the pond. "Horrified at the consequences," Joan convinced a neighbor to help retrieve the rod, which he did, "with a garden rake." But she felt compelled to explain the unfortunate event to her father. Expecting an angry response, a wise father invited her to join him for the next casting club practice, the following Sunday.

This accidental chain of events initiated Joan Wulff's career as a world fly-casting champion. Since then she has won 17 national casting titles, holds the "unofficial" woman's casting record of 161 feet (unofficial because in that competition there were no other women competing), holds the International Women's Fishing Association records for brook trout and Atlantic salmon, is the author of several books and articles on fly casting, writes a regular casting column for *Fly Rod & Reel,* and runs the Wulff Fly Fishing School in the Catskill Mountains, New York State.

Trained as a dancer, and having taught dance for many years, Joan quickly found that the act of casting was similar to dance. "The moves were rhythmic," she says, "and the form of the fly line unrolling was visually beautiful." For that reason, right from the start, fishing always seemed to her "more feminine than masculine." The photograph shown here was taken in 1953 at a national casting tournament in Peoria, Illinois. Joan was 26 then and had decided that although dance was wonderful, casting was glorious! She turned professional.

Travelling around the world, competing in national and international casting competitions, Joan found herself living in a man's world. "But it didn't bother me," she said in a *New York Times* interview in 1988. "I became friends with men who liked to fish and could provide opportunities for me to fish."

Then in 1959 she signed on with the Garcia Corporation, at that time the largest distributor of tackle in the world. Living in Florida at the time, married with a child, her job was to create goodwill for the company and to promote their products "through clinics and exhibitions." One attractive facet of the job was that it required fishing in tournaments around the country. Spending years in competition and exhibition casting, Joan described her fishing knowledge at that time as "broad but shallow." "Just like any other woman, juggling a career and a family left me little time for recreational fishing," she wrote in *Joan Wulff's Fly Fishing: Expert Advice from a Woman's Perspective.* But that was about to change.

A few years later Joan reached another turning point in her life. As part of her job, she received an invitation to appear in a film on giant bluefin-tuna fishing, produced by the famed angler and outdoorsman, Lee Wulff. That was in 1967 and marked the beginning of a partnership that lasted 24 years, until Lee's death in 1991. They not only became a team for Garcia, spreading their talents and creating goodwill around the world, but married and formed their own team as well. In 1979 they started the world famous Wulff Fly Fishing School, attracting students from all over the world. Their love of casting, fishing, fly tying, conservation, and just being outdoors was infectious, placing them among the gurus of the fly fishing world.

Now Joan, 65, is just getting her second wind. She is an attractive woman—strong and warm—and continues to teach the sport she loves and be a role model for the rest of us. "It has taken all of my life," Joan wrote in *Joan Wulff's Fly Fishing,* "for the changes to develop in equipment and attitude . . . there is nothing to stop you now except lack of time."

MOUNTAINEERING

Technique and ability alone do not get you to the top, it is the willpower that is the most important. This willpower you cannot buy with money or be given by others—it rises from your heart.
—*Junko Tabei, quoted in* Women Climbing—200 Years of Achievement

On May 16, 1975, Japanese mountaineer Junko Tabei became the first woman to summit the highest point in the world, Mount Everest, but our mountaineering heritage began long before that. As early as 1808, Frenchwoman Maria Paradis climbed Mount Blanc. A businesswoman, Paradis's specific interest in the climb was for publicity reasons—to attract customers to her tea shop at the base of the peak. It worked!

Mountaineering has always attracted a vast array of spirited (and, yes, sometimes eccentric) characters, and the annals of mountaineering are full of fabulous women. One of my favorites is Annie S. Peck. Nothing held Annie down. A professor of classics at Perdue University and Smith College, her list of first ascents is long and impressive. In 1897 she climbed 17,887-foot Popocatepetl in Mexico—then the highest elevation attained by a woman. In 1906 she made the first ascent of an unnamed 16,300-foot peak in Peru (at the source of the Amazon River). In 1908, at age 58, she made the first ascent of the north summit of Mount Huascaran in Peru (later named Cumbra Ana Peck by the Lima Geographical Society). Further, just to prove she still had it in her, Annie climbed Mount Madison in the White Mountains, New Hampshire at the age of 82.

Englishwoman Lucy Walker is identified in Birkett and Peascod's *Women Climbing—200 Years of Achievement* as the first "real" woman mountaineer. Consistency, not daring, it seems, was Lucy's claim to fame. Making her first climb in 1858 and her last in 1878, along with lifelong mountain guide Melchior Anderegg, Lucy made at least 90 climbs and was the first woman to climb the Matterhorn. (Researching a soon-to-be-published book on the history of women in climbing, writer Sallie Greenwood found that Frenchwoman Henriette d'Angeville climbed Mount Blanc in 1838, and continued climbing regularly for 20 years, which, I guess, would make Henriette the first "real" woman mountaineer.)

THE LADIES' ALPINE CLUB

Banned from the hallowed halls of the all-male Alpine Club, in 1906, the Ladies' Alpine Club was formed. Originating as a special interest group of the Lyceum Club, famed alpinist Elizabeth Le Blond was its first president, followed by Lucy Walker. The Ladies' Scottish Climbing Club followed a year later. These two groups became the focal points for European women climbers to document climbs, form expeditions, socialize, and share stories of the peaks.

With the end of World War I, women had found a new independence. No longer satisfied to "stay in the kitchen," women climbers started striking out on their own, particularly in guideless and manless climbs. To that end, in 1921, a rock-climbing club, the Pinnacle Club, was formed in England. Established by women for women, this organization listed its chief prerequisite for membership as "the proved ability to lead an ordinary climb of moderate difficulty." The founding of this club was considered by some a feminist statement, but it was merely a matter-of-fact way for women to explore and build upon their own unique strengths in a male-dominated sport. These women did not wait around to be guided or led or even to be accepted by their male counterparts. Without mentors, role models, or social sanction, they felt no compunction about establishing their own climbing identities quite separate and apart from those of their mates. Birkett and Peascod have said, "[The] story of women in climbing is more than a history, more than a tale of individual daring or achievement; it is in a very real sense the ascent of woman."

The modern history of mountaineering, from World War I to the present, is peppered with astonishing women of strength and vision, scholarship and pride; women who pioneered new routes, led expeditions, charted new terrain; women who for the most part are relatively obscure but who have forged for us a legacy of adventure, a legacy we can build upon and one with which we can identify with great pride; women such as Annie S. Peck, Fanny Bullock Workman, Elizabeth Le Blond, Miriam Underhill, Dorothy Pilley, Dorothy Thompson, Loulou Boulaz, Nea Morin, Gwen Moffat, Claude Kogan, Molly Higgins, Bonnie Prudden, Wanda Rutkiewicz, Vera Watson, Alison Chadwick-Onyszkiewicz, Arlene Blum, Lynn Hill, Catherine Destivelle, Barbara Washburn, Julie Brugger, Annie Whitehouse, Elizabeth Knowlton, Louise Shepherd, Ruth Dyar Mendenhall, Elizabeth Woolsey, and Kitty Calhoun-Grissom. This is but a sprinkling of women who, through climbing (with both men and women), found adventure, challenge, joy, and camaraderie in the mountains.

Women and mountains is a fascinating subject, and one historically fraught with controversy. The women mentioned above loved to climb and did so when and wherever possible. While most climbed anonymously by choice, and never felt held back in any way, others, especially those involved in extensive mountaineering expeditions, have had to cope with a great deal more than just raising funds. They have had to fight prejudices of every kind, from the most subtle (such as being mentioned in climbing journals and reports by first initial only or not being identified at all) to the most overt, such as when mountaineer Irene Miller joined Sir Edmund Hillary's 1961 Makalu expedition as the only woman member. One member suggested that to be part of the expedition, she should be "willing to sleep with all the men on the team."

Yet obstacles like these have not kept us from the mountains. Instead, it has spurred us on to form our own expeditions to the highest points in the world and to write our own history. In the last 15 years that invincible spirit, coupled with dynamic institutional changes such as the Woman's Movement and the enactment of legislation such as Title IX, has produced a new genre of outdoor women who face few obstacles when calling the mountains their own.

Profiled in *Climbing* (August/September 1990), 33-year-old high-altitude mountaineer Annie Whitehouse says, "Intellectually, I knew that women climbers were probably discriminated against, but frankly, I never was. I can't remember a single time that I was prevented from doing what I wanted because I was female, either on the rock or in the mountains." A powerful statement, and one, we might add, that is heard more often than not these days. But consider Annie's background. As a teenager, her mentor was Margaret Young, a mountaineer, a pilot, a physicist—a vibrant, independent, daring woman who literally showed Annie the ropes. "She was an intense, intimidating woman," Annie adds. "She found being a woman and a climber to be easily congruent, an attitude that I adopted without question. From her I learned that you can often get to the top by sheer perseverance, by just putting one foot in front of the other."

Thirty-two-year-old Kitty Calhoun-Grissom mirrors Annie's view. Climbing the legendary West Pillar of Makalu (27,825 feet) in 1990, and considered one of the foremost mountaineers in America (male or female), Kitty, in *Women's Sports & Fitness,* admits she faces some skepticism by "macho guys just because [I'm] a woman. But instead of telling them about all the things I've done, I like to keep quiet. As soon as we start climbing, they come around fast enough."

WHAT IS MOUNTAINEERING?

Mountaineering is climbing mountains. Mountaineering can encompass anything from several-weeks or months-long assault-style expeditions to the tallest peaks in the world, requiring years of fund-raising and preparation, to Alpine-style ascents that focus on summiting in a day. It makes no difference whether you climb a 4,000 footer in the Adirondacks, a 14,000 footer in the Rockies, or climb to the top of Everest—it is called mountaineering.

Major assault-style expeditions involve establishing several camps at higher and higher altitudes—moving tons of equipment and food and requiring tremendous investments in time and money. Most of us will never be involved in this type of climb.

Alpine-style climbing, marking its beginnings in the Alps in the late 1700s (hence the term "Alpinist") and the style of mountaineering popular today, is a philosophy of traveling light and getting to the top and down quickly without having to carry heavy loads. But, as you might imagine, it is a little more complicated than that. It is also a technical sport, set apart from backpacking/trekking by the necessity for specialized clothing and technical skills and equipment, including knowledge of rope handling, belaying techniques, crevasse self-rescue, glacier skills, and crampon and ice axe use.

Although mountaineering and rock climbing evolved together,

overlapping, today they are considered distinctly separate activities. Mountaineering is likely to include rock climbing, but rock climbing seldom involves mountaineering. Originating in Europe in the latter part of the last century, rock climbing was practiced in Britain, mostly as "training for the Alps," but over the last 150 years has evolved from that simple beginning into a multifaceted, highly technical, and athletic sport today, and many of its stars are women. Direct outgrowths of rock climbing are ice climbing, and competition and sport climbing.

MOUNTAINEERING

Backpacking and trekking become mountaineering when the object becomes to reach summits and not simply to traverse trails and passes. Besides getting you to lofty places, the major attraction of this sport is its constant challenge. Weather conditions often fluctuate dramatically, demanding careful preparation, well-practiced survival skills, and mountaineering techniques, as well as a high level of physical fitness. These are not skills that one just naturally possesses but are skills gained over time, through experience—either with seasoned mountaineers or through courses in mountaineering technique.

In some instances, mountaineering can require rope-handling skills, belaying techniques, and technical climbing expertise. Summits often require the use of ice axes, ropes, snowshoes or crampons, and specialized clothing. Mountaineering is an ongoing process, a series of experiences captured over time—and to many, a life-style. Aside from strictly technical skills, there is no one way to prepare for life in the mountains. "I quickly learned," wrote Julie Brugger in *Rock and Roses,* "that the mountains do not offer their possibilities to the unskilled and unknowledgeable. Their ways must be learned—their weather, how to travel, how to be safe, how to overcome fear, how to respect."

Just as important is being mentally able to handle the added stress of coping with these adverse conditions. "Getting to the top of mountains is mostly just a matter of determination," says Kitty Calhoun-Grissom. To climb successfully, you must "want to." While having the "want to" is certainly the most necessary ingredient to success in any sport, in mountaineering it is critical—being able to tackle one problem after another, developing strategy, then translating that strategy into action until you reach your goal.

Mountaineering can be a team activity. That team brings together the various strengths of its members and utilizes those strengths to ensure the group's success. Those strengths can run the gamut from members who possess the most technical planning skills to those with good old "common sense." As an example, I was part of a group (and the only woman) climbing a trailless peak in the Adirondack Mountains in New York a few years ago. It was winter and there was a good, deep snow cover, requiring snowshoes. But the snow wasn't crusty so breaking trail was difficult and tiring. Halfway up the peak it started snowing and the wind picked up, and I started to find it difficult to keep up. Not realizing what was happening, I sat down in the snow to rest. A member of the party realized I wasn't close behind and came back and found me. He realized immediately that I was suffering from the first stages of hypothermia. He quickly found extra warm clothes in my backpack and helped me on with them, poured a cup of hot soup and held the cup while I drank it, and got me up and walking along at a good pace.

I had reached the point of being out of control. The fine line between healthy and in trouble had been crossed—and that can happen suddenly, and to even the most experienced of us, in mountain conditions. From experience and common sense, my climbing partner was able to assess the situation quickly and knew exactly what to do. That ordeal became an important building block in my mountaineering experience.

Mountaineering is a natural extension for those of you who possess hiking/backpacking skills. Many of the essential skills, such as load carrying, camping, map and compass reading, and survival techniques are those often learned through hiking and backpacking. Summer hiking and backpacking trips are perfect ways to begin to learn those mountaineering basics. Coupled with the proper equipment and formal courses offered by commercial guide services, outdoor organizations and clubs such as National Outdoor Leadership School (NOLS), Outward Bound, the Appalachian Mountain Club, Sierra Club, Colorado Mountain Club, the Mountaineers, Mazamas, and dozens of other regional and local organizations around the country, you'll get off to a great start. These groups not only teach the skills required and offer advice on gear selection, but, just as important, you'll meet others who share your interests.

Joining outdoor organizations such as those listed above (and in the Resources section) will also give you access to used equipment and gear swaps, commonly advertised through organizational newsletters and bulletin boards.

Organizations such as Alaska Women of the Wilderness offer mountaineering courses that include glacier travel, basic mountaineering safety skills, knot tying, orienteering, and equipment selection and care. Rachel Holzwarth, director of this organization, leads trips to Denali and other major peaks and is a great source of information and a good place to start your networking process, if you're interested in an all-woman program. Whatever way you enter the sport, start now. We want to see you on the peaks!

ROCK CLIMBING

Rock climbing is broken down into various categories, and there are various schools of thought as to how to get started. Some say a good way to begin is by bouldering. Bouldering is rock climbing at its most basic—achievable and fun for beginners but practiced and enjoyed even by experts. Any rock face can be used. Its attraction is that a satisfying afternoon can be spent climbing around on a rock while being only a foot or two off the ground. The satisfaction in bouldering comes from finding and utilizing the tiniest nubs and holds, not in the height attained. Bouldering is an inexpensive form of entertainment— the only thing you need is a pair of shoes (such as tennis shoes) that adhere somewhat to the rock.

Others believe, however, that top roping is the way to start—that bouldering can be boring for beginners, that only a more experienced climber can get the most out of that aspect of the sport. Climber Sallie Greenwood likens bouldering for beginners to learning to play tennis by hitting the ball against a backboard. "The experience would be very frustrating, hardly tennis, and they'd probably take up golf," she said. Top-roping is a hands-on approach to climbing. The situation is controlled and the novice gets the benefit of learning to trust the rope, dealing with exposure, and figuring out how to move up within view (and verbal range) of her teacher.

When top-roping, a rope is anchored to the top of a cliff by various methods. Basic safety and rope-handling skills are taught at this time.

You will learn how to tie knots, how to "tie in" to a harness, and how to belay another climber. To belay, your climbing partner wraps the rope that is attached to you around her seat, pulling in the slack as you climb up the rock. If you slip, you can fall only as far as the slack allows, permitting you to climb progressively difficult routes with less risk.

Once you're sure you like rock climbing (and you'll know within the first 15 minutes or so) you will want to purchase your first two pieces of equipment—a pair of sticky rubber-soled climbing shoes and a harness. Available in a vast array of colors and styles, shoes cost between $120 and $160. Less expensive shoes are available but rock shoes are your safety and transportation, so don't skimp on cost! After years of research, Black Diamond Equipment (2084 East 3900 South, Salt Lake City, UT 84124; (801) 278-5533) has produced a harness sized for women called Women's XX Climbing Harness, available by mail for $69.95. Owning your own shoes and harness is a good idea but don't worry about collecting a lot of equipment at first. It takes time and experience to accumulate gear of your own.

If you're still intrigued, the next step is lead climbing. One climber starts at the bottom of a cliff that is more than one rope-length high. The lead climber starts up while the second stays on the ground belaying the leader. As the leader moves along, she puts in protection in the form of nuts or chocks (small metal wedges of various sizes) that fit into cracks in the rock. A carabiner (a metal oval with a spring gate closure) is then attached to the chock and the rope is passed through it. The lead climber can only fall half again as far as her last piece of protection. When the lead climber reaches the top of that rope length, she ties into more protection and belays the second climber up to that point. As the second climber ascends she takes out the protection put in by the leader. Reaching the belay point, she climbs through (past the leader), now becoming the lead climber. This process is repeated until the top is reached.

Rock climbs in the United States are graded for difficulty from 5.0 to 5.14 (easiest to hardest). For example, climbs rated 5.0 to 5.5 are appropriate for beginners. In the ratings of 5.10 and up there are subdivisions of a, b, c, and d, and there is a big difference between a 5.10a and a 5.10d.

Sport climbing is a branch of lead climbing that has gained in-creasing interest over the last few years because of climbers wanting to plumb their highest possible level of skill. Sport climbing made it possible to take the sport to another level and climb not so much to gain a summit but rather to test personal limits, and in some instances, even to earn a living, in which case the climber is considered a competition climber. Lynn Hill is probably the most well-known sport climber today. Featured in magazines and perfume ads, she is paid to climb. Watching Lynn or any sport climber is like watching a gymnast; they possess the same degree of athleticism. This aspect of the sport attracts the most aggressive climbers.

Artificial Climbing Walls

Artificial climbing walls are an extension of sport climbing and a cause of serious concern among the old guard in the sport who believe that the walls, with their artificial holds, merely produce a brand of athlete who relies solely on gymnastics to win, and who has no interest in the rich history of mountain climbing. They argue that the wall is contrived and controlled and is about as far from the essence of the sport as it can be. Then again, others welcome artificial walls and see them as a worthwhile way to defray wear and tear on natural rock face, relieve overcrowding in the more popular climbing areas, and provide ready access to the sport.

Making its debut in the '80s, the climbing wall was developed as a way for climbers to train throughout the year, but its cost and versatility have made it standard equipment in barns and basements and many health and fitness clubs, gymnasiums, and school athletic departments across the country. The glory of the wall is that one wall can possess countless routes (from extremely simple to gloriously complicated) by simply rebolting the artificial holds. In climbing-wall competition, official route-setters bolt the holds, and competitors cannot preview the route or watch any other person climb, and every competitor has to climb the same set of holds.

Writer and climber Susan Rogers notes, "There is a new generation of climbers who are superb wall climbers but who are not comfortable on natural rock. Their dreams are not of El Capitan, but of a 20-foot high wall, with ten ridiculously difficult moves."

Tired of competitive climbing, French world-class climber and mountaineer Catherine Destivelle sheds a somewhat different light on wall climbing. "I don't want to do any more gymnastics," she said in *Outside* magazine (January 1991). "I need more emotions, more adventure. For me, the mountains are more rich."

Competition climbing takes place on rock too, but is different from climbing on artificial walls. Looking at a rock, like looking at a face, every climber sees something different. Recognizing and using those differences is what enables you to win.

As the debate rages on, the artificial wall has found its niche. For some it's a training supplement and for others the wall is the sport. Decide for yourself. Check the Yellow Pages for a wall near you. Usually located in a gym, lessons are inexpensive and it's fun, challenging, and a great workout!

ICE CLIMBING

Ice climbing is the equivalent of lead climbing but it also falls into the realm of mountaineering. Its origins were in the mountains where it was necessary to climb ice on the way to the summit. In the last 25 years, with the development of the curved pick ice axe and hammer, rigid plastic boots, and rigid crampons, ice climbing has developed as a separate sport. These tools allow climbers to tackle extreme vertical ice. Previously, the only way to get up an ice wall was to cut steps with an ice axe, a long and exhausting technique.

In a continuing process, the climber drives the axe and hammer into the ice and hangs on to them as she moves her feet up, reaching up and driving the axe and hammer in again and kicking up one more time, until she reaches the top. As in rock climbing, protection is required and is accomplished using threaded ice screws that are twisted into the ice.

"Climbing is rooted deep in the body," writes climber Pat Ament. "It is gratifying, amusing, healthy to climb." Most of us climbed as kids, so reclaiming those movements is almost instinctive. But as kids, most of us knew little fear. And the most common barrier to women in climbing is fear. In *Outdoor Woman* (June 1990), writer/climber Susan Rogers addressed this issue: "When we climb there are many variables that are out of our control and much fear comes from an awareness of the mountain: avalanches, rock fall, bad weather." Those fears are valid and should be listened to. "Then there is a fear," Rogers adds, "that comes from within. It's a nagging fear, one that can grow slowly if not checked, one that can make you turn back even if there is no visible reason." Those fears are often societal and are harder to brush off.

Fear is an emotion that is difficult to define and can be crippling. But many sports, climbing in particular, "put you there." On the rock or in the mountains, you must deal with each moment, solve that problem, experience that joy and move on. Psychotherapist Dianne Skafte, in a 1987 *Women's Sports and Fitness* article, said, "As women master the severe and elegant lessons of the rock, they learn not only how to cope with fear and other intense emotions, they gain a new yardstick by which to measure themselves." Isn't that what most of us constantly struggle to achieve?

HOW TO GET STARTED

As a beginner, to learn any climbing skill or technique (either rock, wall, or ice), we recommend attending a class offered by a local outing club, professional guide service, or climbing school. While learning with friends may be an option, organized classes teach the sport in a structured manner, starting with the basics and working through more complicated techniques, leaving little room for omissions and assumptions. Most schools have programs for your increasing abilities. There are many good instructors out there, men as well as women, so take your time and find one with whom you feel comfortable.

Hiring a guide is more expensive than learning with a group, but you'll get all the personal attention you want. Guides can run up to $200 or more per day. If you live near a climbing area, check the climbing shops or outdoor stores—they often have bulletin boards and love to give advice and referrals. If you don't have access to an outdoor store, call or write the American Mountain Guides Association (P.O. Box 4473, Bellingham, WA 98227; (206) 647-1167) for referrals of climbing schools and guide services near you. Or get a subscription to *Climbing* magazine (P.O. Box 339, Carbondale, CA 81623), where you will find advertisements for schools, guide services, equipment, and anything else to do with climbing and mountaineering.

Outward Bound offers climbing and mountaineering courses just for women. Call (800) 243-0797 for a brochure. National Outdoor Leadership School (NOLS) also teaches climbing. Check local outdoor groups for their climbing instruction calendars.

Across the country there are organizations that specialize in teaching women to climb. Woodswomen (25 West Diamond Lake Road, Minneapolis, MN 55419) offers climbing at all levels as well as guides for about $175 a day, or you can join a group for a day class or a week-long trip to some popular climbing area such as Joshua Tree National Park in California. Sylvan Rocks (230 Denver, Rapid City, SD 57701; (605) 343-1202), run by Susan Scheirbeck, offers group instruction, guiding, and special classes for women only and for children only at the Needles (within Custer State Park). Maggie Kessel of Personal Challenges (1852 Ashland, St. Paul, Minnesota 55104; (612) 646-2063) offers women-only climbing trips in the Southwest as a way for women to explore their personal limits through climbing—without the pressure of competition or fear of failure.

Once you start networking through a few of these contacts and organizations you'll start to form a group of your own. Those we have mentioned are just the beginning.

WHY DO WOMEN CLIMB?

In an article, "Great Explorations" (*Ms.* magazine, June 1989), Judy Mills addresses this question in part: "For the love of it. To feed unnamed hunger. To face fear. For an all-time high." In other words, for the same reasons men do! Climbing gets you to high, wild, beautiful, and isolated places. It also pushes you beyond your wildest imagination, physically and mentally. It's a learning process that never ends and most of all, it's fun!

Climber Hulda Crooks, on summiting 12,385-foot Mount Fuji at the age of 91, succinctly sums it up: "You always feel good when you've made a goal. You need goals."

Profile: Alison Osius

Alison Osius is one of those lucky people who is able to live her sport 24 hours a day. Her favorite climbing partner is husband Mike Benge; her job is senior editor for *Climbing* magazine; and she holds the number-four slot on the U.S. Climbing Team.

How did Alison manage this wonderful feat? Well, it didn't happen overnight. It began back in college, at a meeting of the college newspaper. "The managing editor was assigning stories and one was on climbing," Alison says. "I opened my mouth and sort of blurted out, 'I'll do that one.'"

Researching her story, Alison struck a chord with the climbers, and they with her. They were modest and funny and told wild stories about climbs they had made. "I wanted to be just like them," Alison says. They invited her on some climbs and remain her friends today. One— Rebecca Upham—became Alison's role model. That was back in 1977, and the rest, as they say, is history.

Alison's history has been a busy and colorful one. Growing up racing sailboats with her family on Chesapeake Bay, even as a kid Alison was driven by a competitive spirit. "We always raced to win,"

Alison Osius.

she says. Then in college Alison not only discovered climbing but women's team sports as well. "I had forgotten how much fun it was to be part of a team. The women on the rugby team were very active, with a lot of interests and I just really liked that camaraderie."

As Alison describes climbing in small groups, you can see how that camaraderie is present on the rock too. "When two or three people make a long ascent together, an almost supernatural bonding takes place because you are trusting and sharing and doing things together."

After college, determined to mine the depths of her skills, to find out what she "could really do," Alison took off for a summer in Wales. Leaving with the goal in mind of staying three months and climbing 5.9s, she returned six months later climbing solid 5.10 + s. For the next three years she worked her way across the United States, climbing every available area in the summer and relying on her journalism skills to see her through the winter.

"I am amazed that I lived through those years, actually," she shrugs. "I had never attended any sort of climbing program and consequently learned a lot of things on my own—through trial and error—and errors aren't good when you're up high." Prodded for a "for instance," she says: "Like being halfway up a cliff and running out of gear—on a lead—not able to move. Instead of downclimbing and going back for more gear, I set up my hanging belay off one big hex. My friend, who was seconding, started to fall and there we were—he was hanging off me and I was hanging off one hex. That was when I thought, 'Boy, I'll bet you're never supposed to belay off just one nut.' "

Although Alison learned to climb with friends, she recommends that others learn with an instructor. "Friends don't usually have a method for teaching and there may be certain things that never get taught (because of oversights and assumptions)—a dangerous thing in climbing."

By nature, Alison searches for answers. That's what makes her a good journalist; it's also what makes her a good climber. "I like being able to figure out all the different techniques to get up a rock wall—putting together all the pieces, like a puzzle."

But by 1982, she had reached a point in her journalism career where the pieces weren't fitting together. She needed some answers—to ethical and moral questions and about style. So she packed up and moved to New York City, to the Columbia School of Journalism.

All that hard work has paid off. After a few years of freelancing and part-time jobs, Alison landed in Carbondale, Colorado at *Climbing* magazine. At the same time she was putting in her time on the rock, bouldering several evenings a week and devoting weekends to climbing. Now she is senior editor at the magazine and holds the number-four slot on the U.S. Climbing Team—and she's just warming up.

Reminiscing, Alison says that it has been exciting to watch her progress over the years, "the letters and numbers kept getting harder and harder—way beyond what I had expected. But maybe my expectations were too low. We didn't have very many women role models then. When I was first climbing in college I knew one other woman climber—Rebecca. I didn't have any idea how good women could get—consequently how good I could ever hope to be. Now that has changed. That's good."

It wasn't until 1985, on her return from Europe, while teaching at International Mountain Equipment in North Conway, New Hampshire, that Alison heard about Lynn Hill and "got a better take on what a woman can do, and it seemed like there was a lot to strive for, hope for, and dream about."

Although Alison climbs with both men and women, her focus now is sport climbing and climbing at her level and in her geographic area. This narrows the field tremendously, so her partners are usually men. "If I lived in a place like Boulder there would be tons of women who climb on my level and who could keep me on my toes," she adds. "It's just geography." Men make up the largest segment of the sport and Alison finds their approach to climbing not only different but often preferable. "Sometimes women are too patient and supportive and it gets in the way; keeps you from not pushing hard enough. If I hesitate on a move when climbing with the guys they say, 'Come on Alison, let's do it! You can do it.' and I think okay, I can do it and I do."

How does she view women in climbing today? "There are a lot of good women now. When I was learning it was rare to see a woman leading a 5.10 and now there are lots of women climbing hard and climbing well. They have good judgment and really good strengths and power."

Her view is mirrored in a *Climbing* editorial. One might say that she's working quietly behind the scenes. "Every once and a while," she says, "our business manager suggests a special issue on women. I immediately say no, I don't want a special issue. Women shouldn't be singled out but covered fairly and evenly—like men."

Alison's philosophy of climbing and journalism can be defined further by something rock climber and guide Rosie Andrews once wrote: "Climbing is climbing, regardless of the gender of the climber. As we all know, the rock really doesn't care. What matters is that particular blend of qualities the individual brings to the sport."

Profile: LaVerne Woods

Why would a corporate tax attorney with degrees from Yale and Harvard want to spend every spare minute at high altitude? "Because it is an isolated, beautiful place," LaVerne Woods explains. "And I like being on snow and ice and being in a threatening-looking place. A lot of the attraction is the aesthetics of being on an icy mountain; I'm a small speck. I like the lack of ambiguity. You know where you are going and you know you're there when you reach the top. It is a linear kind of process that's very satisfying."

Woods has spent time on some of the highest mountains on earth. She was one of three women (and the only American) to participate in the Mount Everest Earth Day 20 International Peace Climb 1990. But she has climbed countless "lesser" peaks as well: Rainier, McKinley, peaks in the Cascades, the Russian Pamirs, in the Alps, in New Zealand, and Hiunchuli and Annapurna IV in the Himalayas.

Where did this love of being in high places originate? LaVerne grew up on a small farm surrounded by the mountains of the Northwest, just east of Seattle. Her parents were climbers and "from a pretty young age" she was dragged along. "It was usually wet and cold and a lot of hard work," she laughs. "I can't say that I cared for it much." But that's where it all started, in the North Cascades, close to home.

While away at college, searching to maintain her connection with the outdoors, she spent some time with the Outing Club at Harvard, "but they were mostly involved in rock climbing," she says. "I'm built for Alpine mountaineering and not for rock. You have to be a lot thinner than I am to be good at rock." And getting to climbing areas required a car, which she didn't own.

But summers off were spent mountaineering with friends back in the Northwest. In 1980 the group climbed McKinley in Alaska, de-

LaVerne Woods on *Annapurna IV: Photo by Don Holle.*

scribed by Woods as, "a climb that easily makes people decide they either love the sport, or that it was fun, but one major mountain is enough." That group went on to do Hiunchuli in Nepal, what LaVerne describes as her "first significant climb."

After completing Harvard Law School, Woods moved to Washington, D.C. "A great place to practice law," she adds, "but I missed the mountains and the wilderness." Then in 1987 she joined a law firm in Seattle, and came home. Shortly after that, her application for the Everest Earth Day Peace Climb was accepted. Jim Whitaker, who in 1963 was the first American to summit Everest, was the organizer, and his plan was to include one woman from each country involved—the Soviet Union, China, and the United States. That climb not only put LaVerne in the hospital, but gave her some fresh perspectives on the sport as well.

The goal of the Everest Earth Day 20 International Peace Climb 1990 was twofold: one was to show the world that through working in harmony, climbers could overcome language and cultural barriers to put at least one person from each country on the top. The other was to deliver an environmental message: in celebration of the twentieth anniversary of Earth Day, the team would haul off piles of garbage left on Everest by various expeditions from around the world.

After choosing expedition members, two practice climbs were held, one on Rainier and one in the Russian Caucasus. LaVerne, Katya Ivanova of the then–Soviet Union, and Gui Sang from Tibet comprised the three women. "I became much more aware of gender than I ever had been before," says LaVerne in an interview in *Outdoor Woman.* "When it's me and a bunch of guys, there aren't a lot of distinctions. They treat me like one of the guys. But when you have three women on an expedition with a group of men, then there are men and there are women."

LaVerne and Katya Ivanova became fast friends and teammates. Gui Sang climbed mostly with the Tibetans. "They were in better condition," notes Woods, "and faster. And since their diet was different from ours, they ate together." This was Gui Sang's second attempt at Everest.

The cultural distinctions among the men of the three countries towards their female counterparts were sometimes glaring. The Soviet and Chinese men tried to make things easier for the three, sometimes even insisting on setting up their tents. The gesture was well-intended and LaVerne found it difficult to discourage that help without seeming ungrateful. The American men didn't cut the women any breaks. "Nor did I want them to," Woods adds. When some of the male climbers assumed that the women would climb together, Katya agreed. She felt that it was a more radical idea for the "women to climb together and show that they were strong enough to do it without men on their rope." Supported by Whitaker, Woods objected. The purpose of the climb, she felt, was for peoples of different cultures, men and women, to climb together as a team, not the men and the women climbing separately.

While the presence of women on a climbing team is sometimes used as a fund-raising tool, that wasn't the case on the Everest climb. Two of the three women summitted. But LaVerne celebrated her team-mates' success from a Bangkok hospital bed, recovering from multiple blood clots in her calf, lungs, and thigh—the result, she believes, of being immobilized in a tent for several days at 23,400 feet, waiting out a storm. The incident, reported by Bev Wessel in *Outdoor Woman,* was frightening. Jim Whitaker, it seems, experienced pain in his calf; team doctors quickly diagnosed him as having a blood clot and whisked him off to a Bangkok hospital. There, doctors found Whitaker's problem to be a pulled muscle.

When Woods complained the same day about a pain in her thigh that wouldn't go away, she felt that the team doctors didn't take her seriously. First, they misdiagnosed her illness as a lymph infection, then pulmonary edema, and then pneumonia. After descending to base camp and experiencing difficulty in breathing, Woods was finally transported to a Bangkok hospital. The doctors told her she may have had as little as 24 hours before the clots broke up and moved to her heart.

Several months later, Woods was back in the office and back to climbing in the Cascades. Was she disappointed at not summiting Everest? "Most people don't get Everest on their first try," she says. "I feel lucky to be alive. We came out all right with 20 people on top and nobody dying." Will she experience blood clots on future expeditions? There's no way to tell. Doctors don't know much about blood clots at high altitude, and they know even less about the physiology of women at altitude.

How does she view women and climbing? Admitting that women climbers can't carry the same amount of weight as men, LaVerne says, "There are not many inherent differences between men and women in climbing. While cardiovascular fitness is sometimes more important than upper body strength, you must be able to carry a pack and use an ice axe. Women climbers can easily be as good as a man if they want to be. It all depends on how badly you want to be there. There are no automatic gender barriers."

Future plans: Right now Woods and her husband are training for the Paris Marathon, but she plans to try Everest again.

ATHLETES WITH DISABILITIES

There are an estimated one million disabled men, women, and children in the United States. Thousands regularly take part in organized sports such as basketball, rugby, tennis, and swimming; others prefer nonorganized sports such as hiking, trail riding, golf, rock climbing, kayaking, canoeing, scuba diving, sailing, snow skiing, and water skiing. There are still others who prefer marathons, bowling, archery, shooting, and weight lifting. Representing each of those sports are organizations and associations through which athletes with disabilities can learn the sport, access information about equipment and events, and network with other athletes. Sounds amazing, doesn't it? Well, it's true!

However, this hasn't always been the case. Historically, the world has been inaccessible to those with limitations. Doctors believed that people with disabilities needed protection and openly discouraged participation in even the least strenuous activities. Can you imagine the look on the faces of those same doctors today if they could see Olympian Diana Golden flying 60 miles per hour downhill, barrelling between the flags, balanced on one ski? Or if they read about paraplegic Mark Wellman, who, after eight days and 7,000 pull-ups, climbed Yosemite's El Capitan? Giving up skiing for mountain climbing, Golden recently climbed Mount Rainier with a group of able-bodied women and is currently at work developing a self-arresting crutch! Wellman, a visitors guide at Yosemite, also kayaks, cycles, swims, and skis (both downhill and cross-country)!

SPACE-AGE WHEELCHAIRS

It was only 45 years ago, with the arrival of wheelchair basketball, that organized athletic events for the disabled were even heard of, but look at the scope of this sport now. Across the country there are 28 conferences, comprising 165 teams—including 12 women's teams. Wheelchair basketball is a business. It has its own national governing body (the National Wheelchair Basketball Association), is officially recognized by the National Basketball Hall of Fame, and since 1991 has been accepted as a voting member of U.S.A. Basketball (an organization made up of the NCAA, NBA, and NAIA).

What added a whole new dimension to the world of disabled athletes, not only highlighting their talents, but amplifying their problems as well, was when the Vietnam veterans came home. Veterans who before the war had enjoyed skiing, running, and every other outdoor activity, wanted to continue having fun and being challenged

Jean Driscoll: *Photo by Delfina Colby of Sports 'n Spokes.*

in the outdoors. Their determination, coupled with new technology, really changed the perception of how the disabled view themselves and their limitations.

However, the major factor in the growth of wheelchair sports is directly attributable to space-age technology. Basketball players began playing in wheelchairs that were "one-size-fits-all." Frustrated by the weight and lack of maneuverability, a few sportsmen began customizing chairs—cutting them down, making them not only lighter but more responsive on the court. Created in garages and basements, such chairs could be located by word of mouth—until a company named Quickie jumped into the void and developed the first mass-produced, high-tech sports wheelchair.

Now, using the lightest-weight metal tubing, precisely machined hubs and ball bearings, and computer-design technology, Quickie and other companies manufacture wheelchairs that address the needs of every specific sport, including tennis, road racing, mountain biking, basketball, and track racing. There are chairs with great knobby tires just like a mountain bike! Using a 15-pound marathon chair, Jean Driscoll did the 26-mile Boston Marathon in 1991 in 1:42.42—a world record! This revolution in wheelchairs has taken place only in the last ten years and has spawned not only maneuverable lightweight wheelchairs but a host of other equipment and adaptations as well.

ACCESSING INFORMATION

Despite gigantic strides in equipment and adaptive procedures, a great difficulty those with disabilities face is the inability to access a central source of information—information on how to get mobile, how to get out of the house and get started, and how to find others with similar interests. It might be that you have had no athletic experience at all and don't have a clue as to what you might like to do or what your abilities might be. This lack of a central source of general and specific information is a dilemma faced by all people with any kind of disability, whether the goal is to learn to water ski or to simply take an outdoor vacation.

Determined to re-enter the paddling sport after her accident, Janet Zeller recounts the difficulties she faced: "There was no central clearinghouse for information—just individuals and groups operating in different areas of the country, each solving their own problems and duplicating a lot of effort."

Joy Stout tells a similar story. A skier before an accident left her a paraplegic, Joy had abandoned all thought of being active again. The chance meeting with a quadriplegic involved in a local ski competition sparked Joy's need to reclaim her athletic self. "I had no idea what was available," Joy says. She is back to skiing and, using a mono-ski, competes in regional ski events. Once she "hooked into the system," Joy found other athletic challenges as well, including tennis, mountain biking, sailing, horseback riding, and water skiing. Recently voted "Player of the Year" by fellow wheelchair tennis players, Joy ranked fourth in the country in wheelchair tennis and took second with a team of other U.S. players at a World Team Cup in 1991.

How do you get into the system? Through networking! You can start by accessing the Resources section in the back of this book. Another great way to begin is to subscribe to *Sports 'N Spokes,* a dynamic magazine (see Disabled Athletes in Resources) published by the Paralyzed Veterans of America. While their focus remains on indoor sports such as wheelchair basketball, this publication covers everything from local fishing tournaments and road racing to world-class ski championships—all with equal enthusiasm. While *Sports 'N Spokes* is aimed at the more aggressive athletes—those who like to work up a sweat and love a real workout—it's a magazine for any athlete with a disability. Jam-packed with great information, fun for everyone to read, carrying truly informative advertising, *Sports 'N Spokes* provides lists of associations and events around the country, all good places to meet others and have fun. It makes you feel good just to read it.

But what about the woman who just wants to be part of the total outdoor scene without devoting herself to a particular sport? Where does she begin the process of reclaiming her physical self and having fun? That information is more difficult to come by. Bonnie Sue Hickson of Truckee, California, has been focusing her energy on solving this problem through a process she calls "The Ripple Effect."

About six years ago, Bonnie Sue organized the first National Wheelchair Tennis Championship, known now as Everest & Jennings Farwest National Wheelchair Tennis Championship. That event quickly blossomed to include an international event—International Wheelchair Tennis Grand Prix—and attracts tennis champions from countries the world over. Bonnie Sue isn't surprised—this is what she calls the "The Ripple Effect." "Drop a pebble into a pool," she says. "The ripples always go farther than you ever expect." She thinks the greatest result of these events is that those athletes go home and establish similar events to include still others and the word about fun and camaraderie spreads, like ripples on the water.

A critical-care nurse by profession, a musician and competitor at heart, Bonnie Sue has suffered from multiple sclerosis for the last 20 years. "I used to be very competitive," she says, "both in skiing and on the tennis circuit. Now the MS has progressed to a point where I can't do that but I love to turn other people on, watch them enjoy the sport and have fun." To that end, Bonnie Sue is developing a healing center—called Farwest Choice—for disabled people in the Donner Lake area. Bonnie Sue describes the program as a "kick start" that recognizes the full spectrum of the person, utilizing the outdoors as a vehicle. "It's a time for persons with disabilities to come up to Truckee and enjoy the mountains," she says. Farwest Choice includes camping, barbecues, singing in the mountains, swimming, and learning how to participate in water sports such as water skiing and adaptive sailing. "We even ride Sardine Peak on mountain bikes," she says, adding, "It's a celebration!"

This all takes place at Donner Lake, about 45 minutes from Reno; costs $25 a day without lodging; and is limited to 25 people. Bonnie Sue is quick to point out that you can stay in the Donner Lake Campground, a fully accessible campground, including ramps on the pier, or at the Donner Lake Village resort.

Another information source is the quarterly magazine *Disabled Outdoors* (see Disabled Athletes in Resources). Its "hook and bullet" format is targeted more toward men than women, but the issues we reviewed had information for everyone. It's worth looking into.

National Handicapped Sports (NHS) is a wonderful start. Organized by a group of Vietnam vets, NHS has 59 chapters nationwide and 24 of those chapters offer ski instruction. Many chapters have a full range of year-round outdoor activities that include mountain climbing, water skiing, and downhill and cross-country skiing. Contact National Handicapped Sports (1145 Nineteenth Street, Suite 717, Washington, DC 20036; (301) 652-7505) for information about programs around the country.

There are many local and regional organizations as well that provide ways for athletes to get out and compete, socialize, and have fun. For instance, the New York Road Runners Club has a special group called the Achilles Track Club. Able-bodied runners from the Club work with runners with disabilities, enabling and encouraging them to participate in local road races, including the New York City Marathon. Triathlete Dinah Day is one of these volunteers, and coached disabled runner Andrea de Mello through two marathons. Having had polio at an early age, Dinah knows the hurdles to be overcome. "It teaches you to be very humble," she says. "You have to completely get out of your own way and focus on someone else's needs." If running is what you want to do, call the Road Runners Club of America (see Sporting Organizations in Resources) to get information about running clubs in your area.

The Bay Area Outreach Program (see Resources) in Berkeley, California, is another starting place. BORP maintains a resource library on disability issues and offers consultation and training.

SKIING

In the '50s, when I was a kid, one of the best skiers on the mountain was a single amputee who skied the most difficult slopes, swooping from side to side while standing on a single ski, using two outrigger skis attached to crutches for balance. Most of us don't possess that fine degree of balance and finesse, and it wasn't until the '80s that equipment was developed that addressed a wide spectrum of skiers with disabilities. At the forefront was the Smith Sled. Patterned after the Norwegian pulk sled (a sled used to carry small children and gear on cross-country ski trails), the Smith Sled was easily adjustable but hard to control and exceptionally fast. It went "just as fast backward," skier Rick Isom notes in *Sports 'N Spokes,* "as it did forward."

The next stage in the equipment evolution was a mono-ski. On a mono-ski, the skier is seated up off the ground, supported by a sophisticated suspension system on a single ski. The skier uses short hand skis, called outriggers, to assist in turning. Turns are initiated by shifting body weight and by changing the edge of the ski you are putting pressure on, similar to the typical Alpine technique. Most new mono-skis can be purchased with a hydraulic mechanism that enables the skier to mount a chair lift unassisted.

The Breckenridge Outdoor Education Center in Breckenridge, Colorado (see Disabled Athletes in Resources) offers ski instruction to anyone, no matter what her level of disability. In conjunction with National Handicapped Sports (NHS), Breckenridge kicked off a program called Disabled Women in Sports, its goal being to get more women and girls into the sport. In 1990, only eight of the 42-member U.S. Disabled Ski Team were female. While it's true that there are more disabled men than women in the United States, it's also true that many women with disabilities still stay behind closed doors, not heard from at all. The week at Breckenridge consists of low-cost clinics for entry-level skiers. Last year it was attended by 29 girls and women who met each afternoon after skiing to share sports concerns, interests, and enthusiasms. All workshops were instructed by female instructors and coaches, including a sports psychologist. In addition to Breckenridge, NHS holds similar clinics in Minneapolis, Minnesota; Bear Mountain, California; Sunapee, New Hampshire; Cleveland, Ohio; Hidden Valley, Pennsylvania; and Beech Mountain, North Carolina. Call NHS for a list of programs for the 1992–93 season.

As with an able-bodied skier, the key to enjoying the sport is finding a ski that fits. In *Sports 'N Spokes,* Rick Isom emphasizes that "whatever equipment you choose should be adjusted to you. The better the fit, the better your performance—and the less chance of injury." Call *Sports 'N Spokes* for a copy of their January/February 1991 issue that includes a ski product review.

KAYAKING AND CANOEING

For a lower limb-disabled athlete a kayak represents complete freedom. Janet Zeller tells an interesting story. "We often put-in and take-out our kayaks on a beach in Maine where other people also paddle. It is not unusual for us to meet and talk to other kayakers during the day on the water and then meet them again at the take-out. They are amazed when someone wheels down my chair after I finish paddling. I often hear the comment, 'We didn't realize you were disabled when you were paddling,' and I can say, 'Well, I'm not disabled when I'm on the water!' "

The American Canoe Association, through the Disabled Paddler's Committee, has devised ways for those who can't grasp the paddle shaft, but who can move it through the water, to grip and strap on a paddle. Adaptations such as these, along with special paddling techniques, supports, and cockpit adaptations, make the paddler a part of the boat, giving her the same maneuverability and control as an able-bodied paddler. Kayaking is an open sport for persons with disabilities. To that end, the U.S. Canoe and Kayak Team's Sports Science and Technology Committee is busy developing adaptive equipment to allow athletes to participate in Olympic-style competition, using radically sleek and fast craft.

To get started in paddling, your very first contact should be the American Canoe Association's Disabled Paddler's Committee (see ACA under Sporting Associations in Resources). They can supply a list of certified instructors near you and paddling groups in your area, and help you find a place to make contacts. Most important, they'll give you information on adapting your boat. Each person with a disability is different and requires different adaptations. A basic primer on the subject, written by Janet Zeller and Anne Wortham Webre and published by the American Canoe Association. It is called *Canoeing and Kayaking for Persons with Physical Disabilities: Instruction Manual,* available from the ACA.

Another possible entry into the sport is to take a canoe or kayak vacation. After a few days or a week on the water, you'll see if you like the sport before investing in costly equipment and adaptive supports. Wilderness Inquiry (1313 Fifth Street SE, Box 84, Minneapolis, MN 55414; (612) 379-3858) provides trips that range from week-long back-country canoe trips to month-long multi-dimensional outdoor trips in Australia or the Arctic. Their successful philosophy of teaming able-bodied and disabled athletes together means their trips may include wheelchair users, blind or deaf individuals, those with mental retardation, and able-bodied athletes as well.

The Nantahala Outdoor Center (41 U.S. Highway 19 West, Bryson City, NC 28713; (704) 488-6737) offers canoeing, kayaking, bicycling, hiking, backpacking, and rock climbing instruction for "People with Mobility Impairment," as well as CPR, first aid, and river and rock rescue courses. NOC also offers year-round retreats that feature a ropes course.

OTHER SPORTS

Adaptive equipment is available for just about every outdoor sport. There are power reels, rod holders, and knot-tying devices for those who love fishing—and waterway access constantly improves. With advanced technology and creative thinking, athletes are taking to the trails on three-wheeled mountain bikes, powered by hand. You've probably read about disabled athletes doing cross-country bike trips. Scuba diving is gaining popularity—a perfect opportunity to be free of the bonds of gravity and the wheelchair. There are 600,000 women scuba divers in the United States, according to Rodale Press, and wet suits are available in women's sizes. Ocean Escapes (3762 Costa Del Rey, Oceanside, CA 92056; (619) 945-7254) and Underwater Discovery (2722 Route 37E, Toms River, NJ 08753; (908) 270-9100) are two places where you can learn to dive. They both lead expeditions for physically disabled divers—so we expect to meet you under the sea!

With the passing of the Federal Americans with Disabilities Act (ADA) in July 1990, a fire was lit under some long-debated issues. Responding to that act and the needs of outdoor enthusiasts across the country, the U.S. Forest Service formulated a Design Guide for Accessible Outdoor Recreation, establishing standards for integrated services, facilities, and programs in national forests and parks. Captioned educational videos for the hearing impaired, printing of large-type and braille brochures, and trail classification systems for wheelchair users and people with mobility impairment will be part of the new guidelines.

National Park Service Access Specialist Tom Coleman, quoted in *Appalachia Bulletin,* says, "ADA has helped people with disabilities become more active. They're saying 'Hey, I want a piece of the pie.' " There will be those who will want to use the outdoors to reach for their limits and test their self-reliance skills, and there will be those who have no further interest than sitting on a grassy hillside with a pair of binoculars, watching herons fish a local pool. But now the whole spectrum of choice is there, and that may be the most important thing to remember—a whole spectrum of choice for a whole spectrum of people. For too long the word "disabled" has categorized many different people into one slot. Janet Zeller is careful to use the term "persons with disabilities" because, she stresses, " 'disabled' lumps everyone together under one word. We are all different, have different needs, talents, ideas, and disabilities. No one is the same." Engineers and architects are sensitive to these needs and are making it possible for persons with disabilities to enter the outdoors like everybody else. The time will come when outfitters such as Wilderness Inquiry will be commonplace and able-bodied and disabled will recreate and have fun together. "We want to be connected," says Bonnie Sue Hickson, "be inclusive, share with others, the able-bodied as well."

I was standing at the counter in our local bike shop recently, complaining to the shopkeeper about the uncomfortable seat on my bike. My goal had been to work out each day, riding a ten-mile circuit, but I was falling behind, and found myself making excuses, one of them being my seat. But even as I stood there complaining, I sensed that the real reason for my failure was all in my head.

Suddenly, like a gust of wind, a beautiful, elegant young woman in a wheelchair breezed through the door, rolling right up to the counter, stopping alongside me. I stared in wonder as she launched into a long conversation with the bike shop owner about her need for special-order tires for the high-tech wheelchair she rode. "Do you change tires on your chair?" I inquired. "Oh yes, these are special racing tires," she said, holding up the tire for me to inspect. Then she reached for her purse, paid for the tire, spun around, and was gone.

I watched her fly out through the door, stunned. "There, now, what can I do for you?" the shopkeeper asked. Jolted out of my laziness, "Not a thing," I replied, literally leaping onto my bike, letting my legs pump their way home.

Attitude is a powerful determinant!

Profile: Joy Stout

Joy Stout of Berkeley, California, has a life-style that would exhaust even the most active person. An avid tennis player, she competes in tournaments throughout the year. She hikes and mountain bikes regularly and skis in Tahoe and Colorado. Weekends are also filled with activities such as sailing, horseback riding, and water skiing. Further, she is the mother of two active teenage sons and owns her own tax preparation agency. What's amazing to most, however, is that Stout does all of this from a wheelchair. She is a paraplegic.

"Physical activity and sports are what shapes my life," says Stout.

"I was a very active person before I was injured. Now it's amazing how many opportunities are open to me."

Though sports were a major part of Stout's life before her accident, it took years before she reclaimed her athletic self. More than 20 years ago, while still in college, Joy was injured in a car accident returning from a ski weekend in Tahoe. She abandoned her former sports self. "I didn't know what was out there, what was available," she says. Stout focused on crocheting, her tax business, and raising her family. While they skied, she waited in the lodge. "We never saw disabled skiers on the slopes or in the lodge," she adds.

Then, eight years ago, in a wheelchair repair shop, she met a quadriplegic man on his way up to Alpine Meadows, a local ski area, to ski in their disabled ski program. "I made arrangements to take lessons," says Stout, who now skis regularly and competes in regional ski events.

"The first skis we used were sit skis, sleds really. They had metal

Joy Stout: *Photo by Kay Barnett of Sports 'N Spokes/Paralyzed Veterans of America 1991.*

runners that were supposed to keep you from sliding sideways, but on very steep slopes they wouldn't hold and down you'd go. We skied with a tether attached to an able-bodied skier. It was very hard on your arms."

But the newer mono-skis are quite different. "It is close to able-bodied skiing," Joy says. "You sit up off the snow and turn by changing edges and by using two outriggers, similar to regular skis. I'm as skilled as anyone else on the slopes, and love being outside!" She does race in competition but is quick to point out that winning is not her sole reason for being there. "Competition has made me grow," she says. "It gives me a challenge, something to work on."

Having such fun skiing, Joy took tennis lessons through the Bay Area Outreach Program. Now she plays two or three times a week through the winter and every day during the summer. Joy has reclaimed her athletic self.

What else is she up to? Well, for one thing she started sea-kayaking. "I've about given up trying to learn to do an Eskimo roll," she laughs, "but I still get out and paddle. Having been a swimmer, I'm comfortable in the water."

"There are many opportunities for the disabled," says Stout. "The problem is connecting the person with the sport." Stout most recently took up mountain biking, using the Cobra off-road wheelchair, made by Up and Over Engineering in El Cerrito, California. "We were on a dirt trail in Tilden Park," says Stout, "and were rolling along at 10 miles per hour, hitting rocks and ruts. If I had been in a traditional wheelchair, it would have been curtains."

"This," she says with a smile, "was great."

Profile: Janet Zeller—
Sport Equals Freedom

"Persons with disabilities who participate in sports are not heroes," Janet Zeller clearly but softly states, "nor do we want sympathy. We have tremendous potential and, like everyone else, just want to have opportunities to participate and to be recognized for our abilities."

Having always been a vigorous outdoor woman, Janet, a quadriplegic whose sport is sea kayaking, is not letting a physical disability rob her of the outdoor experience. "I was not an athlete as a child but we were lucky to spend summers in a rambling old Victorian house in Intervale, New Hampshire, where we did a lot of hiking and mountain climbing. It was there that I developed a real love of the outdoors."

Janet took an unconventional approach to raising a family and getting an education. "I was married soon after high school and had children in my early twenties. Volunteering in the schools that the children attended, I realized that I really liked working in the library. I went back to school and attained first a Bachelor's, then a Master's degree in library science and spent the next 16 years as a school librarian. I guess you could say I found out what I really wanted to do when I grew up."

Canoeing and kayaking have always been a part of her life. In fact, she paddled for 25 years before becoming disabled. "I was paddling at 15 with friends," she says, "and did a lot of white-water and wilderness tripping with my family. We loved open canoe white-water paddling and sea kayaking."

Then, in 1984, Jan fell at work and did major damage to her knee. That injury developed into Reflex Sympathetic Dystrophy, a nerve complication that has caused progressive dysfunction. Because of that injury, she is now a quadriplegic, having some loss of function in all four limbs. "But with minimal left-hand function," she adds, "I'm still able to paddle in a double sea kayak."

Although Janet's paddling preference is white water, she had to make some hard choices. "I loved white-water paddling . . . the high energy of the water . . . the thrill of placing well-executed strokes to make the boat go exactly where you want through a difficult rapid . . . but white water requires kneeling in the boat and with my knee injury I couldn't do that anymore."

By 1987 Janet was in a wheelchair. "I was determined not to lose my sport just because my means of mobility had changed from feet to wheels," she says. While she couldn't do any white-water canoeing, sea kayaking became her connection to the sport. "One major problem with sea kayaking, though, was that I couldn't manipulate the rudder. Another difficulty was in maintaining control of the boat. Control of a boat is, in part, accomplished by shifting your weight, usually by bracing with feet or knees. It is also important to retain balance and stability or, in other words, to 'wear' your boat. How could I adapt the

Janet Zeller.

seat in my kayak so I would stay put? How could I hold onto a paddle with hands that don't grasp so well anymore?

"I was sure that I wasn't the only person trying to deal with these problems, so I put a blurb in a half dozen paddling magazines, asking other people to share their solutions. I heard from 50 people from Maine to Hawaii. They shared information about how their adaptations worked. It became obvious that there was no central clearinghouse for this kind of information, and, given my background in information services, I decided to form a network to exchange information among those 50 people."

Since Janet was the first to start networking with other paddlers with disabilities and those interested in helping them, she quickly drew national attention. "About that time Dave Mason, then head of the American Canoe Association, asked me to work with the ACA in formulating ways to involve folks with disabilities in paddling sports. ACA involvement initiated tremendous changes for persons with disabilities. A committee was formed called the Disabled Paddlers Committee, shortened from the Committee for the Integration of Paddlers with Disabilities. As one of the 12 national committees of the ACA, it is charged with promoting the participation of paddlers with disabilities and integrating those paddlers into all areas of canoe sport from recreation to competition.

"Paddling brings freedom to me," she states. "When I am out sea kayaking, people have told me I don't look handicapped. And I'm not! I still have a disability but I'm part of a sleek craft gliding through the water . . . there are no barriers to stop me. On the water I'm just another paddler enjoying the freedom of paddling . . . water is the ultimate equalizer. That is the message ACA is delivering." Jan has followed up that message in a book she wrote with Anne Wortham Webre called *Canoeing and Kayaking for Persons with Physical Disabilities* (see Bibliography).

The committee's job is to offer training to instructors and information on adaptive equipment to paddlers. "We've developed written materials and offer instructor training. When a person contacts the ACA they are immediately sent information and I promptly follow up. We try to work on a one-to-one basis because everyone has different needs." Janet carefully points out that terms such as "differently abled" or "physically challenged" are misleading and that "the disabled" is too generalized. "The disabled indicates that all persons who have disabilities are alike, which, of course, is not true. The correct terminology is," she gently adds, "a person with a disability . . . the person first, because the person is more important than the disability."

The committee is also very involved in working on equipment, particularly in developing an adaptive seating system. The first question paddlers ask is, "How do I make this work for me?" Instructors who have completed the ACA training program agree that once the paddler is fitted to a boat, using whatever is necessary in adaptive equipment and seating, fundamental instruction is the same. Paddlers who have disabilities can be easily integrated into regular instruction programs.

While remaining Chair of the ACA Disabled Paddlers Committee, Janet has assumed yet another job—on the national level. She now works as Access Coordinator for the U.S. Forest Service in the Eastern Region, covering 14 national forests from Maine to Minnesota to Missouri to West Virginia. "I provide information, training, support, and evaluation for the local access coordinator in each forest," she says. "The Forest Service is the largest provider of outdoor recreation in the country, with 100,000 miles of trails and 10,000 recreation sites, and their mission is to provide outdoor recreation for *all* people. For instance, in the Eastern Region alone we oversee 14 million acres, with recreation opportunities that range from urban to primitive areas.

"I am like other people who want to be able to enjoy easy access to recreation opportunities in developed areas, but who also want to experience the satisfaction of reaching undeveloped areas through my own effort. The Forest Service understands this concept. We are not paving the wilderness, but we are providing opportunities . . . most of all, we are creating awareness."

PACKING TIPS

Remember: this list is merely a starting point. Using this as a beginning, you will quickly develop your own—based on your personal needs.

Sleeping bag
Foam pad
Groundcloth
Tarp or tent

Stove
Cookware
Fuel
Funnel for fuel
Priming items
Matches
Eating utensils
Dishwashing supplies
Thermos

Toothbrush/paste
Toilet paper
Insect repellent
Sunscreen
Lip balm

Hiking boots/socks
Extra socks and underwear
Cold and wind clothes
Sunglasses
Bandannas (use for
   potholder/washcloth/hat)
Wool cap and lightweight wool
   gloves

Medical kit
Signal (mirror/whistle)
Space blanket
Extra matches

Ziploc bags
Water container
Extra-small stuffsack

RESOURCES

S & KAYAKS—MANUFACTURERS & DISTRIBUTORS

Harriman, TN 37748

Feathercraft
4-1244 Cartwright Street
Granville Island, Vancouver
B.C. V6H 3R8 Canada

Keowee Kayak
Aquaterra
P.O. Box 8002
Powdersville Road
Easley, SC 29640
(803) 855–1987

Lightweight kayak.

Kiwi Kayak Co.
10070 Old Redwood Highway
P.O. Box 1140
Windsor, CA 95492
(800) K–4–KAYAK
Ann Dwyer

Lightweight kayaks, paddles, and related gear.

Klepper America
35 Union Square
New York, NY 10003

L.L. Bean Atlantic Coast Sea Kayak Symposium
L.L. Bean, Inc.
Freeport, ME 04033
(800) 341–4341

Demos of every technique imaginable, plus you can test drive dozens of models and brands of canoes and kayaks. Instruction. Held every July.

The Loon Works
525 Orchard Drive
Madison, WI 53711
(608) 231–2192

Tom MacKenzie—maker of custom canoes.

Mad River Canoe
P.O. Box 610
Waitsfield, VT 05673

Necky Kayaks
1100 Riverside Rd.
Abbotsford, B.C. V25 4N2 Canada

Old Town Canoe
58 Middle St.
Old Town, MO 04468

Perception
1110 Powdersville Road
Easley, SC 29640

CATALOGS AND MAIL ORDER FOR WOMEN'S GEAR

Andiamo
P.O. Box 1657
Sun Valley, ID 83353
(208) 788–5444
Underwear with padded crotch and seat—great for biking or rowing.

Beyond Sportswear
4315 Oliver Avenue N.
Minneapolis, MN 55412
(612) 521–1429
Veronica Morgan

Camp Trails/Johnson Camping
P.O. Box 966
Binghamton, NY 13902
Tel: (607) 779–2200
Daypacks, framepacks, child carriers.

Delta Cycle Corp.
166 Tosca Drive
P.O. Box 651
Stoughton, MA 02072
(800) 225–2258
Cycling tools, components, and equipment.

Frostline Kits
2512 W. Independent Avenue
Grand Junction, CO 81505-7200
(800) KITS–USA
Kits to make your own outdoor gear.

L.L. Bean Inc.
Freeport, ME 04033
(800) 221–4221
Backpacks for Baby
L.L. Bean's mountain kid carrier.

Life-Link International Inc.
P.O. Box 2913
1240 Huff Lane
Jackson Hole, WY 83001
(307) 733–2266
Products to make your backcountry skiing safe.

Northwest River Supplies
P.O. Box 9186
Moscow, ID 83843
For every kayaking/canoeing/rafting need.

Outdoor Research
1000 First Avenue S.
Seattle, WA 98134
(206) 467–8197

Patagonia
1609 W. Babcock Street
P.O. Box 8900
Bozeman, MT 59715
(800) 523–9597

Polar Heart Bra
Polar USA Inc.
(203) 359–1966
Sports bra specifically designed for women who use heart-rate monitors.

Quest Outfitters
2590 17th Street, Suite B
Sarasota, FL 34234
(800) 359–6931
Need a zipper for your tent or sleeping bag? Want to make your own? This is the source for fabrics, hardware, grommets, fasteners, and every sewing need for the outdoor adventurer.

R.E.I.
P.O. Box 88125
Seattle, WA 98138-2125
(800) 426–4840

Road Runner Sports, Women's
Edition
6310 Nancy Ridge Road, Suite 101
San Diego, CA 92121
(800) 551–5558

Carries every imaginable design and
make of women's apparel and shoes
for running, swimming, fitness, aerobics, and walking.

Schnaubelt Shorts Inc.
1128 Fourth Avenue
Coraopolis, PA 15108
(412) 262–0993
Cathy Schnaubelt

Biking clothing for women of all
sizes.

Single Track Design
P.O. Box 374
Woolwich, ME 04579
(207) 442–9026
Edie Igelhart

Biking shirts for biking, hiking, tennis, and roller-skating.

Tel-a-Runner
1248 Sussex Turnpike, C-5
Randolph, NJ 07869
(800) 835–2786

Running and workout clothing.

Terry Precision Bicycles for Women
1704 Waynesport Road
Macedon, NY 14502
(315) 986–2103

Title IX Sports
1054 Heinz Avenue
Berkeley, CA 94702
(415) 549–2592

Women's clothing only. For team
sports especially.

Tough Traveler
1012 State Street
Schenectady, NY 12307
(800) 468–6844

Child carriers and outdoor gear for
kids.

Walk USA
6310 Nancy Ridge Road, Suite 101
San Diego, CA 92121
(800) 255–6422

Great, reasonably priced walking,
racewalking, running clothing, and
accessories for women.

Whitewater Specialty
N3894 Highway 55
White Lake, WI 54491-9716
(715) 882–5400

Mail-order canoes and kayaks and all
gear related to river sports.

Womyn's Wheel
540 Lafayette Road, Suite 7
Hampton, NH 03842
(603) 926–4939

Cycling products for women. Cycling clothing for pregnant women,
junior cycling clothes for kids, cycling directory of woman-only rides,
races, and clubs.

WorkAbles for Women
Oak Valley
Clinton, PA 15026-0214
(800) 862–9317
Deborah Evans Crawford

Workboots, rain boots, overalls,
gloves sized for women.

CHILDREN'S HIKING BOOTS

Coleman Co.
250 N. St. Francis
Wichita, KS 67201
(316) 261−3485

Hi-Tec Sports USA, Inc.
4400 N. Star Way
Modesto, CA 95356
(209) 577−1861

Nike
3900 S.W. Murray
Beaverton, OR 97005
(800) 344−6453

DISABLED ATHLETES

Access America: An Atlas and Guide for the National Parks for Visitors with Disabilities, published by Northern Cartographics
P.O. Box 133
Burlington, VT 05402
(802) 860−2886

American Water Ski Association
Disabled Ski Committee
681 Bailey Woods Road
Cacula, GA 30211
(205) 825−9226

Athletics for Blind Leisure
  Enthusiasts
(201) 568−0906
Eileen Goff

Offers hiking, skiing, camping trips to visually impaired people living in the New York/New Jersey area.

Bay Area Outreach Recreation
  Program (BORP)
605 Eshlaman Hall
Berkeley, CA 94720
(510) 849−4663
David Lewis, Executive Director

Blind Outdoor Leisure Development
  (BOLD)
P.O. Box 6
Aspen, CO 81612
(303) 925−7567

Breckenridge Ski Area
P.O. Box 1058
Breckenridge, CO 80424
(303) 453−2368
Toby Quinley

Clothing Concepts
P.O. Box 81
Sun Prairie, WI 53590

Sports clothing for men and women with disabilities.

Disabled Outdoors Magazine
5223 South Lorel
Chicago, IL 60638
(708) 344−5127
John Kopchik

Quarterly magazine covering U.S. and Canada, costing $10, focusing on outdoors. Source for products, new laws and regulations, organizations, instruction.

Enabling Technologies Inc.
2411 N. Federal Boulevard
Denver, CO 80211
(303) 455−3578

Manufacturers of Unique-1 mono-skis and off-road wheelchairs.

Environmental Travelling
Companions
Fort Mason Center
San Francisco, CA 94123
(415) 474–7662
Free brochure.

Farwest Choices
P.O. Box 1681
Truckee, CA 96160
(916) 587–2108
Bonnie Sue Hickson

Spend a week celebrating the outdoors, sailing, riding, mountain biking, birdwatching, and being with friends.

Handicapped Scuba Association
1104 El Prado
San Clemente, CA 92672
(714) 498–6128

International Wheelchair Tennis
Federation
940 Calle Amancecer, Suite B
San Clemente, CA 92672
(714) 361–6811

National Handicapped Sports
4405 East-West Highway, Suite 603
Bethesda, MD 20814
(301) 652–7505
Kirk Bauer

National Park Service
U.S. Department of the Interior
Office of Public Affairs
P.O. Box 37127
Washington, DC 20013-7127

Distributes a lifetime free-entrance pass to federally operated parks, monuments, historic sites, recreation areas, and wildlife refuges to people with disabilities.

National Wheelchair Athletic
Association
3595 East Fountain Boulevard,
Suite L-10
Colorado Springs, CO 80910
(719) 574–1150

Sanctions six sports (archery, shooting, swimming, tennis, track & field, and weight lifting). Regional events.

Outdoor Explorations
P.O. Box 67055
Chestnut Hill, MA 02167
(617) 969–1168

Outfitter offers hiking, canoeing, swimming, snowshoeing, and other sports for persons with disabilities.

Rails to Trails Conservancy
1400 16th Street NW, Suite 300
Washington, DC 20036
(202) 797–5400

Publishes a complete directory of the nation's rail-trails, including names, lengths, endpoints, surfacing material in 35 states. Costs $6.95.

Sports 'N Spokes
5201 North 19th Avenue, Suite 111
Phoenix, AZ 85015
(602) 246–9426

Tahoe Handicapped Ski School
P.O. Box 9780
Truckee, CA 95737
(916) 581–4161

Specializes in adaptive techniques to teach skiing.

U.S. Association of Disabled Sailors
Southern California Chapter
901 Fathom Avenue
Seal Beach, CA 90740
(213) 431–4461

U.S. Rowing Association
Adaptive Rowing Committee
11 Hall Place
Exeter, NH 03833

Up and Over Engineering
1509 Liberty Street
El Cerrito, CA 94530
(415) 233–1328

Makes mountain bikes, among other equipment. Free brochure.

Wilderness Inquiry
1313 Fifth Street SE, Suite 327
Minneapolis, MN 55414
(612) 379–3858

INFLATABLE KAYAKS (IKs) AND RIVER EQUIPMENT

Achilles Inflatable Craft
P.O. Box 2287
1407 80th SW
Everett, WA 98203
(206) 353–7000
or
P.O. Box 517
East Rutherford, NJ 07073
(201) 438–6400 or (800) 722–5232

Produces tough 80 percent Hypalon IKs in one- and two-person sizes.

Sevylor U.S.A.
6651 East 26th Street
Los Angeles, CA 90040
(213) 727–6013 or (800) 821–4645

Manufacturer of Tahiti brand vinyl IKs, Sevytex reinforced vinyl IKs, air mattresses, paddles, etc.

IK INSTRUCTION AND OUTFITTERS

Eastern Professional River
  Outfitters Association
531 South Gay Street, Suite 600
Knoxville, TN 37902
(615) 524–1045

Source for information about dozens of outfitters in the East.

Western River Guides
  Association, Inc.
360 South Monroe, Suite 300
Denver, CO 80209
(303) 377–4811

Source for information about dozens of outfitters across the West.

Wild Water Adventures
P.O. Box 249
Creswell, OR 97426
(503) 895–4465 or (800) 289–4534

Inflatable kayak instruction and schools, all-IK trips on wilderness rivers, raft-supported IK trips on the Rogue, Klamath, and other rivers.

PERIODICALS

Atlantic Coastal Kayaker
P.O. Box 520
Ipswich, MA 01938
(508) 356–0434

Canoe Magazine
Canoe America Associates
P.O. Box 3146
Kirkland, WA 98083
(206) 827–6363

Mainly covers hardshell boats; very seldom features inflatables—kayaks or otherwise.

Currents
National Organization for River
   Sports
P.O. Box 6847
Colorado Springs, CO 80904

River conservation news, political issues such as boater access rights, some adventure, and how-to.

Disabled Outdoors Magazine
(see page 208)

Folding Kayaker, Inc.
P.O. Box 0754
New York, NY 10024-0539

Bimonthly newsletter on foldable kayaks.

Lady Angler . . . Plus
P.O. Box 270479
Houston, TX 77277-0479
(409) 722–8182
Pam Basco

Monthly newsletter covering all aspects of fishing.

Lonely Planet Publications
Embarcadero West
112 Linden Street
Oakland, CA 94607
(800) 229–0122

The best series of guidebooks for out of the country travel. Down to earth and informative, these shoestring guides cover continents or major regions with essential information for travelers on tight budgets. Their phrase books are friendly and easy to use.

The Nature Library
150 Nassau Street, Room 1020
New York, NY 10038-1516
(212) 608–3327

Outdoor books on every sport from backpacking to snorkeling, plus cookbooks and field guides.

River Runner Magazine
P.O. Box 458
Fallbrook, CA 92028
(619) 723–8155

Good source of current IK and general whitewater information. Consult the June 1988 issue for IK specifications comparison chart.

Rower's Bookshelf
Box 440
Essex, MA 01929
(508) 468–4096

Books on rowing.

Sea Kayaker
1670 Duranleau Street
Vancouver, British Columbia
V6H 3S4 Canada
(604) 263–1471

Paddling techniques, and adventure stories for ocean paddlers.

Sports 'N Spokes
(see page 209)

Travel Alternatives
1117 Del Mar Avenue
Santa Barbara, CA 93109
Kristine White

Quarterly newsletter about traveling with respect for the natural, social, and cultural environment.

The U.S. Rowing Association
201 S. Capitol Avenue, Suite 400
Indianapolis, IN 46225
(317) 237–5654

Susan Lezotte's *Sportsperformance* is available through this organization, as are lists of women's rowing clubs across the United States.

Velo-News
5595 Arapahoe Avenue, Suite G
Boulder, CO 80303
(800) 234–VELO

A great biking magazine that gives women fair and equal coverage in cycling. Also sells a complete selection of books on the sport.

Walking Magazine
9–11 Harcourt Street
Boston, MA 02116
(617) 266–3322

ROWING CLUBS

Alden Ocean Shell Association
371 Washington Road
Rye, NH 03870
(603) 436–7402
Ernestine Bayer

Boston Rowing Club
P.O. Box 38
Cambridge, MA 02138
(617) 625–0266
President: Nomi Notman

Buckeye Rowing Association
4200 Royalton Road
Brecksville, OH 44141
(216) 526–7689
President: Nancy Slusarczyk

Janet Spagnoli
55 Broadripple Drive
Princeton, NJ 08542
(609) 924–6449
President: Janet H. Spagnoli

Conibear Rowing Association
12105 NE 33rd
Bell, WA 98005
(206) 883–8716
Chairperson: Mary Joy

Duluth Rowing Club
3614 Minnesota Avenue
Duluth, MN 55802
(218) 723–8435
President: Norine McVann

East Hampton Rowing Club
46 Waterhole Road
East Hampton, NY 11937
(516) 324–7613
Commodore: Linda J. Robbins

Gloucester Women's Rowing
53 Marmion Way
Rockport, MA 01966
(617) 546–9607
Organizer: Pat DeLa Chapelle

Indianapolis Boat Club, Inc.
P.O. Box 30339
Indianapolis, IN 46230
(317) 852–6186
President-elect: Marisa Leach

Litchfield Hills Rowing Club
Box 255, Cathole Road
Litchfield, CT 06759
(203) 567–5251
President: Barbara Francis

Lookout Rowing Club
120 McFarland Avenue
Chattanooga, TN 37405
(615) 267–4797
Secretary: Marian Carney
Commodore: Jenny Mesmer
(615) 757–8410

Mercer County Boat Club
Box 991, Groton School
Groton, MA 01450
(617) 448–2229
President: Janet R. Youngholm

Michigan Rowing Association
P.O. Box 7164
Ann Arbor, MI 48107
(313) 665–5466
President: Lisa Watt McFarlane

Mills Cyclone Crew
Mills College
Oakland, CA 94613
(415) 430–2172
President: Kathy Moeller

Minneapolis Rowing Club
P.O. Box 6712
Minneapolis, MN 55406
(612) 724–6569
Women's Captain: Lisa Fuller

Minnesota Boat Club
1 S. Wabasha—Navy Island
St. Paul, MN 55107
(612) 690–1957
Women's Coach: Miriam Baer

New Bern Boat Club
1706 River Drive
New Bern, NC 28560
(919) 633–3738
President: Ellis F. Mather

New Haven Rowing Club
44 Collier Circle
Hamden, CT 06518
(203) 288–4038
President: Norman Thetford

O.A.R.S.
RD 1, Box 278
Voorheesville, NY 12186
(518) 765–2025

Philadelphia Rowing Program for
   the Disabled
2601 Pennsylvania Avenue #146
Philadelphia, PA 19130
(215) 765–2170
Chairperson: Dorothy Driscoll

Philadelphia Girls Rowing Club
#14 Boathouse Row
Philadelphia, PA 19130
(215) 978–8824
President: Sophie Kozak

Portland Rowing Club
P.O. Box 02370
Portland, OR 97202
(503) 293–0512
President: Lindsay Thompson

Santa Barbara Rowing Club
Univ. of CA/Robertson Gym
Santa Barbara, CA 93106
(805) 683–3008
Master's Coach: Betsy Zumwalt

Sparhawk Sculling School
(November–April)
12336 Westhampton Circle
West Palm Beach, FL 33414
(407) 798–1093
(May–October)
222 Porters Point
Colchester, VT 05446
(802) 658–4799
Pete Sparhawk

Tahoe Rowing Club
Box 1835
Crystal Bay, NV 89402
(916) 546–4723
Assistant Director: C. Anne Cook

The Citykids Coalition Rowing
807 Riverside Drive
New York, NY 10032
(212) 219–4550
Laurie Meadoff

Winsor Crew
Pilgrim Road
Boston, MA 02215
(617) 629–2425
Coach: Jennifer Hale

ZLAC Rowing Club
1111 Pacific Beach Drive
San Diego, CA 92109
(619) 222–2536

SPORTING ORGANIZATIONS

Adirondack Mountain Club
Box 867
Lake Placid, NY 12946

Workshops on hiking, cross-country, and winter mountaineering.

Adventure Associates
P.O. Box 16304
Seattle, WA 98116
(206) 932–8352
Chris Miller and Sandra Braun

Ethical exploring, women in recovery programs. Co-ed and women–only programs.

Alaska Rainforest Treks
P.O. Box 210845
Auke Bay, AK 99821
(907) 463–3466
Karla Hart

Guided hiking adventures. Offers a Women's Week on Herbert Glacier.

Alpine Adventures
Route 73
P.O. Box 179
Keene, NY 12942
(518) 576–9881
Karen Stolz

Rock and ice climbing.

Amazonia Expeditions Inc.
1824 NW 102nd Way
Gainesville, FL 32606
(904) 332–4051
Millie Sangama

A native Amazonian, Millie is the only woman guide in the Amazon. Leads one women's expedition each year.

American Canoe Association
P.O. Box 248
Lorton, VA 22079

American Hiking Society
1015 31st Street NW
Washington, DC 20007-4490
(703) 385–3252
Susan Henley

American Racewalk Association
P.O. Box 18323
Boulder, CO 80308-8323
(303) 447–0156
Viisha Sedlak

Certifies instructors; sponsors races; conducts camps, clinics, lectures and group walks.

American Red Cross
National Headquarters
Washington, DC 20006

Contact your local chapter.

American Whitewater Affiliation
P.O. Box 85
Phoenicia, NY 12464
(914) 688–5569
Phyllis Horowitz

A national organization that promotes whitewater recreation and conversation. Publishes a bi-monthly magazine.

American Youth Hostel Inc.
P.O. Box 37603
Washington, DC 20013-7613

Biking and hiking tours for everyone, including youths.

Artemis Wilderness Tours
P.O. Box 1178
Taos, NM 87571
(505) 758–2203
Mary Humphrey

Wilderness river rafting trips for women.

Bass'n Gal
P.O. Box 13925
Arlington, TX 76013
(817) 265–6214
Sugar Ferris

Bass fishing organization for women. Publishes *Bass'n Gal.*

Big Bend River Tours
P.O. Box 317
Terlingua, TX 79852
(800) 545–4240
Beth Garcia

Some women's river rafting trips.

Blue Moon Explorations
Ecological Adventures in Nature
P.O. Box 2568
Bellingham, WA 98227
(206) 676–4664
Kathleen Grimbley and Randy Olson

Co-ed and women-only outdoor trips dedicated to nature appreciation.

Breckenridge Ski Area
P.O. Box 1058
Breckenridge, CO 80424
(303) 453–2368
Toby Quinley

Call of the Wild/Outdoor Woman's
    School
2519 Cedar Street
Berkeley, CA 94708
Carol Latimer

Colorado Outward Bound
Empowerment Program for Women
(303) 831–6956

Craftsbury Center
Box 31
Craftsbury Common, VT 05827
(802) 586–7767
John Broadhead

An all-around sports center that includes Craftsbury Sculling Center.

Earthwise
Adventures for Women
23 Mt. Nebo Road
Newtown, CT 06470
(203) 426–6092
Lesley Nagot

Explorers at Sea
P.O. Box 51, Main Street
Stonington, ME 04681
(207) 367–2356
Gay Atkinson

Sea kayaking instruction and adventures; island camping.

Femmes de Mer
P.O. Box 6432
San Diego, CA 92166
(619) 221–0142
Barbara King

Sailing instruction for women.

Florida Trail Association
Route 1
Box 896
McAlpin, FL 32062
(904) 362–3256
Sylvia Dunnam

Four Corners School of Outdoor
  Education
East Route
Monticello, UT 84535
(800) 525–4456
Janet Ross

Offers courses in everything from Navajo culture to archaeology to writing and storytelling.

Getaway Vacations for Women
1321 Duke Street, Suite 400
Alexandria, VA 22314
(800) 878–9289
Joelle DeRoche and Lynn Lewis

Great Old Broads for Wilderness
P.O. Box 368
Cedar City, UT 84721
Susan Tixier

A woman's nationwide environmental advocacy group. Send $12 for a fabulous T-shirt.

Hawk, I'm Your Sister
P.O. Box 9109-D
Santa Fe, NM 87504
(505) 984–2268
Beverly Antaeus

Co-ed and women-only wilderness canoe trips.

Heartland Bicycle Tours
One Orchard Circle
Washington, IA 52353
(319) 653–2277
Catherine Lloyd

Co-ed and some women-only bicycle tours.

Her Wild Song
Wilderness Journeys for Women
P.O. Box 6793
Portland, ME 04101
(207) 773–4969

Canoe trips on the west branch of the Penobscot, focusing on herbal study, evoking inner wisdom, meditation, and "for the pure joy of paddling."

K2 Women's Ski Adventures
Box 841
Hood River, OR 97031
(509) 493–4386
Kim Reichhelm

Also runs schools in Crested Butte, Stratton, VT; Bear Mt., CA; Kirkwood, CA

L.L. Bean Cross Country Ski School
Freeport, ME 04033
(300) 341–4341

Instruction from beginner through telemarking, plus waxing clinics.

Lady Bass
P.O. Box 2676
West Monroe, LA 71294
(318) 396–1121
Priscilla Bailey

Mariah Wilderness Expeditions
P.O. Box 248
Point Richmond, CA 94807
Donna Hunter

Co-ed and women-only rafting trips.

Mazamas
909 NW 19th Avenue
Portland, OR 97209
(503) 227–2345

Anyone who has summited a mountain on which there is a living glacier is eligible for membership.

The Metropolitan Canoe and
   Kayak Club
P.O. Box 1868
Brooklyn, NY 11202

The Mountaineers
300 Third Avenue West
Seattle, WA 98119
(206) 284–6310

Conducts courses in mountaineering including mountaineering techniques, glacier travel, and rock climbing.

Nantahala Outdoor Center
41 U.S. Highway 19 West
Bryson City, NC 28713
(704) 488–6737

Instruction in water sports, hiking/backpacking, rockclimbing, mountain biking.

National Outdoor Leadership
   School (NOLS)
P.O. Box AA
Lander, WY 82520

North American Racewalking
   Foundation
P.O. Box 50312
Pasadena, CA 91115-0312
(818) 577–2264
Elaine P. Ward

Publishes very informative and well-written handbooks; supplies individuals, instructors, and clubs with materials and handouts to make their walking programs varied and interesting. Ask about their "Walkabouts."

Off the Gringo Trail
3415 NE 72nd Avenue
Portland, OR 97213
(503) 288–8501
Peggy Sullivan

Muleback adventures in Baja California.

Outdoor Centre of New England
8 Pleasant Street
Millers Falls, MA 01349
(413) 659–3626

Canoe and kayak instruction by women.

Outdoor Leadership Training
   Seminars
P.O. Box 20281
Denver, CO 80220
(800) 331–7238

Break-through adventures in rock climbing, backpacking, ritual ceremony, mountaineering, vision quests. Co-ed and women-only programs.

Outdoor Vacations for Women
   Over 40
P.O. Box 200
Groton, MA 01450
(508) 448–3331
Marion Stoddart

Pack, Paddle, Ski
Box 82
South Lima, NY 14558-0082
Deborah Scordese French

Prairie Women Adventures and
  Retreat
Box 2
Matfield Green, KS 66862
(316) 753-3465
Jane Koger
Learn about prairies on a working
ranch for women of all ages.

Quiet Wanderings
P.O. Box 11
Scotland, CT 06264
(203) 456-4145
Jean Vertefeuille
Women's hiking, horsepacking,
fishing, and canoe trips.

Rainbow Adventures
1308 Sherman Avenue
Evanston, IL 60201
(708) 864-4570
Susan Eckert
Worldwide adventure travel for
women over 30.

Road Runners Club of America
National Office
629 South Washington Street
Alexandria, VA 22314
(703) 836-0558

Rock Women Journeys Home
P.O. Box 6548
Denver, CO 80206
(800) 676-5404
Jane McAuley

Rocky Mountain Sea Kayak Club
P.O. Box 100643
Denver, CO 80250

RVing Women
P.O. Box 82606
Kenmore, WA 98028
(206) 791-1884

An organization for women who
own recreational vehicles. Offers
guides to maintenance, problem
solving, trips, and contacts nationwide.

San Juan Hut System
P.O. Box 1663
Telluride, CO 81435

Huts and guide service Uncompah-
gre National Forest.

SanDee and Friends Wilderness
  Adventures
1817 West Mansfield
Spokane, WA 99205
(509) 327-1712
SanDee Sausville

Horsepacking trips.

Santa Cruz Rowing School and
  Kayak Shop
766 Cathedral Drive
Aptos, CA 95003
(408) 662-8433
Karen Karlson

Sea Safari Sailing
A Women's Sailing School
4835-B Cobia Drive SE
St. Petersburg, FL 33705
(813) 821-6438
Lauren J. Winans/Georgia Hotton

Sea Sense—The Women's Sailing
  School
25 Thames Street
New London, CT 06320
(203) 444-1404
Carol Cuddyer/Patti Moore

Seaskills
37 Geneva Road
Norwalk, CT 06850
(203) 838–9014
Pat Clark/Peg Nelson

Seattle Women's Sailing Association
P.O. Box 17404
Seattle, WA 98107

Sierra Club
730 Polk Street
San Francisco, CA 94109
(415) 776–2211

Southern California Yachting
    Association
1421 Lance Drive
Tustin, CA 92680
(714) 730–1797
Gail Hine

Tenth Mountain Trail Association
1280 Ute Avenue
Aspen, CO 81611

Huts and private lodges, Aspen to Vail—backcountry skiing.

University of Wisconsin Women's
    Rowing
1440 Monroe Street
Madison, WI 53711
(608) 265–6698

Weatherbee's Botanical Trips
11405 Patterson Lake Drive
Pinckney, MI 48169
(313) 878–9178
Ellen Elliott Weatherbee

If you like foraging for wild greens, birdwatching, plant identification, and wetlands, Weatherbee's is for you.

West Broward Freewheelers
P.O. Box 9726
Coral Springs, FL 33075
(305) 755–4918

Encourages women to join. Provides support and encouragement.

West River Sailing Club
Galesville, MD 20765
Women's Big Boat Regatta held every June.

Wintermoon
Sled Dog Adventures for Women
36 Petrell
Brimson, MN 55602
Kathleen Anderson

Womanship
The Boathouse
410 Severn Avenue
Annapolis, MD 21403
(301) 267–6661
Sailing instruction for women.

Womantrek
1411 East Olive Way
P.O. Box 20643
Seattle, WA 98102
(800) 477–TREK
Bonnie Bordas

Worldwide travel adventures for women.

WOMBATS
(Women's Mountain Bike and Tea
    Society)
Box 757
Fairfax, CA 94930
Jacquie Phelan

Women for Sail
326 First Street, Suite 24
Annapolis, MD 21403
(800) 346–6404
Joelle London

Women in the Wilderness
566 Ottawa Avenue
St. Paul, MN 55107
(612) 227–2284
Judith Niemi

Wilderness canoe trips for women. Books about outdoor women.

Women's Club of Hartland
220 West Capitol Drive
Hartland, WI 53029

Sailing club.

Women's Cycling Coalition
523 Park Street
Moosic, PA 18507
(717) 457–7748
Linda Smith

Women's Cycling Network
P.O. Box 73
Harvard, IL 60033
Susan Notorangelo

An organization representing every aspect of women involved in cycling. Publishes a quarterly newsletter.

Women's Sailing Adventures
39 Woodside Avenue
Westport, CT 06880
(203) 227–7413
Sherry Jagerson

Women's Ski Experience
Okemo Resort
Ludlow, VT 05149
(802) 228–4041
Janet Spangler

Women's Ski Seminars
Aspen Mountain
Aspen, CO 81612
(800) 525–6200
Pat Gomes

Woman's Way Ski Seminars
Squaw Valley Ski School
Squaw Valley, CA 95730
(916) 583–0119
Elissa Slanger

Women's Weeks
Telluride Ski Resort
Box 11155
Telluride, CO 81435
(303) 728–4424
Annie Vareille Savath

Women's Yacht Racing
  Association—Miami
P.O. Box 331532
Coconut Grove, FL 33133

Woodswomen
25 West Diamond Lake Road
Minneapolis, MN 55419
(612) 822–3809
Denise Mitten

Worldwide adventures for women.

VIDEOS

Climb the Rockies: A Video Trail Guide to the Colorado Mountains. A guide to ten 14,000-foot mountains. $19.95. (800) 762–7000

Racewalking: A Lifetime Sport. Viisha Sedlak, American Racewalk Association. $29.95 plus $4 postage/handling. (303) 447–0156

WOMEN-OWNED OUTDOOR BUSINESSES

Ciclismo Classico
93 Massachusetts Avenue, Suite 402
Boston, MA 02115
(617) 262–5856
Lauren Hefferon

Bike tours through Italy.

Hurricane Creek Llamas
Route 1, Box 123
Enterprise, OR 97828
(503) 432–4455
Stanlynn Daugherty

Never Summer Nordic
Box 3364
Greeley, CO 80633
(303) 353–2212
Yvonne Brodzinski

Backcountry yurts—great for skiing and hiking in Colorado State Forest.

Noah Llama Treks Inc.
P.O. Box 641
Valle Crucis, NC 28691
(704) 297–2171
Judy Fee

Piragis Northwoods Co.
The Boundary Waters Catalog
105 W. North Central Avenue
Ely, MN 55731
(800) 223–6565

Canoes, packs, paddles, outdoor gear.

Sheri Griffith Expeditions
P.O. Box 1324
Moam, UT 84532
(800) 332–3200
Sheri Griffith

River canoeing trips.

Touring Exchange
P.O. Box 265
Port Townsend, WA 98368
Bonnie Wong

Cycling trips around the globe.

Walking Tours of Southern Vermont
Rt. 2, Box 622
Arlington, VT 05250
(802) 375–1141
Judi Ketels

MISCELLANEOUS

Zinn Cycles Inc.
4715 North Broadway—B3
Boulder, CO 80302

Custom bike builder for women 4'5" and up. Prices start at $1,800.

Kokatat
5350 Ericson Way
Arcata, CA 95521
(800) 225–9749

Foul-weather gear catalog.

Stohlquist
Colorado Kayak
P.O. Box 3059
Buena Vista, CO 81211

Wildwater Designs
230 Penllyn Pike
Penllyn, PA 19422

Alden Ocean Shells
Martin Marine Company
P.O. Box 251
Kittery Point, ME 03905
(800) 477–1507

Maas Rowing Shells
P.O. Box 28117
Seattle, WA 98118
(206) 723–7601

BIBLIOGRAPHY

Abromowitz, Jennifer. *Women Outdoors: The Best 1900 Books, Programs & Periodicals.* Williamsburg, MA: Jennifer Abromowitz, 1990. $28.00.

Allan, Melinda. *The Inflatable Kayak Handbook.* Boulder: Johnson Books, 1991. $10.95

Anderson, Lorraine, ed. *Sisters of the Earth.* Preface by Lorraine Anderson. New York: Vintage Books, 1991. $13.00.

Barker, Harriet. *Supermarket Backpacker.* Chicago: Contemporary Books, 1978. $12.95.

Bird, Isabella L. *A Lady's Life in the Rocky Mountains.* Norman: University of Oklahoma Press, 1960.

Birkett, Bill, and Bill Peascod. *Women Climbing—200 Years of Achievement.* Seattle: The Mountaineers, 1989. $14.95.

Blum, Arlene. *Annapurna: A Woman's Place.* San Francisco: Sierra Club, 1980. $10.95.

Brown, Bruce. *Open-water Rowing Handbook.* Camden, ME: International Marine Publishing, 1991. $14.95.

———. *Stroke! A Guide to Recreational Rowing.* Camden, ME: International Marine Publishing, 1945. $14.95.

Brown, Margaret Duncan. *Shepherdess of Elk River Valley.* Denver: Golden Bell Press, 1982.

Bunnelle, Hasse, and Shirley Sarvis. *Cooking for Camp and Trail.* San Francisco: Sierra Club, 1972. $12.

Cook, Charles. *The Essential Guide to Hiking in the United States.* New York: Michael Kesend Publishing, 1991. $14.95.

Cooper, Gwen, and Evelyn Haas. *Wade a Little Deeper, Dear—A Woman's Guide to Fly Fishing.* Revised edition. New York: Lyons & Burford, 1989. $8.95.

Daniel, Linda. *Kayak Cookery: A Handbook of Provisions and Recipes.* Pacific Search Press.

Darville, Fred, M.D. *Mountaineering Medicine.* Berkeley: Wilderness Press, 1989. $3.95.

Ehrlich, Gretel. *The Solace of Open Spaces.* New York: Penguin Books, 1985. $6.95.

Engel, Claire Elaine. *They Came to the Hills.* London: George Allen and Unwin, 1952.

Fawcett, Ron, Jeff Lowe, Paul Nunn, and Alan Rouse. *The Climber's Handbook.* San Francisco: Sierra Club, 1987. $18.95.

Fleming, June. *The Well-fed Backpacker.* New York: Random House, 1986. $8.95.

Fletcher, Colin. *The New Complete Walker* and *The Complete Walker III.* New York: Alfred A. Knopf.

Fons, Valerie. *Keep it Moving—Baja by Canoe.* Seattle: The Mountaineers, 1986. $15.95.

Ford, Norman D. *Keep On Pedaling—The Complete Guide to Adult Bicycling.* Woodstock, Vermont: The Countryman Press, 1990. $12.95.

Foster, Lynne. *Take a Hike! The Sierra Club Kid's Guide to Hiking and Backpacking.* San Francisco: Sierra Club, 1991. $8.95.

Gibble, Henley, and Ellen Wessel. *Running Women: The First Step.* Alexandria, VA: Road Runners Club of America, 1979, 1991. $1.

Gillette, Ned, and John Dostal. *Cross-country Skiing.* Third edition. Seattle: The Mountaineers, 1988. $10.95.

Gilpatrick, Gil. *The Canoe Guide's Handbook: How to Plan and Guide a Trip for Two to Twelve People.* Freeport, ME: DeLorme Publishing, 1983. $7.95.

Graham, Scott. *Backpacking and Camping in the Developing World.* Berkeley: Wilderness Press, 1988. $11.95.

Gullion, Laurie. *Canoeing and Kayaking—Instruction Manual.* Newington, VA: American Canoe Association, 1987. $15.95.

——. *The Cross Country Primer.* New York: Lyons & Burford, 1990. $14.95.

Hargrove, Penny, and Noelle Liebrenz. *Backpackers' Sourcebook.* Berkeley: Wilderness Press, 1987. $7.95.

Hart, John. *Walking Softly in the Wilderness—The Sierra Club Guide to Backpacking.* San Francisco: Sierra Club, 1977, 1984. $9.95.

Hefferon, Lauren. *Cycle Food: A Guide to Satisfying Your Inner Tube.* Berkeley: Ten Speed Press, 1983. $4.95.

Howe, Ray. *White Water Kayaking.* Harrisburg, PA: Stackpole Books. $15.95.

Isaac, Jeff, P.A.-C., and Peter Goth, M.D. *The Outward Bound Wilderness First-aid Handbook.* New York: Lyons & Burford, 1991. $13.95.

Isler, Peter. *Let's Go Sailing.* New York: Simon & Schuster, 1987. $6.95.

Jackson, Monica, and Elizabeth Stark. *Tents in the Clouds: The First Women's Himalayan Expedition.* London: The Travel Book Club, 1957.

Jacobson, Cliff. *Solo Canoeing.* Chicago: ICS Books. $4.95.

Jacobson, Howard. *Racewalk to Fitness: The Sensible Alternative to Jogging and Running.* New York: Simon & Schuster, 1980.

Jobson, Gary. *Sailing Fundamentals.* New York: Simon & Schuster, 1987. $12.95.

Jeffrey, Nan, with Kevin Jeffrey. *Adventuring with Children: The Complete Manual for Family Adventure Travel.* Marstons Mills, MA: Avalon House, 1990. $14.95.

Knowlton, Elizabeth. *The Naked Mountain.* New York: G. P. Putnam's Sons, 1935.

LaBastille, Anne. *Woodswoman.* New York: Dutton.

Latimer, Carole. *Wilderness Cuisine: How to Prepare and Enjoy Fine Food on the Trail and in Camp.* Berkeley: Wilderness Press, 1991. $14.95.

LeBlond, Mrs. Aubrey. *Mountaineering in the Land of the Midnight Sun.* London: T. Fisher Unwin, 1908.

Leccese, Michael and Arlene Plevin. *The Bicyclist's Sourcebook: The Ultimate Directory of Cycling Information.* Rockville, MD: Woodbine House, 1991. $16.95.

Lezotte, Susan. *Sportsperformance: Rowing Power and Endurance.* Chicago: Contemporary Books, 1987. $7.95.

Martin, Claudine. *The Trekking Chef.* New York: Lyons & Burford, 1989. $14.95.

Miller, Luree. *On Top of the World: Five Women Explorers in Tibet.* Seattle: The Mountaineers, 1976. $10.95.

Moffat, Gwen. *Space Below My Feet.* London: Hodder and Stoughton, 1961.

Morris, Holly, ed. *Uncommon Waters: Women Write About Fishing.* Seattle: The Seal Press, 1991. $14.95.

Myers Bonta, Marcia. *Women in the Field: America's Pioneering Women Naturalists.* College Station: Texas A&M University Press, 1991.

Nichols, Maggie. *Wild, Wild Woman. A Complete Woman's Guide to Enjoying the Great Outdoors.* New York: Berkeley Windhover, 1978.

Niemi, Judith. *The Basic Essentials of Women in the Outdoors.* Merrillville, IN: ICS Books, 1990. $4.95.

Niemi, Judith, and Barbara Wieser, eds. *Rivers Running Free: Stories of Adventurous Women.* St. Paul, MN: Bergamot Books, 1987. $12.50.

Osborne, John Wilcox. *Gourmet Camping: A Menu Cookbook and Travel Guide for Campers, Canoeists, Cyclists, and Skiers.* Brandon, MS: Quail Ridge Press, 1988. $10.95.

Pilley, Dorothy. *Climbing Days.* 2d ed. New York: Harcourt, Brace, 1953.

Prater, Yvonne, and Ruth Mendenhall. *Gorp, Glop & Glue Stew: Favorite Foods from 165 Outdoor Experts.* Seattle: The Mountaineers, 1981. $9.95.

Road Runners Club of America. *Children's Running—A Guide for Parents and Kids.* Alexandria, VA: Road Runners Club of America. $1.50.

Roberts, Harry. *Backpacking.* Chicago: ICS Books. $4.95.

Robertson, Janet. *The Magnificent Mountain Women: Adventures in the Colorado Rockies.* Lincoln: University of Nebraska Press, 1990. $9.95.

Ross, Cindy. *A Woman's Journey on the Appalachian Trail.* East Charlotte, NC: East Woods Press, 1982; Chester, CT: Globe Pequot Press, 1988, 1991; Harper's Ferry, WV: The Appalachian Trail Conference, 1991. $9.95.

——. *Journey on the Crest—Walking 2600 Miles From Mexico to Canada.* Seattle: The Mountaineers, 1988. $11.95.

Royce, Patrick M. *Royce's Sailing Illustrated.* Ventura, CA: Western Marine Enterprises. $14.95.

Savage, Barbara. *Miles From Nowhere—A Round-the-World Bicycle Adventure.* Seattle: The Mountaineers, 1983. $12.95.

Seidman, David. *The Essential Sea Kayaker.* Camden, ME: International Marine. $12.95.

Selters, Andy. *Glacier Travel and Crevasse Rescue.* Seattle: The Mountaineers, 1990. $12.95.

Silverman, Goldie. *Backpacking with Babies and Small Children.* Second edition. Berkeley: Wilderness Press, 1986. $8.95.

Smith, Cyndi. *Off the Beaten Track—Women Adventurers and Mountaineers in Western Canada.* Jasper, Alberta: Coyote Books, 1989. $16.95.

Sumner, Louise. *Sew and Repair Your Outdoor Gear: Expert Tips on Today's Materials, Design & Construction Techniques.* Seattle: The Mountaineers, 1988. $14.95.

Sutherland, Audrey. *Paddling Hawai'i.* Seattle: The Mountaineers, 1988. $12.95.

———. *Paddling My Own Canoe.* Honolulu: University Press of Hawaii, 1978.

Underhill, Miriam. *Give Me the Hills.* London: Methuen and Co., 1956.

Urrutia, Virginia. *Two Wheels & a Taxi—A Slightly Daft Adventure in the Andes.* Seattle: The Mountaineers, 1987. $14.95.

Vause, Mikel, ed. *Rock and Roses.* LaCrescenta, CA: Mountain N'Air Books, 1990.

Venn, Tamsin. *Sea Kayaking Along the New England Coast.* Boston: Appalachian Mountain Club Books, 1991.

Weaver, Susan. *A Woman's Guide to Cycling.* Berkeley: Ten Speed Press, 1991.

Wells, Christine L. *Women, Sport & Performance: A Physiological Perspective.* Second edition. Champaign, IL: Human Kinetics Publishers, 1991. $39.00.

Willard, Frances E., Edith Mayo, and Lisa Larrabee. *How I Learned to Ride the Bicycle: Reflections of an Influential 19th Century Woman.* (Contains three pieces: Edith Mayo's " 'Do Everything': The Life and Work of Frances Willard," and "Women and Cycling: The Early Years," by Lisa Larrabee.) Sunnyvale, CA: Fair Oaks Publishing, 1991. $8.95.

Winnett, Thomas, and Melanie Findling. *Backpacking Basics.* Berkeley: Wilderness Press, 1988. $7.95.

Wulff, Joan. *Joan Wulff's Fly Fishing: Expert Advice from a Woman's Perspective.* Harrisburg, PA: Stackpole Books, 1991. $19.95.

Wulff, Lee. *Trout on a Fly.* New York: Nick Lyons Books, 1986. $12.95.

Zeller, Janet, and Anne Wortham Webre. *Canoeing and Kayaking for Persons with Physical Disabilities: Instruction Manual.* Newington, VA: American Canoe Association, 1990.

ABOUT THE AUTHORS

Patricia Hubbard is editor and publisher of *Outdoor Woman,* the first newsletter of its kind, which is now published nationwide ten times a year. It focuses on the woman outdoors, the connection between herself and her environment. Hubbard enjoys cycling, canoeing, hiking, and jogging. She lives in Nyack, New York.

Stan Wass is an all-around sportsman, instructor, guide, and writer. He contributes to *New York Times Sports, Outside, Canoe, Backpacker,* and *Cross Country Skier* magazines, as well as other sporting publications. He has written two books: *25 Ski Tours in Connecticut* and *25 Ski Tours in Vermont.* Wass has also been on camera as a co-host and producer for WCBS-TV in New York and WBZ-TV in Boston. He lives in West Suffield, Connecticut.

Additional copies of *The Outdoor Woman: A Handbook to Adventure* may be ordered by sending a check for $14.95 (please add the following for postage and handling: $2 for the first copy, $1 for each additional copy) to:
MasterMedia Limited
17 East 89th Street
New York, NY 10128
(212) 260–5600
(800) 334–8232
(212) 348–2020 (fax)

Patricia Hubbard and Stan Wass are available for speeches and workshops. Please contact MasterMedia's Speakers' Bureau for availability and fee arrangements. Call Tony Colao at (908) 359–1612.

OTHER MASTERMEDIA BOOKS

THE PREGNANCY AND MOTHERHOOD DIARY: Planning the First Year of Your Second Career, by Susan Schiffer Stautberg, is the first and only undated appointment diary that shows how to manage pregnancy and career. ($12.95 spiralbound)

CITIES OF OPPORTUNITY: Finding the Best Place to Work, Live and Prosper in the 1990's and Beyond, by Dr. John Tepper Marlin, explores the job and living options for the next decade and into the next century. This consumer guide and handbook, written by one of the world's experts on cities, selects and features forty-six American cities and metropolitan areas. ($13.95 paper, $24.95 cloth)

THE DOLLARS AND SENSE OF DIVORCE: The Financial Guide for Women, by Judith Briles, is the first book to combine practical tips on overcoming the legal hurdles with planning before, during and after divorce ($10.95 paper)

OUT THE ORGANIZATION: New Career Opportunities for the 1990s, by Madeleine and Robert Swain, is written for the millions of Americans whose jobs are no longer safe, whose companies are not loyal and who face futures of uncertainty. It gives advice on finding a new job or starting your own business. ($11.95 paper, $17.95 cloth)

AGING PARENTS AND YOU: A Complete Handbook to Help You Help Your Elders Maintain a Healthy, Productive and Independent Life, by Eugenia Anderson-Ellis and Marsha Dryan, is a complete guide to providing care to aging relatives. It gives practical advice and resources to the adults who are helping their elders lead productive and independent lives. ($9.95 paper)

CRITICISM IN YOUR LIFE: How to Give It, How to Take It, How to Make It Work for You, by Dr. Deborah Bright, offers practical advice, in an upbeat, readable and realistic fashion, for turning criticism into control. Charts and diagrams guide the reader into managing criticism from bosses, spouses, children, friends, neighbors and in-laws. ($9.95 paper, $17.95 cloth)

BEYOND SUCCESS: How Volunteer Service Can Help You Begin Making a Life Instead of Just a Living, by John F. Raynolds III and Eleanor Raynolds, C.B.E., is a unique how-to book targeted to business and professional people considering volunteer work, senior citizens who wish to fill leisure time meaningfully and students trying out various career options. The book is filled with interviews with celebrities, CEOs and average citizens who talk about the benefits of service work. ($9.95 paper, $19.95 cloth)

MANAGING IT ALL: Time-Saving Ideas for Career, Family, Relationships and Self, by Beverly Benz Treuille and Susan Schiffer Stautberg, is written for women who are juggling careers and families. Over two hundred career women (ranging from a TV anchorwoman to an investment banker) were interviewed. The book contains many humorous anecdotes on saving time and improving the quality of life for self and family. ($9.95 paper)

REAL LIFE 101: The Graduate's Guide to Survival, by Susan Kleinman, supplies welcome advice to those facing "real life" for the first time, focusing on work, money, health and how to deal with freedom and responsibility. ($9.95 paper)

YOUR HEALTHY BODY, YOUR HEALTHY LIFE: How to Take Control of Your Medical Destiny, by Donald B. Louria, M.A., provides precise advice and strategies that will help you to live a long and healthy life. Learn also about nutrition, exercise, vitamins and medication, as well as how to control risk factors for major diseases. ($12.95 paper)

THE CONFIDENCE FACTOR: How Self-Esteem Can Change Your Life, by Judith Briles, is based on a nationwide survey of six thousand men and women. Briles explores why women so often feel a lack of self-confidence and have a poor opinion of themselves. She offers step-by-step advice on becoming the person you want to be. ($9.95 paper, $18.95 cloth)

THE SOLUTION TO POLLUTION: 101 Things You Can Do to Clean Up Your Environment, by Laurence Sombke, offers step-by-step techniques on how to conserve more energy, start a recycling center, choose biodegradable products and proceed with individual environmental cleanup projects. ($7.95 paper)

TAKING CONTROL OF YOUR LIFE: The Secrets of Successful Enterprising Women, by Gail Blanke and Kathleen Walas, is based on the authors' professional experience with Avon Products' Women of Enterprise Awards, given each year to outstanding women entrepreneurs. The authors offer a specific plan to help you gain control over your life and include business tips and quizzes as well as beauty and lifestyle information. ($17.95 cloth)

SIDE-BY-SIDE STRATEGIES: How Two-Career Couples Can Thrive in the Nineties, by Jane Hershey Cuozzo and S. Diane Graham, describes how two-career couples can learn the difference between competing with a spouse and becoming a supportive power partner. Published in hardcover as *Power Partners.* ($10.95 paper, $19.95 cloth)

DARE TO CONFRONT! How to Intervene When Someone You Care About Has an Alcohol or Drug Problem, by Bob Wright and Deborah George Wright, shows the reader how to use the step-by-step methods of professional interventionists to motivate drug-dependent people to accept the help they need. ($17.95 cloth)

WORK WITH ME! How to Make the Most of Office Support Staff, by Betsy Lazary, shows how to find, train and nurture the "perfect" assistant and how best to utilize your support staff professionals. ($9.95 paper)

MANN FOR ALL SEASONS: Wit and Wisdom from The Washington Post*'s Judy Mann,* by Judy Mann, shows the columnist at her best as she writes about women, families and the politics of the women's revolution. ($9.95 paper, $19.95 cloth)

THE SOLUTION TO POLLUTION IN THE WORKPLACE, by Laurence Sombke, Terry M. Robertson and Elliot M. Kaplan, supplies employees with everything they need to know about cleaning up their workspace, including recycling, using energy efficiently, conserving water and buying recycled products and nontoxic supplies. ($9.95 paper)

THE ENVIRONMENTAL GARDENER: The Solution to Pollution for Lawns and Gardens, by Laurence Sombke, focuses on what each of us can do to protect our endangered plant life. A practical sourcebook and shopping guide. ($8.95 paper)

THE LOYALTY FACTOR: Building Trust in Today's Workplace, by Carol Kinsey Goman, Ph.D., offers techniques for restoring commitment and loyalty in the workplace. ($9.95 paper)

DARE TO CHANGE YOUR JOB—AND YOUR LIFE, by Carole Kanchier, Ph.D., provides a look at career growth and development throughout the life cycle. ($10.95 paper)

MISS AMERICA: In Pursuit of the Crown, by Ann-Marie Bivans, is an authorized guidebook to the Pageant, containing eyewitness accounts, complete historical data and a realistic look at the trials and triumphs of potential Miss Americas. ($27.50 cloth)

POSITIVELY OUTRAGEOUS SERVICE: New and Easy Ways to Win Customers for Life, by T. Scott Gross, identifies what the consumers of the nineties really want and how businesses can develop effective marketing strategies to answer those needs. ($14.95 paper)

BREATHING SPACE: Living and Working at a Comfortable Place in a Sped-Up Society, by Jeff Davidson, helps readers to handle information and activity overload and gain greater control over their lives. ($10.95 paper)

TWENTYSOMETHING: Managing and Motivating Today's New Work Force, by Lawrence J. Bradford, Ph.D., and Claire Raines, M.A., examines the work habits of the younger generation, offering managers a practical guide to better understanding and supervising their young employees. ($22.95 cloth)

BALANCING ACTS! Juggling Love, Work, Family, and Recreation, by Susan Schiffer Stautberg and Marcia L. Worthing, provides strategies to achieve a balanced life by reordering priorities and setting realistic goals. ($12.95 paper)

THE LIVING HEART BRAND NAME SHOPPER'S GUIDE, by Michael E. De-Bakey, M.D., Antonio M. Gotto, Jr., M.D., D.Phil., Lynne W. Scott, M.A., R.D./L.D., and John P. Foreyt, Ph.D., lists brand-name supermarket products that are low in fat, saturated fatty acids, and cholesterol. ($12.50 paper)

REAL BEAUTY—REAL WOMEN: A Workbook for Making the Best of Your Own Good Looks, by Kathleen Walas, National Beauty and Fashion Director of Avon Products, offers expert advice on beauty and fashion to women of all ages and ethnic backgrounds. ($19.50 cloth)

MANAGING YOUR CHILD'S DIABETES, by Robert Wood Johnson IV, Sale Johnson, Casey Johnson, and Susan Kleinman, brings help to families trying to understand diabetes and control its effects. ($10.95 paper, $18.95 cloth)

STEP FORWARD: Sexual Harassment in the Workplace, by Susan L. Webb, teaches the reader all the basic facts about sexual harassment as well as furnishing procedures to help stop it. ($9.95 paper)

A TEEN'S GUIDE TO BUSINESS: The Secrets to a Successful Enterprise, by Linda Menzies, Oren S. Jenkins, and Rickell R. Fisher, provides guidance for teenagers starting their own businesses or entering the workplace. ($7.95 paper)